The Democratic Coup d'État

The Democratic Coup d'État

OZAN O. VAROL

OXFORD
UNIVERSITY PRESS

OXFORD
UNIVERSITY PRESS

Oxford University Press is a department of the University of Oxford. It furthers
the University's objective of excellence in research, scholarship, and education
by publishing worldwide. Oxford is a registered trade mark of Oxford University
Press in the UK and certain other countries.

Published in the United States of America by Oxford University Press
198 Madison Avenue, New York, NY 10016, United States of America.

© Ozan O. Varol 2017

CIP data is on file at the Library of Congress
ISBN 978–0–19–062601–3 (hbk)
ISBN 978–0–19–062602–0 (pbk)

3 5 7 9 8 6 4 2

Paperback printed by Webcom Inc., Canada
Hardback printed by Bridgeport National Bindery, Inc., United States of America

To my parents, Yurdanur and Tacettin.

For Kathy.

CONTENTS

PART SEVEN   HOW THIS ENDS

The Democratic Coup d'État

PART ONE

FROM SOLDIERS TO POLITICIANS

Don't let the facts disturb the theory.
                                                              —*Unknown*

No argument of mine has generated as much controversy as the one developed in the book you're holding in your hands. My hypothesis is simple: Sometimes democracy is established through a military coup.

That statement alone is sufficient to make people shudder. After all, we widely assume that a coup d'état —French for "stroke of the state"—is inherently bad for democracy. At first blush, you may dismiss the concept as an oxymoron. You may find yourself agreeing with President Recep Tayyip Erdoğan of Turkey, who lashed out against me in a public speech. There is "no such thing as a democratic coup d'état," he argued and compared the concept to the "living dead," calling it a figment of my imagination.[1] You may also worry that you are about to read an advocacy of human rights abuses by military leaders, a how-to guide for legitimizing coups, or a celebration of CIA-backed attempts to topple unfriendly regimes in foreign countries.

But that's not what this book is about. Instead the book attempts to answer a set of seemingly simple questions that popped into my head as I sat in my apartment in Chicago in early 2011 watching the Arab Spring unfold. In Egypt the military had just seized power from the authoritarian government of Hosni Mubarak and promised democratic elections. Although Egypt's democratic transition later took a turn for the worse, the military coup enabled the first ever democratic elections in a country that has been around since before Christ. In Tunisia the military enabled a democratic transition by refusing orders from the dictatorship to use force on its rebellious population. On some accounts, it was Rachid Ammar, chief of staff of the Tunisian Armed Forces, who said "Tu est fini" (You are finished) to the Tunisian dictator Zine el-Abidine Ben Ali and sent him running to Saudi Arabia for refuge.[2]

As my television set unveiled these events in bright colors and mass confusion, I began to ponder: Why do we assume that militaries inherently pose a problem to democracy? Can a military coup serve the counterintuitive function of toppling a dictator and establishing the foundations of democratic rule? Over the ensuing six years I devoured innumerable historical and contemporary sources, trekked to Egypt and Turkey for interviews and research, and wrote articles in search of answers to these questions. That search culminated in this book.

I first coined the term *democratic coup d'état* in an article published in 2012 in the *Harvard International Law Journal*. The article received considerable praise and criticism, and the term became an integral part of the nomenclature in law and political science. It was widely cited—both positively and not so positively—in the academic literature and assigned to courses in law schools and graduate schools. The article made headlines across the globe in major media outlets.

Despite the waves it generated, the 2012 article was only a preview; this book is the feature film. It completely revamps the article and substantially expands on the original treatment I offered. It covers scores of additional case studies and explores the rich nuances and consequences that I could not cover in the article. In addition, the article was written for an exclusively academic audience, whereas I wrote this book for a general audience with intellectual curiosity.

In many ways I am an unlikely author of a book that considers coups with democratic potential. I was born in Istanbul, Turkey, at a time when the nation was under military rule. In 1980, the year before my birth, the Turkish military seized power from a civilian government in a brutal coup. In the ensuing two years, the coup makers disbanded the Parliament, drafted a repressive constitution, and committed widespread human rights abuses. Numerous civilians were forced into exile, jailed, tortured, or executed after receiving trumped-up charges and sham trials. To escape being jailed as communists, my parents burned all of their books that had even a semblance of leftist ideology. Although the military returned power to civilians after two years, the ravages of the coup reverberated for two decades. Having personally witnessed these events, I was, for the majority of my life, quick to condemn all military coups.

Yet the events of the Arab Spring also led me to reflect on an earlier coup in Turkey—a coup of a much different caliber—that my grandparents lived through. In 1960 the Turkish military toppled an authoritarian government and turned power over to democratically elected leaders. Under the military's supervision, Turkey emerged from an eighteen-month transition process as a genuine, multiparty democracy with a thriving civil society and what is widely accepted as the most liberal constitution in Turkish history.

I began researching whether there were other coups that fit this latter, paradoxical pattern and came across numerous examples that no serious academic can dismiss as measurement errors or extreme outliers. These coups dispute the clean, comfortable narrative that dismisses all military coups as detriments to democratic development. They prove that an event as undemocratic as a military coup can, in some cases, lead to democracy.

I picked a broad set of cases to feature in this book, from different time periods and world regions, to analyze why and how democratic coups happen. The book covers events from the Athenian Navy's stance in 411 BC against a tyrannical home government to military coups in the American colonies against corrupt British governors and to twentieth-century coups that toppled dictators and installed democratic rule in countries as diverse as Guinea-Bissau, Portugal, and Colombia. The stories of these coups are both fascinating and troubling. They involve bargains, conflict, trade-offs, and backstabbing, both literal and metaphorical.

In the following pages I unpack these stories in detail. I try to refrain from telling a single story or creating a grand theory. The chaotic reality of a coup d'état is too rich to be reduced to a one-size-fits-all paradigm that pretends to explain events at the expense of the facts. Although my focus is on the military, I also examine the relevant events from the point of view of those who stand outside it.

You'll find that my approach is neither blind admiration nor blanket condemnation. I bristle when I see the mindless glorification of militaries or military coups, yet I also chafe at blanket dismissals of all militaries and all military coups as unyielding threats to democracy. In the end, my aim is to bring much-needed nuance to the discourse on civil-military relations.

One of the many challenges of writing a book on military coups is the dearth of reliable information about events and actors. I agree with these sentiments of an Egyptian activist: "The military is a black box, and no one knows what happens inside."[3] Secrecy only increases during the planning of a coup. Coup makers rarely shout their plans from mountaintops, and the military's decision-making process is notoriously shrouded in secrecy. In putting together the case studies for this book, I relied on a combination of primary sources—news stories, contemporary interviews with relevant actors, official statements, and the like—as well as secondary sources that summarize the relevant events. I also personally conducted interviews in Turkey and

Egypt, two countries featured prominently throughout this book. These discussions were not formal field research but simply an attempt on my part to cut through the noise and get a better grasp of the relevant events on the ground instead of speculating from my comfortable academic chair in the United States. Even the sum total of these sources wasn't sufficient to resolve all ambiguities. But they helped me to comprehend what seemed incomprehensible and place myself in a better position to evaluate the credibility of the sources I used.

Coups are not the domains of idle academics. Although this book is written by a professor, its subject is practically and politically significant because military coups are attempted regularly around the globe. As recently as July 2016, when I was writing this book, factions within the Turkish military staged an ill-fated coup attempt against the incumbent government. (I'll return to this coup in due course.)

The book is ultimately a study of individual behavior and humanity's eternal struggle with power, as it grapples with several baffling questions: Why would militaries that loyally serve a dictatorship turn their arms against the dictator? After seizing power from a dictator, why would imposing generals—armed with tanks and guns and all—voluntarily surrender power to civilian politicians? What distinguishes militaries that help build democracies from those that destroy them?

The book is also a cautionary tale about the risks of blindly accepting comfortable yet demonstrably wrong societal assumptions. It's about the importance, to paraphrase Mark Twain, of pausing and reflecting whenever you find yourself on the side of the majority. It's a story of how our society developed a theory condemning all military coups before analyzing the facts, which, if you know your Sherlock Holmes, is the worst mistake an investigator can make. Once the theory was created, reinforced, and retweeted, it became the truth. And we have refused to let the facts disturb it. As a result, a simple idea supported by hard, historical data—that democracy sometimes comes with a coup—has come to prompt immediate visceral reactions at the expense of human knowledge.

I hope this book will serve as a reminder of the vices of consensus, the urgency of questioning the standard narratives about our world, and the imperative of engaging with all ideas, no matter how controversial.

December 1, 2016
Portland, Oregon

1

Love Ballads, Carnations, and Coups

The most difficult subjects can be explained to the most slow-witted man if
he has not formed any idea of them already; but the simplest thing cannot be
made clear to the most intelligent man if he is firmly persuaded that he knows
already, without a shadow of a doubt, what is laid before him.
— Leo Tolstoy, *The Kingdom of God Is Within You*, 1897

The Eurovision Song Contest is an annual spectacle thoroughly mocked but also adored by millions of viewers.[1] The contest is produced annually by the European Broadcasting Union, whose membership includes fifty countries that expand beyond the borders of Europe. Each country nominates one song produced by a local artist, and national juries award points during a live event to the songs nominated by other countries. These points are then tallied to determine the winner.

As a child growing up in Turkey, I vividly recall being glued to the TV during each year's Eurovision Contest. I'd munch on popcorn and listen to my parents discuss conspiracy theories about why other countries are always loath to vote for Turkish songs. Eurovision has been around since 1956—long before *American Idol* or *The Voice*—and continues to inspire bizarre performances, music of highly questionable quality, and fierce nationalism as political battles get settled on the musical stage.

In 1974 Portugal's nominee for Eurovision was a ballad titled "E Depois do Adeus," or "After the Farewell." Penned by the singer Paulo de Carvalho, it depicts the end of a romantic relationship. The song performed abysmally in the Eurovision Contest, coming in fourteenth in a field of seventeen. Yet Carvalho's deep disappointment must have morphed into utter astonishment when his love ballad served as the signal to launch a military coup d'état in the heart of Europe.

In the Western world, military coups are ordinarily relegated to the fantasy realm. Coups are supposed to happen in backward, faraway lands, in countries riddled with corruption and incompetence, and in nations that end with *-stan*. But on April 25, 1974, Western Europeans awoke to a coup in their own backyard.

At the time of the 1974 coup,[2] the now democratic Portugal was home to a brutal dictatorship. Although it was dubbed the Estado Novo, the New State, the dictatorship was anything but new. António de Oliveira Salazar established the regime in 1933, and Marcelo Caetano took over the reins after Salazar suffered a stroke in 1968. By the time of the coup, the dictatorship had been around for over four decades, which gave it the dubious honor of being Western Europe's oldest authoritarian government. Although the regime held periodic elections, opposition political parties were generally outlawed, except for a brief period immediately before the elections. This act of democratic window dressing left little opportunity for political parties to organize and mount effective election campaigns. With "sadistic efficiency," the regime's reviled political police, known as the International Police in Defense of the State (Polícia Internacional e de Defesa do Estado), censored, imprisoned, tortured, and outright assassinated dissidents.[3]

Under the Estado Novo, Portugal became the last European power to cling to colonial adventures in Africa. Colonies in Angola, Guinea-Bissau, and Mozambique, among others, provided Portugal with gold, diamonds, and cheap raw materials and furnished an easy market for the export of Portuguese wines and textiles. To continue its lucrative colonial exploitations, the dictatorship committed Portugal to costly and disastrous wars in the colonies. These wars isolated Portugal from the international community, damaged its already ailing economy, and ruined its military.

During the dictatorship, Portugal was the most underdeveloped nation in Western Europe, with many Portuguese living in abject poverty. Portuguese workers were the most poorly paid in Western Europe; wages in Portugal were seven times less than Swedish wages and five times less than British wages. Labor unions and strikes were prohibited. Although the nation was ailing and disaffection was widespread, the regime prevented the opposition from catalyzing meaningful changes, and its stronghold on power showed no signs of abating.

In this corrupt dictatorship, the military was the only state institution with significant levels of popular support. In contrast to many nations, where the military is isolated from society, Portugal's continuous colonial wars made isolation impossible. To supply the military machine from a small population, the regime mandated a two-year military service for all men. By 1974, 1.5 million Portuguese had served overseas, and one in every four adult males was in the armed forces. Further, the low pay levels of military officers required them to work in the civilian sector to supplement their income while off duty, which kept them in frequent contact with civilians. Over time, in a very real sense, the armed forces became the Portuguese society.

For many years the military was a mere pawn in the Estado Novo. The armed forces participated in Portugal's colonial wars and carried out most regime demands. But as dissatisfaction with the regime grew rampant, the military became the player that moved the pieces.

On April 25, 1974, devastated by unwinnable colonial wars as well as low pay and prestige, two hundred military officers decided to take action. The officers initially called themselves the Captains' Movement, which they later renamed the

Armed Forces Movement to portray the image of broader support throughout the military. Their plan was to topple the dictatorship, fully restore civil liberties, hold elections for a constituent assembly to write a new constitution, abolish the political police, find a diplomatic solution to the colonial wars, and turn power over to democratically elected leaders. Although it was junior officers who planned and staged the coup, they picked a senior officer, General António de Spínola, to serve as its figurehead. Spínola was a well-respected war hero who had penned a controversial book, *Portugal and the Future*, which argued that a military victory in the colonies was impossible and instead proposed a political solution that granted the colonies limited autonomy.

The signal to launch the coup was two songs broadcast on two different radio stations. Precisely at 10:55 p.m. on April 24, a radio station would play Paulo de Carvalho's "After the Farewell," Portugal's ill-fated nominee for the 1974 Eurovision Contest. Less than two hours later, at 12:25 a.m. on April 25, it would be followed by a second song, "Grândola, Vila Morena," referring to a town in southern Portugal as a swarthy or sun-baked town. This song was composed by Zeca Afonso, whose works were banned by the regime for advocating communism.

As "Grândola, Vila Morena" began to hum on radios across Portugal, the coup plotters moved into action. The soldiers first seized public news sources, followed by the Lisbon airport. Tanks rolled into Lisbon's Praça do Comércio, a central square situated on the Tagus River. Other units seized the Salazar Bridge across the Tagus to prevent any possible resistance from the South. Army officers loyal to the regime were quick to put down their guns after they realized they were significantly outnumbered. With his end in sight, the ruling dictator, Caetano, relented and called General Spínola to arrange for a transfer of power. Caetano and other prominent regime officials were forced into exile.

The forty-year-old dictatorship collapsed with remarkable speed. The coup was peaceful; there were no executions. But there were new sheriffs in town.

Following the coup, thousands immediately flocked to the streets in celebration. The crowds picked up carnations from the Lisbon flower market, a central gathering point, and placed them in the gun barrels of soldiers as symbols of support. Car horns honked the rhythm of "Spín-Spín-Spínola." During the May Day celebrations in Lisbon, which took place within a week of the coup, a banner that read "THANK YOU, ARMED FORCES" was unfurled in a soccer stadium packed with a crowd of 200,000 to hear speeches by leftist leaders who had returned from exile. In the following weeks, red carnations became ubiquitous across Portugal, displayed everywhere from buttonholes on men's jackets to women's blouses. The April 25 coup came to be known as the Carnation Revolution.

The day after the coup, on April 26, General Spínola delivered a brief statement on public television. He introduced the ruling military junta, a group of seven high-ranking officers from the army, air force, and navy. The junta would guide the transition process to democracy, establish and run a transitional government, hold democratic elections, and transfer power to a civilian government. On May 15, following his official inauguration as the president of the Republic, Spínola appointed Adelino da Palma Carlos, a politically moderate former law professor, as his prime minister. Carlos's government would work toward what came to be known as "the three Ds"—decolonization, democratization, and development—with the ultimate objective of integrating Portugal into the European community.

Soon after the coup political parties began to form, and within a few months approximately fifty parties were competing for power in the newly minted democratic marketplace. The military abolished censorship of the press and permitted freedom of expression. As a result, meetings and demonstrations—once completely banned—became a visible part of daily life. Political prisoners jailed during the Estado Novo were freed. The coup also ended Portugal's costly colonial adventures in Africa, with the ruling military granting independence to the colonies.

To achieve democratization, the military strove to win the hearts and minds of the rural population, which required increased levels of interaction between the military and civilians. For example, the military organized a rural development program called the Cultural Dynamization Campaign to educate the population about the ongoing democratization process. The campaign sought to ensure that the largely illiterate rural population would not be manipulated into reelecting an authoritarian regime. The campaign was run primarily by soldiers, though civilian singers and artists also participated. Through its "sessions of enlightenment," the campaign delivered information on a variety of political issues, such as decolonization and the upcoming democratic elections. The military brought its dynamization campaign to more than 1.5 million peasants, workers, and shopkeepers. These interactions, in turn, kept the military in touch with civilian values.

Like most transitions from dictatorship to democracy, the coup also brought social and economic turmoil to Portugal. When dictatorships fall, they fall hard. The Portuguese transition to democracy produced six provisional governments, three elections, and two coup attempts. After decolonization, the textile industry, which employed about 120,000 people at the time, lost its supply of raw materials and access to convenient markets in the colonies. The reduction in the size of the armed forces following the end of the colonial wars also swelled the ranks of the jobless. The newfound freedom of expression and freedom to strike prompted intense demonstrations, and once-forbidden strikes affected all sectors of the economy. Workers took over factories, and students revolted in schools. Even the Carnation Revolution produced a few thorns.

As promised, the ruling military junta held democratic elections for a constituent assembly to write a new constitution, which were symbolically scheduled for the first anniversary of the coup, April 25, 1975. These elections were the first in Portuguese history to feature universal suffrage and a secret vote, and the first meaningful elections in Portugal since the 1920s. The turnout was an impressive 92 percent. Following parliamentary and presidential elections, the coup leaders, successful in dismantling the dictatorship, turned over power to democratically elected leaders. In addition to creating a democracy in Portugal, the coup instigated a global wave of democratization known as the Third Wave across more than sixty countries.[4]

The date of the coup became, and remains, a national holiday in Portugal. Along with many other streets and squares in Portugal, the iconic Salazar Bridge in Lisbon over the River Tagus was renamed the April 25 Bridge (Ponte 25 de Abril). In 1999 an exhibition opened to commemorate the twenty-fifth anniversary of the military coup and to celebrate the establishment of Portugal's still thriving democracy.

One of the two songs that triggered the April 25 coup, "Grândola, Vila Morena," came to symbolize the coup and the beginning of democratic rule. In February 2013 protesters sitting in the public gallery of the Portuguese Parliament interrupted Prime Minister Pedro Passos Coelho's speech with a rendition of the same song, to protest his government's economic and social policies. To his credit, the prime minister calmly awaited the removal of the protesters before commenting, "Of all the ways work might be interrupted, this would seem to be in the best possible taste."[5]

When we think of military coups, the first images that pop into our heads are not the establishment of Western democracies, carnations, or soccer stadiums filled with jubilant fans celebrating the gift of liberty. Rather the term "coup d'état" brings to mind coups staged through corrupt backroom plots by power-hungry generals. Coups remind us of Muammar Gaddafi, Augusto Pinochet, Omar al-Bashir, and scores of other ruthless military dictators who wreak havoc on their local populations and set their national progress back by decades.

These military dictators, and others like them, abuse public trust and overthrow the existing regime not to democratize but to concentrate power in their own hands. Once they assume power, they stay in power. They disband parliaments, suspend constitutions, impose curfews, declare martial law, censor the media, ban protests, crack down on dissidents, commit atrocious human rights abuses, and instill fear in every corner of the country. *This* is the image that fits comfortably in our preconceptions of coups: brutal, ruthless, and *bad*.

The modern study of civil-military relations developed largely in response to these types of antidemocratic military interventions. The experts reached a consensus that all coups inherently present a menace to democracy, and we were told to move along—nothing to see or dispute here.[6] As a result, when we think of military coups, we tend to do so in a homogeneous fashion: coups look the same, smell the same, and present the same threats to democracy.

It's a powerful, concise, and self-reinforcing idea.
It's also wrong.

In this book I challenge this consensus about military coups. Distilled to its core, my hypothesis is this: *Sometimes a democracy is established through a military coup.*

That simple statement conceals many complexities, which I will unravel in each chapter. I begin with an introduction to the basics.

A democratic coup occurs when the domestic military, or a section of it, turns its arms against a dictatorship, temporarily takes control of the government, and oversees a transition to democracy. The transition ends with free and fair elections of civilians and the military's retreat to the barracks.

Of course a military coup itself is an undemocratic event. In a coup, the military assumes power not through elections but by force or the threat of force. I use the term democratic to refer to the regime type the coup produces.

The target of a democratic coup is an authoritarian government. Under this definition, a coup staged against democratically elected leaders is not democratic. Many coups have been perpetrated against supposedly corrupt, inefficient, or short-sighted politicians. These coups are not democratic because there is another avenue, short of military intervention, for getting rid of these politicians: vote them out of office. A coup may be considered democratic only when the incumbent politicians do not permit competitive elections.

Foreign interventions, in the name of democratic regime change or otherwise, are also excluded from my definition of a democratic coup. The 2003 U.S. invasion of Iraq serves as a poignant reminder of the unique set of problems generated through interventions by foreign powers. In democratic coups it's the domestic military that topples the dictatorship and oversees a transition to democracy.

At this introductory stage, the reader may object to even considering the questions I raise in this book. If we succeed in explaining how military coups may produce democracies, will that not legitimize military coups? Doesn't the phrase democratic coup falsely glorify coups at the expense of preferable methods of regime change?

Ideally, of course, enlightened civilians, not military leaders, would oversee a transition process from authoritarianism to democracy. But often the conditions necessary for that ideal transition are absent. The civilian leaders at the helm may be unwilling to give up power. The dictatorship may crush popular movements before they take root. Worse, civilian elites may be in cahoots with the authoritarian government and lack interest in democratic progress. The press and civil society may be malfunctioning under the oppressive might of an authoritarian state.

In these cases we may have to expand our aperture to include an institution traditionally assumed to hamper, not promote, democracy: the military. If other paths to democratization have been blocked by a dictator, the armed forces, equipped with sheer military might, may be the only institution capable of toppling the dictatorship and installing a democracy. In some cases the second-best option in theory may be the best option in practice.

The democratic coup remains the exception, not the norm. Many military coups continue to pose impediments to democratic development and pave the way for military dictatorships. But the democratic coup is *not* an extreme outlier. Countries as diverse as Portugal, Mali, Colombia, Burkina Faso, England, Guinea-Bissau,

Guatemala, Turkey, Egypt, Peru, and the United States have all undergone democratization after their militaries turned their arms against the incumbent government. Each of these cases is a major snag in the standard thinking on coups.

Although I cover a diverse set of cases in this book, democratic coups are also not limited to these cases. According to an empirical study, in the post–cold war era, 72 percent of coups (31 out of 43) were followed by democratic elections within five years.[7] As the authors of that study note, "the new generation of coups has been far less harmful for democracy than their historical predecessors."[8] According to another study of coups in African countries from 1952 to 2012, authoritarian states in Africa are "significantly more likely to democratize in the three years following coups."[9]

A democratic coup is like chemotherapy: an extreme measure reserved for extreme cases. It can be highly effective in curing an authoritarian patient, but it can also have significant side effects, at least in the short term. Far from glorifying coups and the military elites that stage them, this book addresses not only their potential benefits but also the problems they generate. Although numerous coups have produced meaningful democracies, the standard disclaimer still applies: Past performance does not guarantee future results.

Some readers may feel that I am offering a rather rosy—even naive—account of military coups. After all, why would soldiers armed with guns ever submit to politicians in suits? How could an event as undemocratic as a coup lead to democracy? As Lord Acton famously quipped, "Power tends to corrupt and absolute power corrupts absolutely." Military leaders may echo the rhetoric of democracy or mimic its rituals, but surely they cannot have any altruistic commitments to democracy that transcend the immediate lure of absolute power.

I am under no false pretenses about the coup makers' intentions. Although coups can produce democracies, the agendas of even democratic coup plotters tend to be self-serving. As I'll explain in later chapters, altruism is not the primary driver of the phenomenon I describe here. Where the interests of the military elites and a dictatorship are aligned, the military will tend to support the dictator. Where, however, conflicts emerge between the military leadership and the dictatorship, or where popular opposition to the dictator becomes powerful enough to thwart the regime's suppression efforts, the military's incentives may change. Faced with a wobbling authoritarian government, the military might stage a coup, seize power from the regime, and oversee a transition process that ends with the transfer of power to the people. That option allows the military to establish a more stable regime, emerge in the eyes of the people as a credible state institution, and preserve its own interests during a transition process that the military leaders themselves control.

In this introductory chapter, I provided a general overview of democratic coups and a flavor of the ideas that will be unpacked in the book. In the next chapter, I'll take a step back and more broadly explore the universe of democratic transitions.

I'll explain why we tend to romanticize democratic transitions like most romantic comedies glamorize love: The people gather in a central square, start protesting, topple the dictatorship, hold elections, and live happily ever after. I'll explain why the on-the-ground facts often fail to live up to this simple ideal, why history is littered with failed attempts to democratize, and why even successful democratic transitions are often painfully long and violent. In doing so my hope is to inject a healthy dose of reality into our soaring expectations about emerging democratic movements, which, if unrestrained, can blunt our capability to appreciate alternative avenues for democratic regime change. The perfect should not be the enemy of the good, particularly since the perfect is often unattainable.

From there I'll explain why the military plays a decisive role in almost all revolutions and why, in some cases, the military may be the only actor available to ignite democratic regime change. I'll also provide a brief crash course on democracy and authoritarianism and explain what sets apart democratic coups from their nondemocratic counterparts. Along the way I'll discuss why the popular American television sitcom *Hogan's Heroes* explains the U.S. State Department's reluctance to use the "c" word (coup) to describe the 2013 military intervention in Egypt, and how a coup staged by a soldier named Mustafa Kemal founded the Turkish Republic.

The book will then take the reader on a chronological journey through the life of a democratic coup. I'll begin with the military's overthrow of an authoritarian government and discuss several "why" questions: Why would a military ever turn its arms on a dictatorship? Why are some militaries more likely to support a dictatorship and others more willing to turn their arms against it? I'll explain why democratic coups tend to occur in countries with mandatory national conscription, where civilians serve in the military for a defined term, usually one to three years, before returning to civilian life. I'll discuss how the social experiments of a Holocaust survivor shed light on why conscript militaries are less likely to shoot at protestors; why the Glorious Revolution in England is more accurately described as the Glorious Coup; why the assassination of Julius Caesar provides key insights into why a modern military may turn its arms against a dictator; and how military coups in the American colonies laid the foundations for the American Revolution and the later birth of the modern United States.

This will take us into the next phase of the transition process to democracy. Having deposed a dictator, the military will have two primary choices: keep power and establish a military dictatorship or give up power to civilian leaders and pave the way for democratic regime change. Some militaries opt for the former, and others—the subjects of this book—pick the latter. I'll discuss why the military may benefit from democracy, and how, in some cases, democracy may benefit from the military. I'll also explain, however, that the military may not desire all trappings of democracy and could engage in strategic gamesmanship during the transition process to protect its interests, rig the rules in its favor, and secure exit benefits.

I'll close with reflections on the aftermath of a democratic coup. This type of coup ends with the election of democratic leaders and the military's retreat to the barracks. In some cases the coup may produce only a fragile democracy, teetering on the brink of collapse. Democratic institutions may not fully mature, and the military may roar back to life after a superficial exit from civilian politics. But in other cases the budding democracy created by a coup can eventually blossom into a genuine liberal democracy, as it did in the case of the 1974 Portuguese coup. The establishment of democratic institutions—however unwittingly—can open up a democratic Pandora's box that even the military leadership itself cannot contain. Once ignited, democracy may persist, despite any attempts to extinguish it.

2

The Romance of Democratic Transitions

You can't nudge history forward in the way a child would when wishing to make a flower grow more quickly: by tugging at it. . . . We must patiently plant the seeds and water the ground well, and give the plants exactly the amount of time they need to mature.

—President Václav Havel of the Czech Republic,
"Speech to the Academy of Humanities and Political
Sciences," Paris, October 27, 1992

The Lore of Democratic Transitions

It's a cold winter day, but the cool air feels liberating. The dawn has yet to break, but thousands have already lined up on the streets. Many have taken the day off from work to live the moment that history books will surely discuss for decades, if not centuries. There is laughter, yet also anxious conversation, about what has been and what has yet to be. Amid the crowds Western reporters are busy seeking English-speaking interview subjects for thirty-second sound bites. "The beginning," one newspaper headline boldly declares. "I vote, therefore I am," says another.

The elections—the country's first after decades of authoritarian rule—proceed in an orderly fashion. Aside from minor scuffles, there are no voting irregularities, no stuffing of ballot boxes, no voter intimidation, and no buying of votes. When the victors are declared, all parties accept the results, and the newly elected leaders take their seats without resistance. These elections are decidedly free and fair. Western politicians stumble over each other to place congratulatory phone calls to the electoral victors. "Welcome to the club," they say, "glad to have you here." After an inclusive process, the country ratifies a democratic constitution with a plethora of individual rights modeled after Western constitutions and establishes a constitutional court to keep the politicians in check. Stripped of its authoritarian shackles, the economy begins to thrive, unemployment falls, gross domestic product rises, and crime rates plummet.

This story of the typical democratic transition has become lore. We have come to romanticize transitions to democracy like most romantic comedies glamorize love: Two strangers serendipitously meet, fall in love, overcome all obstacles, and then live happily ever after. We have faith in the crowds gathering in squares from Cairo to Kiev to overthrow their dictators.[1] We believe in the people's ability to shame tyrants into being sensible, upend the status quo, wipe the slate clean, and rebuild their nation's foundations on the bedrock principle of Western governments: the rule of the people. We trust the power of the ballot box and assume that democratization is the best, and perhaps the only, hope for societies emerging from a dictatorship. As a result we equate the collapse of an authoritarian government with the establishment of democracy, assuming that nations liberated from dictatorship inevitably gravitate toward democratic rule just as the arc of the moral universe bends toward justice. Once a democratic transition has been ignited, we expect it to spread like wildfire and clear an unobstructed path for economic growth, employment opportunities, and robust individual rights.

This fanciful image has been nursed in part by politicians. *Democracy* has become a word used primarily for its political selling power. This political trend dates back to Woodrow Wilson's declaration that the purpose of World War I was to make the world "safe for democracy."[2] Even where the United States tolerated—and outright supported—undemocratic regimes, twentieth- and twenty-first-century American politicians still invoked the rhetoric of democracy. This unyielding, albeit hypocritical, commitment to democratization culminated in the Washington Consensus in 1989, which articulated the belief that democracy, free markets, and the rule of law would develop in unison.[3] A 2000 U.S. State Department report declared that global experiments with authoritarianism had failed. At long last, it continued, "democracy is triumphant."[4] The 2003 U.S. invasion of Iraq was justified in part in democratic terms. "The concerted effort of free nations to promote democracy," argued President George W. Bush, "is a prelude to our enemies' defeat."[5] After the Libyan dictator Muammar Gaddafi was toppled with NATO assistance, President Barack Obama was quick to announce that the "dark shadow of tyranny ha[d] been lifted" over Libya.[6]

Journalistic opinion has also contributed to this narrative. In recent years the public's insatiable hunger for breaking news has been fed by around-the-clock news coverage of revolutions, protests, and experts speaking confidently of new waves of democratization. Writing in the *Weekly Standard*, Max Boot predicted that the 2003 invasion of Iraq would be the "moment when the powerful antibiotic known as democracy was introduced into the diseased environment of the Middle East, and began to transform the region for the better."[7] The use of social media during the 2011 Arab Spring took the media's romanticization of democratic transitions to new heights. Tools previously used for sharing cat photos became the agents of democratic change and enabled revolutions to proceed at exceptional speed. It took Egyptians eighteen days to topple Hosni Mubarak's three-decade-old dictatorship. Old-school autocrats could not keep pace with the power of mouse clicks, status updates, and tweets. Aided by technology, utopian possibilities began to trump cold, hard historical realities.[8]

If you doubt the ubiquity of this democracy myth, just glance at the media headlines. Summing up the 2011 Egyptian revolution for the *New York Times*, Thomas Friedman wrote with satisfaction, "This was a total do-it-yourself revolution. This means that anyone in the neighborhood can copy it by dialing 1-800-Tahrir Square."[9] Other headlines celebrated "Twitterlutions" and "Egypt's Revolution by Social Media."[10] Making the ultimate leap, one newspaper pondered, "Could the Internet Unleash Democracy in China?"[11]

Academic scholars have also played a role in perpetuating this lore. Many academics in law and political science have a normative outlook. They replace how things are with how things ought to be, creating false visions of possibilities. For example, several prominent scholars have argued that a revolutionary moment generates, in the words of Bruce Ackerman, "a political constellation that allows for the mobilization of deep and broad support for a liberal constitution."[12] These arguments presume a sane transitional moment, ripe for cool and calm reflection. Transitions, however, are more often marked by passionate and destabilizing conflict.

It's not just distant politicians, reporters, and academics who idealize democratic transitions. Even domestic revolutionaries seeking to overthrow a dictator can operate under a reality-distortion field and become overly confident that democracy alone will solve all problems. But celebrations can prove sadly premature as democratic aspirations meet on-the-ground realities. Revolutionaries rarely see beyond the overthrow of a dictator to the later challenges of creating a "happily ever after." They assume that once the dictator is deposed, life will inevitably improve. After all, if eighteen days is all it takes to depose an entrenched authoritarian such as Mubarak, why should it take much longer to establish a democracy?

Take, for example, the public reaction to Sultan Abdulhamid II's restoration of the Ottoman Constitution.[13] Abdulhamid had suspended the Constitution, along with the Parliament, in 1878. Under pressure from military officers, he restored the Constitution in 1908, unleashing a surge of celebrations unparalleled in the empire's history. According to one observer, "men and women in a common wave of enthusiasm moved on, radiating something extraordinary, laughing, weeping in such intense emotion that human deficiency and ugliness were for the time completely obliterated."[14] The public believed that the Constitution's reinstatement would cure the problems plaguing the empire. A speaker among the crowds confirmed this belief: "Constitution is such a great thing that those who do not know it are donkeys."[15] But, as we'll see in later chapters, the Constitution turned out to be far from the advertised panacea.

This romanticization of civilian-led democratic transitions partially explains why we have a strong distaste for the idea of military coups as potential agents of democratic change. Military coups insert ambiguity and uncertainty into our vision for a smooth, peaceful democratic transition orchestrated by the masses. After all, if democratic transitions proceed as they should in our romantic ideals, why resort to an event as horrid as a military coup to depose a dictator and oversee a transition to democracy?

But we have to ask: What is our point of comparison when we decide that military coups are "horrid" or "bad"? The condition of "bad" rarely exists in the abstract. One thing is bad compared to *something else*. If that something else is the romantic ideal of a democratic transition, then the standard narrative—that military coups are bad for democracy—makes perfect sense.

But the reality, of course, is more complicated than the lore.

Reality Strikes

Here's the hard truth: History is a graveyard for failed democratic transitions. Most attempts at democratization fail, and the establishment of a constitutional democracy is the least likely outcome of an intended democratic transition.[16] The march toward democracy is often painfully slow, and a well-functioning political marketplace does not emerge overnight. Constitutions are not written in succinct 140-character tweets, and nations cannot immediately overcome decades of repression, instability, and inexperience in democratic politics. Most emerging democracies can't cope with the mounting international pressure "to make it happen"—to create effective political institutions, stop sectarian infighting, resolve culture clashes, join international alliances, and get the military out of politics.[17]

Conflict and full-fledged violence often go hand in hand with a democratic transition. Peaceful, orderly transitions to democracy are the exception, not the norm. Ambitious authoritarian leaders with an iron grip on power rarely surrender voluntarily. Faced with a popular opposition, they often dig in rather than give in. Democratic movements can be crushed by a ruthless dictator, or the forces of democracy and dictatorship may become locked in a stalemate with no end in sight. As the nation descends into revolutionary chaos, enthusiasm for democracy can quickly fade. What's more, sectarian tensions controlled under the stronghold of an autocratic leader can detonate when that leader is deposed, generating further instability, if not all-out civil war. The 2003 U.S. invasion of Iraq, to cite one example, unleashed brutal sectarian conflict. Once Saddam Hussein was toppled, the can of worms exploded.

Consider also the attempted democratic transitions that followed the 2011 Arab Spring. In Libya, Gaddafi fought to the bitter end to eliminate what he called the "cockroaches" daring to challenge his rule. He appeared likely to hold onto power until NATO cruise missiles came to the rescue. Gaddafi was eventually overthrown, but the nation soon spiraled into anarchy, as the divergent factions that had coalesced to topple him turned on each other.[18] The country turned into a "basket case" and a breeding ground for al-Qaeda operatives and human traffickers.[19]

Thousands of Libyans died trying to cross the Mediterranean to escape the anarchy at home. A brutal civil war began in Syria, where a dictator relentlessly hunkered down, causing over 450,000 deaths at the time of this writing. Yemen is mired in serious armed conflict, as regional power brokers Iran and Saudi Arabia are settling old debts by aiding opposing revolutionaries. Egypt's experiment with democracy came to a halt when the military deposed President Mohamed Morsi. Even the democratic transition in Tunisia—widely hailed as the most successful of the Arab Spring—teetered on the brink of complete collapse after two opposition leaders were assassinated in February and July 2013, prompting massive protests and economic and social instability.

It's become commonplace to wonder why the Arab Spring has turned into an Arab Fall. But the more puzzling question, given historical experience, is why we were so convinced that the Arab Spring would succeed in the first place.[20]

Even where successful, revolutions can also produce unintended, and potentially dangerous, consequences that challenge the revolutionaries' democratic aspirations.[21] For example, the French Revolution of 1789 overthrew the monarchy and established a republic, but it also eventually brought Napoleon to power as dictator. Only after World War II—150 years after its revolution—did France become a liberal democracy.[22] The Russian Revolution of 1917 that overthrew the tsarist dictatorship likewise began with democratic aspirations but culminated in the establishment of a communist dictatorship. As the French revolutionary Mirabeau warned, "When you undertake to run a revolution, the difficulty is not to make it go—it is to hold it in check." What begins as a democratic transition can easily turn south as antidemocratic forces ride the waves of the revolutionary movement to the establishment of another dictatorship. As in nature, in democratic transitions the fastest predator takes home the fattest prey.

The American Revolution is often cited as the rare example of a successful democratic transition in the eighteenth century.[23] But the American path to democracy was anything but smooth. The United States was not a democracy, at least not by modern standards, when its Constitution was ratified in 1789. Slavery was legal in many states. Women and minorities could not vote. On its march to democracy, the United States fought a disastrous Civil War that claimed over 600,000 lives, experienced a bitter Reconstruction, and adopted several constitutional amendments to expand the electoral franchise. That still wasn't enough. By many accounts the United States did not meet the bare minimum criteria for democracy—free and fair elections with universal adult suffrage—until the Voting Rights Act of 1965 outlawed racial discrimination in voting, nearly two centuries after the colonies broke away from England.[24] And critics continue to identify various dysfunctions in the American democratic process, from gerrymandering, where a political party draws legislative districts to its benefit, to the corrupting influence of big money in elections.

Sober Awakening

When the reality of democratic transitions fails to meet our unreasonably high expectations, we begin the blame game. When the initial successes turn sour, the roadblocks hamper progress, the forward momentum is lost, we shift blame from one institution to the other. We blame the lack of democratic momentum on international meddlers, the inept or corrupt local politicians, the apathetic civil society, the vestiges of the dictatorship, or the military. We hail one politician as a democratic savior, only to condemn him or her the next week. We express constant consternation over the inability of these "backward" societies to deliver instantaneous democratic results. Throughout this roller-coaster ride, our only constant is the homage to democracy and the steadfast commitment to our ideal democratic transition. We believe that there is something wrong with *this* democratic transition because it doesn't fit what we have come to expect.

The history of failed democratic transitions brings us to a sober awakening. War may be hell, but so are most transitions to democracy. There is no easy recipe for democracy and no objective playbook for how to create it. Democratization is a messy process; it involves backstabbing, politics, posturing, greed, instability, and often violence. Democratic development also takes time, despite an epidemic of impatience that tends to affect both domestic and global observers. Attempts to accelerate the process by tugging at it are likely to fail or, worse, backfire.

Nations evolve and democratize in ways that continue to challenge our models and assumptions.[25] Since it remains open to serious debate whether our aspirations even accurately describe how the Western world democratized, we should hesitate before imposing them in starkly different contexts. Even though our own history rebuts it, we cling to the outmoded yet comfortable ideal of the democratic transition. We tend to neglect the bad for the good, recalling the facts that confirm our preconceptions and ignoring those that dispute them. We subject fledgling democracies to stringent standards that most Western nations would have failed a handful of decades ago.

At this juncture the reader may believe that while disputing the lore of democratic transitions, I have fallen to romanticism and nostalgia of my own by naively casting military coups as agents of democratization. But recall that the theory of the democratic coup involves a second-best choice. As later chapters detail, *democratic* as used in the term *democratic coup* does not mean unproblematic. Each mode of democratic transition presents its own set of challenges, and military coups are no exception. Ideally, of course, it would be enlightened civilians—not military leaders—who would depose an authoritarian government and promote, in concert with civil society, the conditions necessary for democratic development. But in many cases civilian institutions are unable or unwilling to enable democracy, leaving the military to take charge as the one-eyed man in the land of the blind.

3

In the Land of the Blind

In the land of the blind, the one-eyed man is king.

—Proverb

Given the numerous challenges that budding democracies face, the question is not why democratic transitions fail. Rather the question is why they succeed at all.[1] What is the glue that makes democracy stick? How does one ensure that an unelected dictatorship does not become, to paraphrase Thomas Jefferson, an elected dictatorship? What actors, laws, and institutions ensure that a new, fragile democracy becomes and remains a constitutional democracy?

Politicians and the Masses

As we saw in the previous chapter, the lore of democratic transitions idealizes civilian political leaders who, in conjunction with civil society, lead their country on a steady march toward democracy. And there are plenty of historical cases that come close to this ideal. Nelson Mandela, South Africa's first black president, oversaw the dismantling of apartheid and a transition to a more pluralistic democracy. Václav Havel, a Czech playwright who spent years in jail for his political activities, played a prominent role in toppling the communist regime in Czechoslovakia and became its first democratic president. Mahatma Gandhi employed nonviolent civil disobedience to free India from the shackles of British colonial rule.

Why can't we routinely rely on the Mandelas, Havels, and Gandhis of the world to enable democratic regime change? As a practical matter, without intervention by the domestic military or a foreign power, civilian leaders may not have the necessary resources to topple a defiant government armed with all the might of an authoritarian state. To be sure, dictators are occasionally overthrown by the masses. In South Korea, for example, protests in 1987 forced the incumbent dictatorship to relent and hold elections. But in many other cases, popular movements by themselves aren't powerful enough to topple an autocracy. A dictator can often nip a democracy movement in the bud before it gathers sufficient popularity to generate meaningful change.

In some cases civilian elites may owe their allegiance to an authoritarian government and remain uninterested in promoting democratic progress. Politicians, bureaucrats, and judges may be ineffective or, worse, serve as blunt instruments of authoritarian rule. The press and civil society may be silenced. It is therefore unsurprising, albeit unfortunate, that most democratic transitions fail. When the glue that makes democracy stick is missing, tyranny becomes inevitable.

Even if civilians manage to depose an authoritarian government, the civilian leaders who assume power may have ulterior, antidemocratic motives. For every Mandela, Havel, and Gandhi, there is a Hugo Chavez, Recep Tayyip Erdoğan, and Vladimir Putin. As James Madison argued, one cannot always rely on enlightened leaders because "enlightened statesmen will not always be at the helm."[2] Madison also famously dismissed the possibility that moral obligations superior to short-sighted self-interest would be sufficient to prevent tyranny: "If men were angels, no government would be necessary. . . . If angels were to govern men, neither external nor internal controls on government would be necessary."[3] At the hands of self-interested politicians and a pliant majority, constitutional limitations on government power can be neglected at will and the rights of the politically weak suppressed.[4]

The One-Eyed Man

Where other paths to democracy have been blocked by a dictatorship, military intervention may be the only way forward. An authoritarian regime extinguishes or significantly stifles the press, political opposition, civil society, and other reformist institutions, but it often leaves the military intact. The armed forces, after all, are necessary for the survival of most nations. As a result the military may be the one-eyed man in the land of the blind—the only available institution relatively independent of the dictatorship and capable of cracking its edifice. What's more, soldiers, properly disciplined and trained to use coercive force, are more capable of translating courage into action than most civilians.[5] As the Oxford economist Paul Collier puts it, "A truly bad government in a developing country is more likely to be replaced by a coup than by an election."[6]

Collier's view is an exception to that of most scholars, who seem reluctant to concede this point. Many intellectuals have a deep-seated yet seldom acknowledged antimilitary bias.[7] They too have been infected with centuries of dogmatic thinking on democratic transitions, which, rather misleadingly, has shunned the military as a relevant actor in moments of democratic change. For the most part, as the political scientist Richard Hamilton explains, "the army, despite its massive size and manifest power, is an institution that is regularly omitted from discussions of macro theory."[8]

Although scholars may be ignorant to the military's role in effectuating regime change, dictators are not. They are well aware that their own military often poses the only credible challenge to their rule. To keep the threats from the military at bay, they appoint loyalists to the top brass, shower them with substantial salaries and benefits, and attempt to keep a tight leash on potential troublemakers among the junior ranks. These strategies reduce the risk of a military coup, but they do not eliminate it.[9]

The historical reality is that the military plays a role in almost all democratic transitions—and that role is often a decisive one. In some cases the military's role is destructive. The military may heed regime demands and crush a budding revolution, as in the case of the 1989 democratic protests in Tiananmen Square. The Chinese soldiers dutifully carried out regime orders to enforce martial law and suppress the protests, massacring hundreds of civilians. Likewise the military in Bahrain sided firmly with the government in the wake of the 2011 Arab Spring and suppressed the revolutionary movement.

But in other cases the military may refuse orders to suppress a popular opposition and instead turn its arms against the regime. Recall the 1974 coup in Portugal.[10] At the time of the coup, the Estado Novo dictatorship ensured that the popular opposition remained too disorganized, socially and politically, to play a primary role in deposing the government. The military offered the only place where individuals could discuss politics relatively free from regime oversight. As the disastrous colonial wars dragged on, the political conversations in the officers' mess increased in frequency and openness, eventually culminating in a democratic coup.

Likewise, in three distinct periods in Turkish history, the military was the only available weapon against an authoritarian government.[11] As I'll discuss later, the military took the lead in rallying against the repression of dissidents under Sultan Abdulhamid II in the early 1900s, forming a representative republic from the ashes of the Ottoman Empire in the wake of World War I, and deposing the authoritarian Democrat Party government in 1960.[12] In all three periods the Turks could credibly ask, "If the army does not do this job, who will?"[13]

Across the Mediterranean, in Egypt, Lieutenant Colonel Gamal Abdel Nasser spoke in similar terms after toppling King Farouk in 1952: "The state of affairs singled out the armed forces as the force to do the job. The situation demanded the existence of a force set in one cohesive framework, far removed from the conflict between individual and classes, and drawn from the heart of the people: a force composed of men able to trust each other, a force with enough material support at its disposal to guarantee swift and decisive action. These conditions could be met only by the army."[14]

Consider also Tunisia, where the 2011 Arab Spring began after a fruit vendor set himself on fire to protest government corruption.[15] Although the events in Tunisia were celebrated as the triumph of the people over a corrupt regime, instigated by the selfless act of this fruit vendor, a closer look at the events reveals an important and decisive role played by the military. In response to rapidly escalating protests against his rule, the Tunisian president Zine el-Abidine Ben Ali ordered the military to open fire on the protesters. If the military had obeyed the order, the Arab Spring would have been over before it even began. But the army chief of staff, General Rachid Ammar, refused to follow Ben Ali's orders. Instead the army turned its arms against the police and the presidential guard, which were shooting at the protesters. According to some accounts, it was General Ammar who forced Ben Ali out, marking the end of a dictatorship that had lasted nearly a quarter century.[16] After Ben Ali fled to the comfort of Saudi Arabia, the military stepped back and let Tunisian civilians take the reins of the democratic transition process.

As the Arab Spring spread from Tunisia to Egypt, a similar scenario played out. After protesters gathered in droves in cities across Egypt, Hosni Mubarak called on the military to intervene. Much to Mubarak's dismay, the military did not share his eagerness to end the protests. Instead of quashing them, the military's presence seemed to enliven the protesters. An army jeep veering toward Tahrir Square was stopped short by a group of demonstrators who frantically asked, "Are you here to shoot us?" The colonel "descended from the vehicle and wrapped his arm around a demonstrator's shoulders and replied: 'You have nothing to fear. We would cut our hands before firing one bullet. Your demands are legitimate. Go ahead and don't turn back.' "[17] If the Egyptian military hadn't sided with the protesters, as the political sociologist Hazem Kandil explains, "it is doubtful that the revolt would have persisted long enough to convince the political leadership to step down."[18]

Decisive Inaction

In these examples and many others I discuss in future chapters, the military played an active role in the democratization process by staging a coup against a dictatorship. In other cases the military's role in the democratic transition is more passive. Military leaders may refuse regime orders to suppress the protests and let the revolution take its course, but without deposing the dictator themselves. Even in these cases, however, the military's role is often decisive. By refusing to step in the way of a popular revolution, the military may allow the uprising to succeed.

In Serbia inaction by the military led to the ouster of its dictator, Slobodan Milošević, in October 2000.[19] Milošević first came to power in the late 1980s, drawing on rising Serbian nationalism and presenting himself as a champion to the oppressed Serbs. He kept the opposition in check through violence, arrests of dissidents, and tight control of the media. He carried his people into war for a "Greater Serbia," committing war crimes, including genocide, during military campaigns in Bosnia, Croatia, and Kosovo. When Milošević lost the popular vote in 2000 to his pro-democracy rival, he contested the election results in a bid to retain his seat. What prompted him to give up his seat, however reluctantly, was the military's withdrawal of support from his government following persistent street protests. Deprived of military backing, Milošević had no choice but to acknowledge defeat.

Consider also the role of the military in Romania's transition to democracy in 1989.[20] At the time, the regime of Nicolae Ceaușescu was one of the most oppressive dictatorships in the world. Endorsing his own brand of communism, Ceaușescu was resolute in his determination to pay off Romania's foreign debt. But the burden of reconciling the balance of these accounts was placed squarely on the backs of every man, woman, and child residing in Romania. In an effort to increase cash flow from the export of foodstuffs, Ceaușescu's government thrust rationing upon the people in 1981. Shortly thereafter, Ceaușescu, who was fanatical about his own dietary habits, claimed Romanians were too fat and introduced the Rational Nourishment Commission to implement a "program of scientific nourishment" designed to limit the country's caloric intake. The rest of the decade was marked by widespread food shortages.

The strict policies and isolationist rhetoric of Ceaușescu galvanized the masses to action. After many years of oppression and hardship, nationwide popular dissent powered the Romanian uprisings of 1989 and embroiled the country in a revolution that overthrew the dictatorship.

But the revolution was made possible only by the withdrawal of the military forces tasked with suppressing the rebellion and protecting the regime. Although the military and police forces initially squared off against the civilian protesters, they were eventually overwhelmed by the tide of discontent and quietly stepped aside to enable the overthrow of the regime in favor of democracy. The minister of defense, Victor Stănculescu, didn't carry out Ceaușescu's order to escalate the repression of civilians.[21] Instead he ordered the armed forces to retreat to the barracks.[22] After Stănculescu's "de facto coup," the Romanian military, similar to its Tunisian counterpart in the 2011 Arab Spring, allowed the civilians to take control of the transition process.[23]

After Stănculescu's defiance of his order, Ceaușescu and his wife fled the capital by helicopter. But they never made it to a safe haven. The pilot, Lieutenant Colonel Vasile Maluțan, landed the helicopter after warning the dictator that it was possibly being tracked by radar and could be shot down. The army arrested the Ceaușescus the same day.

Three days later the regular television broadcast was interrupted by an announcement from a representative of the new provisional government, the National Salvation Front (NSF). The representative declared that, after a trial by "an extraordinary military court" for "particularly grave crimes against Romania," Ceaușescu and his wife had been found guilty of genocide. The punishment was death. By the time the NSF's television announcement aired, the Ceaușescus had already been executed by firing squad. A new provisional civilian government took office and paved the way for Romania's transition to democracy. Although the transition was messy—and at times violent—Romania managed to establish a democracy, joining the ranks of NATO in 2004 and the European Union in 2007.[24]

No Military, No Democracy

Vladimir Lenin was a brutal dictator. But he got one thing right: "No revolution of the masses can triumph without the help of a portion of the armed forces that sustained the old regime."[25] The political theorist Hannah Arendt was similarly firm in her conviction: "Generally speaking, we may say that no revolution is even possible where the authority of the body politic is truly intact, and this means, under modern conditions, where the armed forces can be trusted to obey the civil authorities."[26]

In his groundbreaking book, *Social Origins of Dictatorship and Democracy*, the American political sociologist Barrington Moore Jr. presented his conclusion in four simple words: "No bourgeoisie, no democracy." At the risk of simplicity, the argument in this chapter can also be distilled to four words: "No military, no democracy." The military is the levee that keeps democratic movements at bay to protect a dictatorship. Only if the military breaks can the river of democracy jump the banks.

Although salvation from tyranny may lie with the military, it is easy to overstate this point. The belief that only the military can do the job may serve as a convenient rationalization for replacing the civilian dictatorship with a military one. In Egypt in 1952, for example, the military toppled King Farouk with promises of civilian rule, but the new president, Nasser, quickly consolidated power and established an authoritarian government, as I'll discuss in later chapters.

When we accept the premise that revolutions cannot succeed without the military's express support, or at least its implied acquiescence, then the relevant question changes. The question is *not* whether the military *should* play a role in democratic transitions, as the military almost always does. Instead the question is under what circumstances do militaries support rather than hamper democratic transitions.

Before turning to that question, the next chapter will address a crucial preliminary issue relating to semantics. In this context the words we choose to describe the relevant events can be critical.

4

Hogan's Heroes

I hear nothing, I see nothing, I know nothing!
— Sergeant Hans Schultz, *Hogan's Heroes*
(American television show), 1965–1971

A Game of Taboo

On July 3, 2013, the Egyptian military, led by Minister of Defense Abdel Fattah el-Sisi, toppled Egypt's first democratically elected president, Mohamed Morsi. The overthrow came on the heels of determined and widespread national protests against economic stagnation and power consolidation under Morsi's watch. After assuming power, the military suspended the constitution and appointed an interim government to oversee a fresh set of elections.

We'll return to examine the rich inner dynamics of this military intervention in future chapters. But for present purposes, let's travel six thousand miles away from chaotic Cairo to the relatively calm environment of the Harry S. Truman Building in Washington, D.C. Originally built to house the Department of War, the Truman Building is now home to over eight thousand employees of the State Department. On July 3, 2013, in response to the news of the military intervention and the resulting social and political unrest in Egypt, the State Department took the usual precautions. A travel advisory was issued, and all nonemergency U.S. government personnel and family members in Egypt were evacuated.

After tending to these immediate necessities, State Department officials turned to another pressing question: What do we call this event? The military intervention certainly looked like a coup. After all, the military illegally removed Morsi from power against his will. But here was the rub: Branding the event as a coup would require the United States to suspend all aid to Egypt under a federal law that prohibits the provision of federal aid to a country whose duly elected head of government has been deposed by a military coup.[1] The United States would be bound to cancel, among other financial assistance, the $1.3 billion provided annually to the Egyptian military as part of the 1979 Camp David accords that cemented a peace treaty between Israel and Egypt. The suspension of this aid would jeopardize U.S. relations with the new government of a significant regional ally and produce a host of other collateral consequences. If, on the other hand, the United States declared that the military intervention was *not* a coup, that would bring legitimacy and a powerful endorsement to the military's actions from the paragon of democratic countries.

Stuck between a rock and a hard place, State Department officials chose to walk a middle ground. Specifically they decided to avoid using the "c" word to describe what happened in Egypt. The comedian John Oliver, then a *Daily Show* correspondent, depicted the U.S. government's approach as a game show where State Department officials had to describe the events in Egypt, but if they used the word *coup*, they would lose the game.[2] This delicate balancing act required U.S. diplomats to twist themselves into positions, particularly during press briefings, that even seasoned yogis cannot hold.

Take, for example, a July 8 briefing, where the following exchange took place between a journalist and State Department Spokeswoman Jen Psaki. To make sense of this exchange, a brief primer on the American television show *Hogan's Heroes* is necessary. The show depicts an Allied prisoner-of-war camp in Germany during World War II, where soldiers use the camp to conduct espionage against the Nazis. One of the prison guards, Sergeant Hans Schultz, routinely accepts bribes for turning a blind eye to the prisoners' clandestine activities, often repeating his memorable catchphrase, "I hear nothing, I see nothing, I know nothing!" With that background, let's tune into the State Department briefing that took place five days after the coup in Egypt:

QUESTION: *[To make] a legal determination that a coup happened would require a suspension or cutoff in all non-humanitarian assistance to Egypt, including the 1.3 billion in FMF [foreign military financing]. Is that correct?*

PSAKI: *Well, Matt, because we're not there, we haven't made that determination.*

QUESTION: *I know, but the—that determination would trigger a cutoff or suspension of the assistance; is that correct?*

. . .

PSAKI: *Well, that is—there is a broad legal definition that is applicable in many cases, right, Matt? But we're also looking at what happened here on the ground. There are millions of people on the ground who do not think it was a coup. We factor lots of factors in. We're in the analysis process right now, and I'm not going to get ahead of where that may or may not go.*

QUESTION: *So I just—will you let us know when the heat from the flames of the burning hoops that you're jumping through to avoid taking a position on this get too hot, or will that just be obvious from what you're saying at the podium?*

PSAKI: *Matt, if you're having a good time today, I'll be back here tomorrow. We'll do this again.*

As promised, the semantic tail-chasing continued in a July 26 briefing:

PSAKI: *The law does not require us to make a formal determination—that is a review that we have undergone—as to whether a coup took place, and it is not in our national interest to make such a determination.*

QUESTION: *Okay. Can you explain to me, or to all of us, how it took this crack team of warriors three and a half weeks to come up with a determination that essentially sounds like something that Sergeant Schultz would have said on "Hogan's Heroes," or that we might all know as being the motto that is underneath pictures of three monkeys covering their ears, mouth, and—*

PSAKI: *I am not a big "Hogan's Heroes" fan. (Laughter.) But—*

QUESTION: *Yeah. Well, if you don't get the cultural reference, it's, "I know nothing; I see nothing", and—*

PSAKI: *I understood the monkey reference.*

Yes, State Department briefings are far more entertaining than you imagined. But more important, the quandary that U.S. diplomats faced illustrates the importance of terminology in this context. Throughout this book I employ emotionally charged and contested terms, such as *democracy, authoritarianism, coup d'état,* and *revolution.* To avoid any rhetorical struggles, this chapter will define the key terms that are often misused in popular discourse. Before proceeding, however, a cautionary note is in order.

It's tempting to overemphasize the importance of terminology. Yes, terminology is important, and some lines can be drawn in this field, but be forewarned that there will be ambiguous cases. Although classifications are often appealing in the abstract, the complex reality of a revolution, coup, or democratic transition rarely fits within neatly defined categories. Classifications can oversimplify and mask important nuances. Although I will devote this chapter to terminology, I don't intend to force case studies into classifications where they don't necessarily belong. Rather I will explain when terminology fails to capture reality.

What Is the Military?

The military, also known as the armed forces, is the state institution responsible for defending a nation's borders.[3] A typical modern military comprises the army, air force, and navy, and when I use the term *the military,* I refer collectively to all three services. As we'll see in later chapters, in some coups these three branches will act in unison, but other coups will pit them against each other, with some branches maintaining loyalty to the regime and others disavowing it.

Generally speaking, the military includes rank-and-file soldiers, junior officers, and senior officers. As used in the book, the term *junior officer* includes lieutenants, captains, majors, lieutenant colonels, and colonels. Senior officers make up the military's top brass; they are the generals, admirals, marshals, and the like.

Importantly, the military is a separate institution from the state's security forces. Although journalistic and historical accounts often conflate the military with the security forces, they serve distinct functions.[4] That distinction may become blurred in some cases, but typically the security forces include the police, the political police, and intelligence services. Unlike the military, whose focus is on external threats, these security forces serve as political watchdogs that keep domestic threats at bay. This distinction will be significant in later chapters where I'll discuss why many dictatorships use their security forces instead of their militaries to suppress popular rebellions. As a result many democratic coups end up pitting the military against the internal security forces.

For the military to fulfill its responsibility of fending off external threats, the state must supply the military with the means to use force. This creates a paradox: Guns and tanks are necessary for the military to defend the country, but they can also be turned against the same regime that empowered the military's existence. As the political scientist Peter Feaver puts it, "The very institution created to protect the polity is given sufficient power to become a threat to the polity."[5] Although most nations employ various measures to keep the military subservient to the civilian government, those measures are effective only if the military chooses to follow them.[6] When the military disregards those measures and unleashes its coercive power against the sitting head of state, the result is a coup d'état.

Although I frequently refer to "the military" throughout this book, it would be a mistake to assume that the military is a singular, homogeneous institution. The military tends to display a higher degree of coherence than many other institutions because of its hierarchical command structure. The U.S. Republican Party may be unable to get its Tea Party wing to toe the party line, but inferior military officers usually follow orders from their superiors. Yet even in a military hierarchy there are bound to be opposing factions as well as divisions within and between senior officers, junior officers, and rank-and-file soldiers. For example, as was the case in Turkey in 1960, junior officers may stage a coup without the knowledge or against the explicit directions of their superiors. What's more, the interests of these military officers may change over time. For example, as we'll explore later, what began as an alliance of convenience between the Egyptian military and the Muslim Brotherhood in early 2011 quickly frayed, culminating in a coup against the Muslim Brotherhood's leader, Morsi.

Similarly terms like *civilians, the people,* and *citizens* provide a convenient shorthand, but they need to be used with care. Divisions may also exist among the civilians, as was the case in Egypt following Morsi's ouster in July 2013. Some Egyptians believed the event was an antidemocratic coup that returned Egypt to military rule, but others celebrated the intervention as a triumph of popular will over a defiant political leader.

All of this makes it misleading to speak in a collective manner of "the military's motives" or "the civilians' interests." There is no such thing as a singular "interest" or "feeling" of institutions as complex as the military or collective bodies as diverse as civilians. Rather than glossing over these nuances, I highlight instances of fissures within both the military and civilians. These fissures surely complicate matters, but they also bring richness to the inquiry.

What Is a Military Coup?

What exactly is a military coup, and how does it differ from other methods of regime change? As used in this book, a military coup occurs when the domestic military, or a section of the domestic military, overthrows the sitting head of the state using illegal means.[7]

Under this definition, what was the answer to the question that sent State Department officials jumping through hoops? Was the 2013 intervention by the Egyptian military against Morsi a coup? The answer is yes. The Egyptian military ousted a democratically elected president through the use of illegal and unconstitutional means. That's surely a coup d'état.

Although I focus only on coups staged by the military, coups can also be staged by other entities within the government, including civilian politicians. Consider, for example, a 1992 coup that took place in Peru. President Alberto Fujimori dissolved the Parliament and illegally assumed all of its powers. Although the military supported Fujimori's actions, it was Fujimori himself—not the military—who was calling the shots. As a result the 1992 coup in Peru is an example of a presidential, not military, coup.

The definition of a military coup also excludes regime changes perpetrated by foreign powers. For example, neither the 2003 U.S. intervention in Iraq that toppled Saddam Hussein nor the NATO intervention in Libya in 2011 that resulted in the overthrow of Muammar Gaddafi were coups. To be sure, in staging a coup the domestic military may have the financial and military backing of foreign powers. But I set aside cases of foreign-mandated regime change, as in the case of Iraq and Libya, which raise unique problems compared to the overthrow of the regime by the country's own military.

Popular Revolutions

The definition of a coup ordinarily requires that its perpetrators come from a state institution such as the domestic military. Although many features of coups are also present in revolutions and popular movements, the definition of a military coup excludes these events because they are perpetrated by the masses, not members of the military.[8] As we'll see in the next chapter, however, popular opposition to the regime may precede a military coup.

At this juncture the reader may wonder why we should draw a distinction at all between coups and popular revolutions. If both a revolution and a coup can lead to regime change, why not study the substantive outcome rather than the process by which a nation gets there? There is some merit to this argument, but studying the process is important for two reasons. First, the process has been misunderstood. The standard narrative has assumed that a coup cannot lead to democratization. To correct that misunderstanding, the process must be analyzed. This is why I decided, with some reluctance, to introduce a new term, *democratic coup*, to a field of inquiry that is already overcrowded with jargon in order to draw attention to a neglected process through which democratization can take place. Second, the process is also important because it can affect the substantive outcome. To comprehend how various methods of democratization generate their own unique benefits and challenges, we need to take a hard look at the process.

Although I draw a boundary between military coups and popular revolutions, the boundary is admittedly imperfect. A democratic coup is often preceded by popular opposition—including massive protests—against the incumbent dictator. A broad coalition of support for a democratic coup from diverse segments of society can lead to the emergence of more inclusive political institutions. But as long as the actors that accomplish the overthrow are members of the military, the event is a coup, not a popular uprising. Consider the following example.

Mustafa Kemal's Coup

The ss *Bandırma* was one tough ship. Built in 1878 in Scotland, the forty-seven-meter cargo ship first sailed the seas as a freighter and then served as a mail ship in the Ottoman Empire.[9] During its life the ss *Bandırma* experienced two serious injuries: an accident with a private ship in 1891 and a torpedo attack by a British submarine during World War I.[10] As if to presage the fate of the uprising it would later come to represent, the ss *Bandırma* sank in both incidents but floated again. This small but resilient vessel was exactly what a thirty-seven-year-old military officer in the Ottoman Empire by the name of Mustafa Kemal needed to topple the Ottoman sultan.

On May 16, 1919, Mustafa Kemal boarded the ss *Bandırma* from the empire's capital, Istanbul, and set sail to Samsun on the northern coast of Turkey. His mission: Lead a coup against the Ottoman Empire.

When the ss *Bandırma* departed Istanbul, the empire was in dire straits. At the height of its power the Ottoman Empire had spanned three continents: Asia, Africa, and Europe. But by 1919 it had been demoted to "the sick man of Europe." It had just been crushed alongside Germany in World War I. The Allied Powers partitioned the empire into different sectors and occupied major cities, including Istanbul. The empire agreed to surrender most of its landmass to the Allies. Great Britain would take the Arabian Peninsula and Mesopotamia; France would take Syria and southeastern Anatolia (also known as Asia Minor); Greece would take Izmir and eastern Thrace; and Italy would occupy western Anatolia. An independent Armenian state would be formed in northeastern Anatolia, and an autonomous Kurdistan would be established in southeastern Anatolia.

The Ottoman sultan's complicity in the empire's demise moved Mustafa Kemal to action. Starting in Samsun, where the ss *Bandırma* had left him after a perilous three-day voyage from Istanbul, Mustafa Kemal started touring the battered nation and organizing the remnants of the Ottoman Army against the sultan and the Allies.

But this was no easy feat. To many the uprising that Mustafa Kemal hoped to ignite was an exercise in futility. Before he assumed command, the resistance movement was composed of irregular guerrilla forces. Ammunition, uniforms, and other battle supplies were woefully lacking; soldiers were difficult to recruit among the impoverished and skeptical Anatolian peasants; and the irregular militias were unwilling to accept the discipline of a regular army. These fledgling militias bore a striking resemblance to the men George Washington had been asked to command in 1776 against Great Britain. And it would take a commander of Washington's caliber to transform them into an organized army.

Mustafa Kemal was no stranger to difficulty. He had fought in the First and Second Balkan Wars and the First World War. He had been wounded in the Battle of Gallipoli during World War I by shrapnel, but he cheated death when the shrapnel hit a pocket watch his father had given him, barely missing his heart. But even for the bravest of commanders, the task Mustafa Kemal faced seemed insurmountable. He had managed to create a central army (Kuvayı Milliye) for the resistance, but the newly formed army paled in size, equipment, and experience when compared to the veteran armies of the occupying Allied Powers. Worse yet, Mustafa Kemal's novice army had to confront the Allies on three different fronts: Armenia on the eastern front, Great Britain and Greece on the western front, and France on the southern front. To top it off, Mustafa Kemal was fighting not just the Allied Forces but also the Ottoman Empire, which sided with the Allies throughout the Independence War.

After a series of seemingly miraculous military victories over the course of three years of battle, Mustafa Kemal's army managed to defeat the Allied Forces and the Ottoman Empire. The signing of the Treaty of Lausanne marked the end of the Turkish Independence War and the formation of the modern Republic of Turkey. In 1922 Turkey abolished the position of sultanate, and Vahdettin, who was the Ottoman Empire's last sultan, swiftly fled to England. The Republic of Turkey was officially declared on October 29, 1923, and Mustafa Kemal was elected its first president. He was later given the surname Atatürk (meaning "the father of all Turks") by the Turkish Parliament.

The newly established Turkish state, like many others at the time, was not a full-fledged democracy. Women could not vote. A political party that Atatürk formed, the Republican People's Party (Cumhuriyet Halk Partisi), governed the nation in a single-party framework. Despite attempts to establish a multiparty parliamentary system during Atatürk's presidency, these experiments were all short-lived, as the country repeatedly reverted to the stability of a one-party government.

But the coup laid the foundations for democracy, with a series of swift reforms aimed at democratic progress. The Parliament abolished Sharia courts and Sharia law, replacing it with a system based on the Swiss Civil Code. Under this new civil code, men and women were equal under law, with equal rights in divorce, custody, and inheritance. In 1933 women obtained the right to vote in all elections, long before their counterparts obtained the same right in Western countries like France, Italy, Canada. In 1935 eighteen women were elected to the Parliament. Atatürk was also a fierce advocate of military subordination to civilian authorities. After taking office he required all politicians active in the military to resign from military service. Although he attempted to instill a culture of balanced civil-military relations, these attempts, as we'll see in later chapters, ultimately failed.

Many Turks know this episode in Turkish history by heart. One history teacher after another has taught Turks that their ancestors, under the heroic leadership of their quasi-divine leader, Mustafa Kemal, toppled a broken regime and its allies against all odds and established the modern Turkish state. This was the Turks' David and Goliath moment, one that is celebrated each year through not one but three distinct national holidays: May 19, 1919 (when Mustafa Kemal arrived in Samsun on the ss *Bandırma*), August 30, 1922 (when Turkey emerged victorious in the Independence War), and October 29, 1923 (the official declaration of the Republic of Turkey). To say that the Turks are proud of their success in the Turkish Independence War would be a gross understatement.

There is a significant difference between the standard narrative about the Turkish Independence War and the story I've provided. I described the relevant events as a coup, and, as far as I can tell, I am the first one to do so. The standard narrative assumes the Turkish Independence War was a popular revolution, and many Turks will vigorously dispute my characterization of it as a coup. Classifying the events as a coup does a disservice, many will argue, to the role that the Turkish people played in this transformational moment in their history.

But a close look at the events suggests a more complex reality. Many of the leaders of this "revolution" were soldiers in the Ottoman military disenchanted with the sultan. Undoubtedly the military leadership had significant civilian support, and any military officer worth his salt knows that a coup is more likely to succeed with popular backing. But it was the military leadership that orchestrated the uprising, reorganized the remnants of the Ottoman Army, and turned them against the sultan. Commander Mustafa Kemal's transformation to President Atatürk, and the birth of the modern Republic of Turkey, is more accurately described as a military coup against the sultan, not a popular revolution staged by the masses.

Each society puts its own anthropological spin on history. Turks decided to call their Independence War a revolution because we assume a military coup—stroke of the state—kills nations; it does not give birth to them. But when a dictator is at the helm, a stroke is precisely what the country may need. Coups that accomplish that result—what I call democratic coups—are a different kind of stroke.

5

A Different Kind of Stroke

Those who make peaceful revolution impossible will make violent revolution inevitable.

—John F. Kennedy, address on the first anniversary
of the Alliance for Progress, March 13, 1962

As the Egyptian military prepared to stage a coup on July 3, 2013, I happened to be just across the Mediterranean getting ready for my wedding. My wife-to-be and I were hosting the event in the city of my birth and my wife's favorite destination, Istanbul. Friends and family traveled from near and far, and we spent most of the day getting ready, greeting guests, and trotting around old Istanbul for photographs. Lost in my own reality, I was blissfully unaware of the events taking place in Cairo. Right before I went to bed, I pulled up the *New York Times* on my phone to catch up on the news of the day. As I read the headline, my jaw dropped to the floor: "Army Ousts Egypt's President: Morsi Is Taken into Military Custody."

The coup garnered many strong opinions. I was inundated with questions from reporters during our honeymoon (sorry, honey). As you might recall from earlier chapters, I had written an article titled "The Democratic Coup d'État" in 2012, which featured, among other case studies, the 2011 Egyptian coup against Hosni Mubarak. The reporters who reached out to me after the 2013 coup posed the same questions: Was Morsi's ouster a coup? Was it "good" or "bad" for democracy? Did this event fit within my definition of a "democratic coup"?[1]

Other reporters rushed to their own conclusions. A Turkish journalist writing for the newspaper *Star* suggested that I was partially responsible for what happened in Egypt.[2] The coup leaders, he argued, had clearly followed the steps outlined in my scholarship to legitimate their illegitimate intervention. Notably the newspaper is owned by a wealthy businessman with close ties to Turkey's then-prime minister, Recep Tayyip Erdoğan.[3]

Aside from the highly amusing image of Egyptian generals poring over esoteric law review articles, this argument may seem persuasive at first blush. After all, the generals had staged their coup in the name of saving democracy from President Morsi's tyrannical hands, and my article was about coups that generate democratic regime change. Prime Minister Erdoğan was also moved by this argument. He criticized my scholarship in a public speech, lashed out against the Egyptian military for removing Morsi, and argued that a democratic coup is the same as the living dead: a figment of our imagination.[4]

Was the coup against Morsi a "democratic" coup? To answer that question, we must take a closer look at the operation of democratic coups. So far, in providing brief examples of democratic coups in the context of larger discussions, I have painted with relatively broad strokes. This chapter will slow things down a bit and break down a democratic coup into the following three components:

1. The military overthrows an authoritarian government. Coups that target democratically elected governments are inherently not democratic.
2. After the overthrow of the authoritarian regime, the military supports the transition to democracy and prepares for elections.
3. The transition ends with the free and fair elections of civilian leaders and the military's retreat to the barracks.

In listing these fundamentals my goal is not to create a universal one-size-fits-all theory of democratic coups or an elegant theoretical model disconnected from reality. As I noted, the chaos of a coup d'état rarely fits within neat categories. Coups tend to involve a range of different motivations, actors, and outcomes. The objectives of the military, as well as the outcome of the coup, will often be context-dependent. We will explore these nuances in later chapters, but for now, let me begin with the basics.

The Target

The target of a democratic coup is an authoritarian government. But what exactly is authoritarianism, and how does it differ from democracy? Although this difference is often taken for granted, the boundary between democracy and authoritarianism is blurry and imperfect.[5] As a result most scholars have adopted a spectrum approach to conceptualizing democratic and nondemocratic regimes.[6] If regime types are placed on a one-dimensional spectrum, democracy and authoritarianism would appear at its polar ends.

Democracy

"Democracy" is a term that gets thrown around frequently in both academic and popular discourse, often without careful definition. The word is based on the Greek composite *demos kratos*, or the power (*kratos*) of the people (*demos*). That simple statement conceals considerable variation and conflicting definitions. Rather than adopt a singular definition that can't capture democracy's diverse forms, most academics accept that democracy itself exists on a spectrum. On the polar ends are "procedural democracy" and "liberal democracy." A procedural democracy refers to a regime whose political leaders are elected in free and fair elections with universal adult suffrage. This definition has two dimensions: contestation and participation.[7] Contestation means that candidates freely compete for the contested seat of the incumbent.[8] Participation requires that virtually all of the adult population be allowed to vote.[9] Procedural democracy is the bare minimum required to consider a government democratic.

At the other end of the spectrum is liberal democracy, also called constitutional democracy. This is the democratic theorist's holy grail. Although definitions vary, a liberal democracy ordinarily is a regime with a vibrant political marketplace where multiple parties compete in free and fair elections; the electoral playing field is reasonably level; protection of civil liberties—such as the freedom of press, speech, and association—is high; and government actors generally respect the legal boundaries that restrain them. Even liberal democracies may occasionally violate some of these criteria, but the violations are not sufficiently systematic to fundamentally distort the electoral competition between political parties.[10]

Authoritarianism

Authoritarianism is located at the other end of the spectrum from democracy. The term traditionally refers to a regime whose ruling party has eliminated political, social, and economic pluralism. Political loyalty is valued above the law, corruption is rampant, and abuse of state resources is commonplace. In authoritarian regimes, it is prohibitively difficult to unseat the incumbent party through elections. Regime change is possible only with a revolution, coup, foreign intervention, or pacted transition, where the incumbent regime voluntarily agrees to step down. Modern-day authoritarian regimes include Zimbabwe under Robert Mugabe, Syria under Bashar al-Assad, and Cuba under Fidel and Raúl Castro.

Hybrid Regimes

There are also regimes that lie somewhere between the polar ends of the democracy–authoritarianism spectrum and combine features of both. Scholars have branded these regimes "competitive authoritarianism," "electoral authoritarianism," "semi-authoritarianism," "hybrid regimes," or, more creatively, "Frankenstates."[11] Although definitional differences distinguish these brands,[12] most bear the same hallmark: There are real, competitive elections, but the electoral race is unfair because the incumbents enjoy numerous and substantial advantages compared to their opponents. Incumbents may abuse state resources, harass political dissidents, threaten journalists and opposition politicians, and deny the opposition equal opportunity to air their views on media. As a result incumbents tend to stay in power indefinitely, and a core purpose of democracy—competitive elections and the resulting turnover of government power—becomes significantly impaired.[13] But at the same time, competitive authoritarianism differs from full-scale authoritarianism because elections in competitive authoritarian regimes still provide a real, albeit flawed, method for unseating the incumbents.[14] Although these cases are subject to contestation, modern-day competitive authoritarian or hybrid regimes include Russia under Vladimir Putin, Turkey under Erdoğan, Venezuela under Nicolás Maduro, and Hungary under Viktor Orbán.

The argument of this book should be clear at this point, but it bears repeating: A coup can be democratic only if it topples an authoritarian government. Democratic coups occur only in extreme circumstances, when the use of legal and democratic avenues for deposing an authoritarian leader are futile. As a result a coup staged against a nonauthoritarian government is not a democratic coup under this framework.

What if the coup's target is a competitive authoritarian government, one that is neither fully democratic nor fully authoritarian? Competitive authoritarian governments are *not* legitimate targets of a democratic coup. Many coups have been perpetrated with the ostensible purpose of toppling politicians that military leaders view as corrupt, inefficient, or shortsighted. This pattern has been common in Pakistan, to cite one example, where the military routinely ousts politicians for failing to govern effectively. Those coups fall outside the democratic coup framework because Pakistanis could instead depose incompetent or corrupt politicians by voting them out of office.

A coup is an extreme remedy. Even as a democratic coup cures the authoritarian patient, it has the capacity to generate significant side effects, as we'll explore in later chapters. Therefore the legitimate target of a coup must be defined carefully and narrowly. Only when elections are not a meaningful mechanism for deposing a political leader—because that leader refuses to permit competitive elections—can a coup become a potentially legitimate mechanism for regime change. Although a competitive authoritarian regime rigs the electoral field in favor of the incumbents, elections still remain a viable, albeit difficult, mechanism for replacing incumbent politicians.

Broadening the definition of a democratic coup to include competitive authoritarian regimes as legitimate targets may inspire premature coups. Unless we limit acceptable coups to fully authoritarian governments, the edges can creep inward and exceptions can begin to multiply. What's more, an opposition movement gathering strength to oust the incumbents in a competitive authoritarian system may be nipped in the bud if the military steps in to administer a quick fix. Through overreliance on military coups, the polity may not develop the ability to fight political pathogens on its own. And without that ability, democracy may never fully mature.

In light of this discussion, how do we answer the questions that numerous reporters posed to me: Was the coup against Morsi in July 2013 democratic? Did the generals use my scholarship as a roadmap in staging their coup?

If the generals did reference my articles, they skipped the very first point: A democratic coup begins by toppling an authoritarian government. The government that the Egyptian military toppled, however, was not authoritarian. President Morsi had been elected only a year before in elections that most characterized as free and fair. To be sure, the military responded to the demands of a massive protest movement against an immensely unpopular and defiant president. There was much to criticize about President Morsi's majoritarian governance style, which routinely sidelined the opposition. But speculations aside, there was no indication at the time of the coup that Morsi would refuse to relinquish power upon an electoral loss or that any elections under his government would be rigged, as they were under Morsi's predecessor, Mubarak. If the military had not forcibly removed Morsi, opposition groups may have been able to capitalize on his unpopularity to oust him at the ballot box. The military's preemptive quick fix short-circuited the established democratic procedures and significantly jeopardized the future of Egypt's democracy.

Transition

After a coup deposes an authoritarian government, the military temporarily governs the nation as part of an interim government that rules only until democratic elections of civilian leaders take place. During the transition, the military must oversee a number of housekeeping tasks to prepare the nation for democratic elections. For example, the military may create the infrastructure for political parties to form, organize, and campaign. The military may hold elections for a constituent assembly to draft a new constitution (as did the Portuguese military following the 1974 coup), or it may handpick a group of constitution drafters (as did the Turkish military following the 1960 coup).

One of the most important priorities during the transition is to set a date for democratic elections of civilian leaders.[15] As the political scientists Juan Linz and Alfred Stepan have noted, "the strongest democratic countervailing power to the nondemocratic dynamic of an interim government is free elections with a set date."[16] The promise of elections "presuppose[s] a democratic regime in formation."[17] A fixed date for elections is necessary to create a new marketplace for democratic political actors, organizations, and institutions.[18] Elections can also provide some legitimacy to the interim military government. By setting a date for elections, the temporary military government acknowledges the limited nature of its role and signals that its term in government is, in fact, temporary. For example, the Portuguese military, in a statement issued the day after its 1974 coup, committed itself to holding democratic parliamentary and presidential elections within two years.[19]

To meet the definition of a democratic coup, the military must serve as a relatively neutral caretaker for these elections. Political parties must be able to freely organize, campaign, and compete—with the possible exception of the political party associated with the deposed authoritarian regime. In some cases that party is dissolved following the coup and therefore doesn't participate in the democratic elections—at least not under the same name. For example, following the 2011 coup against the Egyptian dictator Mubarak, political parties were allowed to freely establish themselves and participate in parliamentary elections, but Egypt's High Administrative Court dissolved Mubarak's National Democratic Party for monopolizing power and manipulating elections.[20]

At times the elections may bring to power a former military leader. There is a tendency in both popular and academic commentary to conclude that a regime governed by a politician with a military background is a military dictatorship. But this conclusion is misleading. As long as the election was free and fair, the election of a former military officer who abandons his or her uniform for civilian office doesn't necessarily render the coup nondemocratic. France under Charles de Gaulle was not a military dictatorship, nor was the United States under George Washington, even though both men had served their country in uniform. It's only where the coup produces a military regime run by an unelected group of officers, rather than freely elected by the people, that the coup becomes nondemocratic.[21]

In democratic coups, elections tend to happen within a few years. A military determined to transfer power to democratically elected leaders typically wants to get out of the unfamiliar business of governing a country and get back to what it knows best: defending the nation from external threats. For example, the Turkish and Portuguese militaries, which staged democratic coups in 1960 and 1974, respectively, both returned power to democratically elected leaders within two years.

Outcome

Coups against dictatorships can be categorized into two admittedly simplified groups: those that produce democratic regime change and those that do not.

The first type of coup—which, for ease of reference, I call the "nondemocratic coup"—conforms to our preconceptions of military coups as antidemocratic events. Coup leaders replace the incumbents with military officers, but the dictatorial form of government remains unaltered. In a nondemocratic coup, the objective of the military officers is to concentrate power in their own hands and rule the nation indefinitely as dictators. Prominent examples include Muammar Gaddafi's overthrow of the Libyan regime and Augusto Pinochet's coup in Chile.

The second category of military coups against dictatorships produces a different outcome. These coups overthrow an authoritarian regime and catalyze structural regime change by facilitating fair and free democratic elections.

A coup that fails to produce at least a procedural democracy is not democratic under my definition. I considered whether more advanced forms of constitutional or liberal democracy should serve as the metric. But I settled on fair and free elections as the proper outcome because constitutional democracies don't emerge overnight. They can take decades—even centuries—to develop, particularly in countries that have suffered through decades of dictatorship. Although the rather minimalist form of democracy that is procedural democracy can't be a panacea to all societal ills, I use it as the baseline because almost all democracies begin here.

In the case of a democratic coup, the regime type that emerges can be viewed as a procedural democracy with an asterisk. Although military leaders relinquish power to civilians following free and fair elections, they may reserve legal and political prerogatives for themselves to perpetuate their influence even after they retreat to the barracks. For example, the military may retain autonomy over its budget, obtain a veto power over the appointment of the secretary of defense, or establish a loyal constitutional court to strike down laws and regulations inconsistent with the military's interests even after it gives up power to civilians. The procedural democracy that emerges from a military-led democratic transition may therefore look slightly different than its civilian-led counterpart. Although the civilians may be in charge after the military exits politics, the military can still possess authorities that, in some cases, impede long-term democratic development.

Later chapters will take a hard look at the aftermath of a democratic coup. Like any mode of democratic transition, a democratic coup poses a unique set of challenges to a budding democracy, and those challenges can be formidable. A democratic coup may produce only a fragile democracy that wears thin over time and invites further coups by a powerful military armed with legal and constitutional prerogatives. In other cases a procedural democracy may blossom into a robust, liberal democracy, with the civilians emerging triumphant over the military.

The categorization of a coup as democratic is inherently retrospective. Democratization is not the inevitable outcome in coups that begin with the overthrow of a dictatorship. A coup may start out on a democratic path, but stagnate. Actions undertaken with the expectation of democratic progress can produce the opposite. Military leaders who tear down an authoritarian government with the promise of democracy may be less than sincere in their aspirations; they may become drunk with power and grow reluctant to relinquish it. For example, Chile's Pinochet staged his coup in democratic terms, declaring that he was taking upon himself "the moral duty of deposing the illegitimate government."[22] Not everyone bought this line, of course, and subsequent events exposed Pinochet's initial promises for the lies they were. As this example suggests, a coup cannot be declared democratic until free and fair elections are held and military leaders transfer power to elected civilians. Although several factors can influence the democratic path of a coup—and I analyze these in later chapters—one can conclusively determine whether a coup is democratic only at its end, not its beginning.

Having provided a broad overview of democratic coups, I'll now take the reader on a chronological journey through the life of a democratic coup, beginning with the military's overthrow of a dictator. The next part will explore why militaries stage democratic coups and betray the dictatorships they are supposed to defend. Along the way I'll explain why the motives of Julius Caesar's assassins shed light on the intentions of soldiers who topple dictatorships, why garrisons that doubled as pig farms became the breeding grounds for the Romanian military's discontent with the Ceaușescu regime, how the Egyptian military threw in with the Muslim Brotherhood before deciding to throw them out, and why King James II's own army and daughter abandoned him in his hour of need.

PART TWO

BRUTUS AND CASSIUS

Et tu, Brute?

—Julius Caesar, in Shakespeare's *Julius Caesar*

On October 6, 1981, President Anwar Sadat of Egypt raised his head to gaze upon his shiny new military jets thundering across the Cairo sky.[1] The scene was the annual victory parade that celebrated Egypt's crossing of the Suez Canal during the 1973 war with Israel. This parade was to be the most illustrious of its kind and serve as a testament to Sadat's achievements during his ten years in office. It would showcase brand-new weapons acquired from Western allies, signifying Egypt's rapprochement with the West following two decades as a Soviet ally. Endless columns of soldiers marched in unison and saluted Sadat, their supreme commander, as he stood next to high-ranking state officials and foreign dignitaries.

As Sadat was admiring his new jets, an armored vehicle broke away from the parade and sped toward the reviewing stand. Sadat recoiled in shock as four assassins leaped out of the vehicle and began lobbing grenades and firing rifles in his direction. In forty seconds Sadat was dead.

During the assassination, Sadat's vice president, a former commander of the air force named Hosni Mubarak, was also wounded but escaped death. Following Sadat's death, Mubarak automatically assumed the presidency. He would go on to become the longest-serving president in Egypt, completing nearly thirty years in office until a coup d'état removed him from power in February 2011.

Mubarak was a typical dictator. His party, the National Democratic Party (NDP), dominated the government throughout his term in office, consistently winning landslide majorities in the People's Assembly. Mubarak tolerated little political pluralism and relied on repressive and fraudulent measures to silence opposition voices and keep his competition at bay. He routinely denied the opposition access to broadcast media and other campaign resources, shut down television stations, forced critical talk shows off the air, and pushed opposition journalists out of their jobs. These strategies effectively paralyzed the opposition parties' efforts to publicize their views. Where cutting off access to campaign outlets wasn't enough, the NDP jailed opposition leaders. For example, immediately before the 1995 elections, eighty-one members of the Muslim Brotherhood were imprisoned on trumped-up charges of inciting violence to preclude their participation as independent candidates in the upcoming elections.

The NDP's repressive and fraudulent electoral practices led to widespread apathy toward parliamentary elections. Although all adult citizens were eligible to vote, they viewed the NDP's victory as a foregone conclusion. As a result few bothered to vote. Voter turnout for the 2010 parliamentary elections—the last before Mubarak's fall—was a meager 27 percent.[2]

In addition to manipulating legislative elections, the Mubarak regime also stifled the opposition in presidential elections. Elections for president took place by referendum every six years for a single candidate (Mubarak) until 2005, when multicandidate elections were instituted in response to domestic and foreign pressure. Although opposition presidential candidates were permitted to run, Ayman Nour—the distant second-place finisher after Mubarak, with 7.3 percent of the vote—was convicted of falsifying government documents and sentenced to five years' imprisonment. Nour's conviction sent a loud and clear message to other presidential candidates: Stay away.

Throughout his thirty years in office, Mubarak kept an emergency law in place. The law permitted arbitrary arrests and searches, indefinite detention without trial, censorship, and trials of civilians by military tribunals, which were infamous for handing out swift and severe punishments with few procedural safeguards. The emergency law also prohibited gatherings of more than five people—an extraordinary restriction on the freedom of association. In accordance with this law, the Mubarak regime jailed thousands of opposition figures, dissident journalists, and ordinary citizens. By 2010 Egypt had an estimated seventeen thousand political prisoners.

Mubarak's rule is often characterized—misleadingly—as a military dictatorship. It was not. Although Mubarak had previously served in the military, as Hazem Kandil convincingly argues, during Mubarak's reign Egypt "decisively evolved from a military to a police state."[3] Located a few minutes' walk from the U.S. Embassy in Cairo, the Interior Ministry oversaw this police state. The Ministry included many branches, including the intelligence services, the paramilitary Central Security Forces, and the regular police. The

Interior Ministry enjoyed a budget of billions of dollars and wielded equally enormous clout. Writing in 2010 the journalist Adam Shatz observed, "Very little of consequence gets done without the ministry's agreement: the appointments of university professors, judges and journalists all require approval from the ministry's security officers; so does anyone who wants to set up an NGO, a school or a television station."[4] Even military officers were placed under constant surveillance to detect and eliminate politicized elements that might pose a threat. In 2010 the longtime speaker of the Parliament, Fathi Sorour, summed up the Interior Ministry's power in the following terms: "I have worked with the president for 25 years, but lately I felt that the Interior Minister was running the country."[5]

The evolution of Egypt into a police state had begun under Mubarak's predecessors. In 1977, four years before Mubarak became president, the size of the paramilitary Central Security Forces rapidly increased from 100,000 to 300,000. In 1979 alone the Central Security Forces were provided with 153,946 tear-gas bombs, 2,419 automatic weapons, and 328,000 bullets. Sadat prioritized policemen rather than military officers in the appointment of provincial governors.

The expansion of police powers came at the expense of the military. Colonel Muhammed Selim summarized the sentiment of his colleagues in the following terms: "We understood that the general strategy was to weaken the army and strengthen the police force. . . . We lived to see the day when the interior minister became the most powerful man in Egypt. . . . We were quickly becoming dispensable. And there was nothing we could do about it."[6]

By the time Mubarak took office in 1981, the balance of power in Egypt had tilted decisively toward the security institutions. From Mubarak's perspective, the security institutions were loyal and reliable—precisely what a dictator needed to remain in power. So he continued to fortify the powers of his reliable allies. The size of the police force alone skyrocketed from 150,000 in 1974 to more than 1 million in 2000. Overall, during the last decade of Mubarak's rule, the entire security apparatus comprised approximately 2 million people in a population of approximately 80 million.

Mubarak's massive security apparatus had its hands full. It managed the regime's daily repression activities, including screening applicants for membership in the NDP, investigating and intimidating citizens, and rigging elections to guarantee victory for the NDP. As Shatz reported in 2010, "The average Egyptian can be dragged into a police station and tortured simply because a police officer doesn't like his face. The tortures to which Egyptians are subjected in police stations have been well documented and include electric shocks to the genitals, anal rape with sticks, death threats, suspension in painful positions and 'reception parties,' where prisoners are forced to crawl naked on the floor while guards whip them to make them move faster."[7]

Rising corruption and political repression rendered the regime increasingly dependent on the Interior Ministry. As a result the security forces began to perceive themselves, in the words of a security chief in 2011, as the "masters of the country." These masters had a symbiotic relationship with authoritarianism: The authoritarian state wouldn't exist without the Ministry, and the Ministry wouldn't exist without the authoritarian state.

While top regime officials and members of the security apparatus increased their clout and wealth, much of the public suffered. A popular saying in Egypt was "Anyone who hasn't begged in the time of Mubarak will never beg." Mubarak and his family carefully nurtured a wealthy business elite at the expense of other citizens. Although Egypt's GDP increased from $92.4 billion to $187.3 billion between 2000 and 2009, much of this increase accrued to corrupt regime officials and their cronies. To cite one example, Interior Minister Habib al-Adly and his immediate family owned "nine villas, seven apartments, [approximately seventy-eight acres] of agricultural land, thirteen construction sites, a shopping mall in Sharm el-Sheik, and four Mercedes automobiles."[8] In 2006 the World Bank reported that nearly half of the Egyptian population lived on less than $2 a day. In 2010 the estimated unemployment rate stood at roughly 26 percent.

Many expected Mubarak to remain in office until his death. At that point power would presumably pass to his son and heir-apparent, Gamal Mubarak, whom he had been priming to be the next pharaoh of Egypt.

On January 25, 2011, inspired by the revolts that toppled President Zine el-Abidine Ben Ali in nearby Tunisia, thousands of Egyptians protested across the nation. In Cairo the protest began symbolically in front of the Interior Ministry, located three blocks away from the aptly named Tahrir (Liberation) Square. The demonstrations were largely nonideological, and the protesters hailed from all facets of Egyptian society. Women and men, Muslims and Christians, secularists and Islamists, the poor and the wealthy all joined hands across Egypt. The date, January 25, coincided with Egypt's National Police Day, which commemorates the police officers killed or wounded during their resistance on January 25, 1952, to the British troops that had occupied the Suez Canal city of Ismailia. But by the time of the 2011 uprising, the police had transformed from national heroes into the dictatorship's reviled weapon of choice. The protesters were clear in their

demands: "The people want to topple the regime" was the revolution's unifying slogan. President Mubarak did his best to portray the crowds as a few,
unthreatening rabble-rousers. In reality they were anything but.

As the protesters grew in number and fervor, Mubarak called in the black-
clad riot police, notorious for their brutal repression tactics. First came the
tear gas. This weapon had little effect on the determined protesters, who had
learned from their Tunisian counterparts that gas masks and vinegar would
mollify its adverse effects.[9] Tear gas was eventually replaced with rubber
bullets, and rubber bullets were replaced with real bullets. The riot police
entered Tahrir Square on camel and horseback and opened fire on the protestors. The bullets from the ground were accompanied by Molotov cock-
tails and sniper fire from atop nearby buildings. The government shut off
the Internet and disrupted mobile service to disable the protestors' primary
lines of communication: Facebook, Twitter, and cell phones. Security forces
even enlisted an unlikely ally—prison inmates—to counter the protesters.
They opened the gates to numerous prisons and let convicted criminals
roam freely in city streets, hoping that aroused criminals would terrorize the
citizens and force the people back into their homes.

Mubarak also stirred up a feeble pro-regime movement. Government-
owned media launched a "campaign of love for the president," and Mubarak
organized his own demonstrations in support of his rule. However, none
of these measures was sufficient to disperse the defiant protestors. "Leave,
leave," they continued to chant, "Down, down with Mubarak."

For Mubarak, the worst was yet to come. With the police forces unable
to handle the hundreds of thousands gathered in Tahrir Square, Mubarak
called on the military to intervene. At this point the script should have been
predictable: The military would enter the square and clear out the protesters,
and life in this authoritarian country would go back to business as usual. The
military once counted Mubarak among its ranks (he served as commander
of the air force), and the military institutions had supported him during his
three decades in office. But something went wrong. The expected script was
turned on its head.

Recall that there was no love lost between the Egyptian military and the
security forces. The protests in Tahrir Square pitted these hostile institutions
against each other, as military vehicles moved as a shield in front of the protesters engaged in a fight with the Egyptian riot police. The defense minister
made it clear to Mubarak that "The soldiers are not going to strike against
demonstrators; . . . they are there to protect, not assault them."[10] As the political economist Tarek Osman explains, "For many Egyptians, the appearance

of the army's tanks and armored vehicles in the streets of Cairo, Alexandria, and other cities brought a sense of security. Unlike the police, the army was highly revered and respected by the people."[11] The rank-and-file soldiers in Tahrir Square were primarily conscripts who serve one to three years in the military before returning to civilian life. These soldiers were well aware that their friends, relatives, and neighbors were among the protesters that the government had ordered them to disperse.[12]

One of the protesters told me during interviews I conducted in Egypt that the crowds erupted in celebration at the sight of the first military tank that entered the square. With the soldiers' consent, the crowds drew anti-Mubarak graffiti on military tanks. The protesters began to express hopes that the military, having refused to turn its arms on the people, would instead turn its arms on the Mubarak regime and stage a coup d'état. In what must have been a first in world history, a well-known opposition leader, Mohamed ElBaradei, expressly called for a military coup on Twitter: "I ask the army to intervene immediately to save Egypt."[13]

Confronted with growing numbers of protesters and an astonishingly defiant military, Mubarak implemented cosmetic measures as an appeasement. He fired his cabinet and appointed Omar Suleiman, the intelligence chief, as his vice president. But that did little to mollify the crowds, who merely added Suleiman to their resignation chants. Mubarak then promised to step down following presidential elections in September and to appoint a committee to propose constitutional amendments, but the protesters, all too familiar with his broken vows, refused to relent.

When Mubarak announced that he would give a televised speech on Thursday, February 10, the crowds widely expected him to use that venue to resign. But a defiant Mubarak appeared instead and vowed to finish his term as president, promising to hand over only the functions, but not the title, of the presidency to Vice President Suleiman. Mubarak's stubborn hold on power enraged the crowds in Tahrir Square, sending a million Egyptians onto the streets of Cairo.

On Friday, February 11, the sign of hope that the crowds had been awaiting came in the form of a communiqué from the military, declaring that it was intervening to protect the country and "sponsor the legitimate demands of the people." The military announced "that [it]—not Mr. Mubarak, Mr. Suleiman or any other civilian authority—would ensure the amendment of the Constitution to 'conduct free and fair elections.'"[14] According to the communiqué, democracy would be established "within defined time frames," and at the end of the transition process the military would hand off its authority to a "free democratic community." The military leadership affirmed its commitment to repeal the much-despised emergency law "as soon as the current circumstances are over" and promised immunity for the protestors, whom it called "the honest people who refused the corruption and demanded reforms." Hours after the release of the communiqué, Vice President Suleiman announced that Mubarak had resigned and the Supreme Council of the Armed Forces—the body of Egypt's most senior military officers—had assumed power.[15]

The initial reaction to the military coup was ecstatic. The crowds "hugged, kissed, and cheered the soldiers, lifting children on tanks to get their pictures taken."[16] The soldiers likewise honored the protesters by attaching to their tanks photos of the protesters killed during the revolution. Some soldiers relinquished their posts to join the crowds in celebration.

In the words of a popular chant in Tahrir Square, the people and the army were "one hand."

After the corrupt dictator was toppled, then came his punishment. Mubarak was charged with corruption and ordering the Egyptian riot police to fire on the protesters during the uprising. His sons, Alaa and Gamal, were also arrested and charged with corruption.

I was in Cairo on August 3, 2011, the historic first day of Mubarak's trial. This was a rare occasion when an Arab dictator was scheduled to be tried by his own people. In the days leading up to the trial, many Egyptians were skeptical that Mubarak would even appear in court. He had made no public appearances in the nearly six months since the coup. Rumors were widespread around Cairo that the ruling military was reluctant to punish him and would see to it that he evaded a criminal trial.

A convention center in downtown Cairo was initially selected to host Mubarak's trial, but for safety reasons the trial was moved to the outskirts of the city, to a police academy that ironically once bore Mubarak's name. On the day of the trial, the streets of Cairo resembled a movie set: They were eerily barren; the crowds had emptied, and the ordinarily unbearable traffic seemed almost sane. I walked in downtown Cairo and saw Egyptians crowded into stores to watch the trial of the century on TV. The normally persistent storekeepers barely noticed me when I entered one of the stores to observe the trial with the locals.

When Mubarak appeared in court on a stretcher in a metal cage, many of the locals erupted in celebration. He was accompanied by his two sons, who were both prominently carrying the Quran. Some viewed this as a cheap trick, but others considered it a sign that the sons, despite their not-guilty pleas, were repenting. One local pointed out to me that Mubarak had been picking his nose throughout the trial—a sign that, despite all appearances, the impervious latter-day pharaoh of Egypt was perhaps human after all. Some thought Mubarak's frail appearance on a stretcher was a ruse, designed to arouse the sympathy of the Egyptian public. They despised what they viewed as the special treatment he had been receiving in detention and wanted him to be treated as an ordinary citizen (or, according to one local, "worse than an ordinary citizen").

But not all Egyptians had the same visceral reaction to Mubarak. Surprisingly, several locals felt sorry for him, despite acknowledging that he was a corrupt dictator under whose reign the Egyptian people languished. Some pointed to his old age and others to his service—however corrupt—to the Egyptian nation. Perhaps the patriarchal Egyptian society had viewed Mubarak, despite all his wrongdoings, as the father of their nation for three decades.

After a series of trials and appeals, Mubarak and his two sons were eventually convicted of corruption and given prison sentences. Gamal and Alaa were later released, but, at the time of this writing, Mubarak remains in detention in a military hospital.

Captivating as it is, Mubarak's downfall is not the most celebrated story of a dictator toppled by his once-loyal compatriots. That honor belongs to Julius Caesar. In 44 BC, on the Ides of March, Caesar was stabbed twenty-three times by members of the Roman Senate. The assassination followed Caesar's appointment as *dictator perpetuo*, or dictator in perpetuity. Among the assassins was Caesar's good friend and protégé, Marcus Junius Brutus. Brutus betrayed Caesar because his loyalty to the people of Rome trumped his loyalty to Caesar. "Not that I love Caesar less," Brutus declared in Shakespeare's depiction of the events, "but that I love Rome more."[17]

Contrast Brutus's altruism to the less palatable motivations of his co-assassins. For example, Gaius Cassius Longinus, one of the most active in the conspiracy, was driven by a longing for revenge. He was deeply troubled that Caesar had appointed his junior, Brutus, to the governorship of Syria, and Caesar's murder was his vengeance.[18]

We know something about why Brutus and Cassius betrayed Caesar. But why did the Egyptian military support Mubarak during his three decades in office and then abandon him in his hour of need? Was the military like Brutus, moved primarily by altruism and a commitment to the greater good of their compatriots? Or were the coup-makers more like Cassius, with their own self-serving reasons for bringing down Mubarak?

Although this part began with recent events in Egypt, these questions apply more generally: Why do militaries support dictatorships? And more paradoxically, why do militaries turn their arms against a tyrant and stage a coup?

Before I proceed, one caveat is necessary. Recall that, despite all appearances to the contrary, the military is not a single, monolithic beast. Although the military is more cohesive than most other institutions because of its hierarchical command structure, each military is composed of thousands of individuals—senior officers, junior officers, and rank-and-file soldiers—with divergent interests. Some members of the military may defend the authoritarian regime, while others may defect. In addition, the interests of these individuals are not static and may vary over space and time. The same officer may support the dictatorship one day and turn against it the next. Just as one cannot come up with a singular, unifying reason for why Caesar was betrayed—there were nearly sixty conspirators involved—it's impossible to discern a singular reason for why the military supports, or abandons, a dictatorship.

As a result my argument is not that militaries have an inherent interest in supporting dictatorships or an inherent interest in turning their arms against them. There is no such thing as *the* "inherent interest" of an institution as vast and complex as the military. Rather my aim is to explain why the military may support dictatorships if and when they do so and why militaries turn their arms against dictatorships if and when they do so. Inevitably, numerous interests will be at work and animate military officers in their decision to support or abandon a dictator.

Friends with Benefits

*Friendship is but another name for an alliance with the follies and the mis-
fortunes of others. Our own share of miseries is sufficient: why enter then as
volunteers into those of another?*
—Thomas Jefferson, letter to Maria Cosway, Paris, October 12, 1786

Put simply, militaries will tend to support dictatorships when their interests are
aligned. Even where the military doesn't share the dictator's ideology, military
officers may hold their nose and support him if the dictator is willing to protect
their interests. Support can be active or passive. The military can actively support
an authoritarian government by taking affirmative steps to fend off domestic and
foreign threats. Support can also be passive, as when the military merely tolerates
the dictatorship and refrains from toppling the regime even though the opportunity
presents itself.

The military's loyalty can be purchased. The dictator may shower the armed
forces with social and financial perks, such as salary increases, better training, modern equipment, and promotions.[1] Particularly when the rest of the population is
deprived of similar benefits, soldiers may have significant incentives to support a
regime that treats them well. For example, in Kenya, President Daniel arap Moi provided land grants to military officers in the 1980s to ensure their support. Following
a 1982 coup attempt against his government, he granted generous salary increases
amounting to 30 percent for officers and 15 percent for enlisted soldiers.[2]

Take also the Egyptian military. Military industries constitute somewhere
between 5 and 15 percent of Egypt's economy, which Egyptians refer to as the "military economy." The military has enormous political and economic privileges and
owns vast commercial interests. In many respects it functions like a civilian business,
engaging in real estate development, engineering, and tourism and running its own
social clubs and shopping centers. The revenue from these extracurricular activities goes directly into the military's budget without any state oversight. Egyptian
officers are regularly trained in the United States and participate in joint military
exercises with American soldiers. Their arsenal includes state-of-the-art equipment,
from M1A1 Abrams tanks to F-16 Falcons. Officers also enjoy benefits—such as

officers' clubs, discounted apartments and vacation homes, food subsidies, and a boat on the Nile for the air force—that are beyond the reach of most Egyptian citizens. What is more, the military receives $1.3 billion in annual aid from the United States as a dividend of the Camp David peace agreement between Egypt and Israel.

The military has an obvious interest in preserving these substantial privileges. And for most of his rule, Mubarak had no intentions of interfering with these privileges, which provided the military with significant incentives to support his regime. These benefits accrued in large proportion to the military's top brass—who, unlike the junior officers or the rank and file, enjoyed lavish salaries and other benefits— giving them a stronger incentive to back Mubarak. During the 2011 protests against Mubarak's rule, the military leadership gave him every benefit of the doubt, whereas the lower-ranked soldiers appeared to sympathize with the protesters more readily.

Some dictators go beyond simply providing financial and social perks to the military and engage in active social engineering to ensure its loyalty. Many dictators routinely purge officers who pose a threat of disloyalty and promote those with organic links to the regime—through race, ethnicity, community, religion, or otherwise.[3] For example, after taking office in 1978, President Moi of Kenya transformed the ethnic makeup of the military to ensure that it was dominated by his ethnic group, the Kalenjin.[4] As a result of his transformation efforts, by the mid-1990s the Kenyan Army was "Kalenjin at the bottom, Kalenjin at the middle, and Kalenjin at the top."[5] Likewise Saddam Hussein favored Sunnis in military promotions since he was a Sunni himself and felt threatened by the Shias in his majority-Shia country.[6] Hafez al-Assad, who ruled Syria from 1971 until 2000, ensured that every combat unit was commanded by officers from the Alawi sect of Shia Islam, tied to him by "blood or bonds of allegiance."[7] The military units stationed around big cities and charged with the defense of the dictatorship were also primarily staffed by Alawites.[8]

The military may also remain loyal to a dictatorship where the regime is strong and stable. Militaries rarely stage coups against stable governments. Only when a dictatorship begins to wobble does a coup become a possibility. The reasons are simple. Coup attempts against stable regimes are quite risky because they are more likely to fail. If and when they fail, the attempted coup makers can expect the worst: discharge from service, prison, torture, or outright execution for treason. A failed coup can also prompt the government to reduce military autonomy and implement greater oversight to coup-proof the institution. For example, following a failed coup in Turkey in July 2016, the government swiftly moved to arrest tens of thousands of soldiers and military officers and shut down prominent military academies, including the 171-year-old Kuleli Military High School in Istanbul.

In addition, most militaries have an intrinsic interest in preserving stability, not disrupting it.[9] An unstable regime distracts the military from its primary task: defending the nation from external threats. The toppling of a stable regime may usher in chaos, violence, and even civil war, which can drag the military into a domestic quagmire or render the nation vulnerable to foreign threats. Where the dictatorship is sufficiently powerful, the military will often yield to the regime to preserve stability.

Stability in authoritarian states may arise in part from domestic support for the regime.[10] For example, many monarchies, such as Saudi Arabia, rely primarily on family and kinship to perpetuate their rule against domestic resistance.[11] They base their power on historical or religious grounds, which serve as a substitute for adopting the trappings of the democratic, modern nation-state.[12] These historical or religious claims may bolster popular support for the regime and ensure the perpetuation of monarchical rule. Economic success can also create stability. Well-fed populations and well-paid military officers rarely bite the dictatorial hand that feeds them.

In some cases divisions within the military may also hamper any coup attempts against a dictator. As noted earlier, some officers may support the dictatorship while others oppose it, producing a deadlock within the military. Even when the officers are relatively united in their opposition to the regime, they may bicker over how to stage the transition and who will lead it. These internal squabbles may cause the officers to spend their time and energy fighting each other rather than the dictatorship.

External threats may also motivate the military to side with a dictator. In some cases the military may face retaliation by a foreign invader if it decides to topple the incumbent dictatorship. France, for example, is famous for guarding the rulers in its ex-colonies against attempted coups.[13] In 1996 France intervened when the military in the Central African Republic rebelled against President Ange-Félix Patassé after he failed to pay military salaries and attempted to amend the constitution to increase his powers. Although the French were successful in protecting Patassé in 1996, the military managed to topple him in 2003, after his abysmal economic performance and continuous attempts to circumvent the rule of law completely undermined his domestic legitimacy.

This brings us to the more difficult questions: Why might a military that once supported a dictatorship turn against it? Why would a military voluntarily choose to abandon the comfort and certainty of a dictatorship for the uncertain and messy reality of democracy?

With Friends Like These

For Brutus, as you know, was Caesar's angel:
Judge, O you gods, how dearly Caesar loved him!
This was the most unkindest cut of all

—Shakespeare, *Julius Caesar*

Relationships are fickle things. They have a tendency to change, for better or for worse. What begins as an alliance of convenience between the dictatorship and the military can atrophy over time. When that happens, the same military that supported a dictatorship may turn against it.

At the risk of oversimplifying matters, let's create a caricature of two military officers: Officer Brutus and Officer Cassius. Officer Brutus is the warrior with a soul. He seeks to depose a dictator because it's the right thing to do ("for the love of Rome"). This altruistic officer puts the welfare of society above his own and aids his fellow citizens in their hour of need by toppling a dictator. He risks everything—including his own power and prestige—to install the beginnings of democracy. In contrast, Officer Cassius is motivated by self-interest. He sides with the dictatorship when it's in his interests, but he won't hesitate to turn against the dictator when the dictator no longer serves him.

It's tempting to believe that the Officers Brutus of the world are responsible for toppling dictators. And certainly there are bound to be some heroic officers with the Brutus mindset who act primarily out of altruism in turning against an autocrat. Yet to insist that altruism is the overriding motivation for a military's decision to topple a dictatorship is to ignore reality.

Some readers may believe that I am presenting an overly cynical take on military behavior. But if these Brutus-like soldiers were the driving forces in democratic coups, one dictator after the next would be toppled by domestic militaries. If altruism and the interests of society reigned supreme, the Egyptian military, to cite one example, would not have turned a blind eye to decades of brutal repression and widespread corruption under Mubarak's rule. If there were any Officers Brutus in the Egyptian military, they were overwhelmed for three decades by the Cassius-like majority. Just as Cassius tolerated Caesar until Caesar denied him that coveted governorship in Syria, the Egyptian military stood by Mubarak's side until Mubarak no longer served its interests.

To be sure, the contrast between Cassius and Brutus is somewhat overstated. Many soldiers won't fit squarely within either of these two camps and may be motivated by a combination of interests—partially altruistic and partially self-centered—in toppling a dictatorship. And for some self-proclaimed altruists, Brutus-like positions declared for public consumption may be convenient window dressing for a more selfish reality lurking beneath the surface. Although the Cassius-Brutus caricature oversimplifies matters, it's a useful way of illustrating the competing interests at work and explaining why the Cassius mindset often predominates.

Paradoxically, then, democracy promotion is often not the principal driver of democratic coups. Militaries stage coups primarily to depose a regime unfavorable to the military's interests. The establishment of democracy is merely the means through which the military achieves its intended result.

That bring us to the next question: Why might the relationship between the military and the dictatorship fray? Just as it's not possible to devise a singular reason for why the interests of the military and the dictatorship may align, it's also not possible to come up with a singular reason for the partnership's demise. A multitude of interests are likely to be at work. And at times a seemingly insignificant factor can be the straw that breaks the camel's back.

Bruised and Battered

Most obviously the relationship may turn sour where the dictatorship begins to pose a threat to the military's interests. If the regime doesn't treat the military well, the soldiers may set aside their previous loyalty and identify more with the protesters' grievances. Mistreatment can come in the form of low-level, outdated military equipment; costly and unpopular military conflicts; or military defeat, for which military officers may blame the political leadership.[1]

Before the Portuguese military toppled the Estado Novo dictatorship in 1974, there was widespread disenchantment within the military with the regime's lengthy colonial wars.[2] After a decade of fighting, even the senior officers had begun to show signs of dissatisfaction with the status quo. The enormous desertion rate underlines the pervasive antiwar sentiment within the military: Between 1961 and 1974 an estimated 110,000 conscripts dodged military service. The conscripts and the officers alike were tired of fighting and feared that they would be blamed for Portugal's inevitable defeat. They viewed the colonial wars as detrimental to their personal interests, as well as the interests of the military as an institution.

The colonial wars also flooded the military with amateur conscripts, whom the regime attempted to promote on a fast track. These university-educated conscripts could assume permanent officers' commissions only after taking a short training course. This fast-track promotion system devalued years of career training that regular officers had undergone, which caused resentment and bruised their professional vanity.

Junior officers suffered from low income and skyrocketing costs of living in the colonies where they fought the regime's colonial wars. It was the junior officers who battled in the jungles and bore the burden for the senior officers' errors, while the senior officers collected lucrative paychecks for moonlighting as board members of large companies. As Captain Rodrigo Manuel Lopes de Sousa e Castro lamented, "The army is always blamed for anything which goes wrong in this country. We were blamed for everything when we were in Africa. For 13 years the soldiers . . . were belittled and exploited in the war. Personally, I can say that as a sub-lieutenant in the combat zone I earned 4,500 escudos, less than a porter at the Imperial Cinema in Luanda. As a captain commanding a company in Mozambique I earned less than a barber in Nampula, 10,000 a month. And I went months on end without seeing my family or my friends." The low levels of pay translated into the declining prestige of the military. As one Portuguese officer put it, "A policeman in the street could humiliate a captain at any time and get away with it. They gave orders to officers in uniform. We had no money, no prestige, and nothing from the country."

From the junior officers' perspective, the coup served as a convenient tool for bringing the colonial wars—which, for them, were a question of life or death— to a swift end. The fragmented Portuguese officer corps, whose membership varied across the political spectrum, united over their resentment of the colonial wars and the regime that supported them. These complaints prompted the formation of the Captains' Movement among the junior officers, which eventually toppled the regime in April 1974.

The fall of the Ceaușescu dictatorship in Romania in 1989 also illustrates why the alliance of convenience between a dictator and his military can break down.[3] Although the military was the primary tool Ceaușescu used to impose his agenda on the masses, soldiers were not insulated from his oppressive policies. The army, which contained roughly 140,000 men, received inferior salaries, privileges, and basic resources compared to those given to members of the Securitate, or Security Police, which had nearly 40,000 members. Because the hardships the military experienced were similar to civilians, it was viewed as a "popular army," not a privileged group with a stake in Ceaușescu's survival.

The inferior compensation and lack of resources were only small contributions to the discontent running through the ranks of the Romanian Army. The senior army generals were also unhappy with Ceaușescu's foreign and military policies. Defense budgets were largely on hold throughout the 1980s, and consequently conscripts were not rigorously trained to fulfill their roles as soldiers. Instead the state utilized the whole cadre of draftees as free labor, forcing them to work in various roles in agriculture and construction. Additionally Ceaușescu was adamant that each unit should supply its own food, which "meant that many garrisons doubled as chicken or pig farms, surrounded by the omnipresent cloud of stench."[4] Military personnel were so displeased with Ceauşescu's policies that whispers of plans to depose the dictator had been heard as far back as the mid-1970s. When a popular uprising finally shook the country in 1989, the military was content to withdraw its support from the dictator, leading to his demise.

Consider also two coups that took place in Egypt.[5] In 1952 the military ended King Farouk's rule after he imposed a series of ill-conceived measures that antagonized the military leadership. In October 1944 he changed the army's motto from "God, Country, and King," to "God, King, and Country," symbolizing his near-divine authority. He appointed incompetent cronies to senior leadership positions within the military, including a prison warden who was known for forcing prisoners to cultivate the king's land for free. In 1948 he sent Egyptian soldiers on a costly military adventure against the new state of Israel. The king framed the operation as a defense of the Palestinian people, but in reality it was a power play to elevate his prestige in the Arab world.

But the military was reluctant to fight Israel. The military leadership expressed concerns that the army was unprepared, and training and equipment were woefully lacking, but the king disregarded them and marched the military toward a devastating defeat. Gamal Abdel Nasser, the mastermind of the coup against Farouk, wrote in a letter to a school friend that the soldiers were "dashed against fortifications . . . using defective arms which had been purchased by the king's cronies, a collection of petty crooks who profited from the war by realizing huge commissions from arms deals."[6] He went on to lament that his battalion had no maps, tents, or logistical support and, to top it off, had been subject to inconsistent orders from the king. Mohammed Naguib, another leader of the coup against Farouk, was wounded twice during the war. Both Nasser and Naguib, and other officers like them, came to believe that the real enemy was sitting in the palace in Cairo.

The 2011 coup in Egypt was motivated by similar concerns. Although the military enjoyed enormous social and economic privileges in Egypt, by the time of the 2011 coup these privileges had unraveled. President Mubarak's aggressive privatization policies had begun to encroach upon the military's economic domain, and the social privileges of the security institutions had begun to outshine those of the military. After Mubarak was toppled in 2011, a *Financial Times* commentator, Yezid Sayigh, reported that the military's "reputed economic 'empire' . . . is considerably more modest in volume than is commonly believed, and has probably shrunk in proportion to a national economy that has grown by more than 3 per cent annually since 2003."[7] As a result, when the massive uprising was ignited against Mubarak in 2011, the military had lost many of its incentives to stand by his side. The writing was on the wall. The military was simply waiting for the right moment to strike.

In England it was the religious aspirations of the Catholic King James II that turned his military against him in the 1660s.[8] After taking office, James quickly

began to replace Protestant officers with men whose sole qualification was their
Catholicism. Catholic officers were concentrated in strategic posts across the
empire, and many of the army's Protestant officers feared both for their religion
and their personal security. As more Protestant officers were replaced by Catholics,
many shared a growing concern that Catholicism would soon be imposed by force
and private property would revert back to the Roman Catholic Church. Eventually
these officers staged a coup against James in an event known as the Glorious
Revolution, which I will cover in due course.

A Wobbling Dictatorship

The military may also turn against a dictator if the dictatorship is no longer stable. At
some point during the dictator's rule, the power dynamic between the regime and
the people might change, and popular opposition may become powerful enough to
thwart suppression efforts by the authoritarian leaders. That opposition ordinarily
takes the form of a popular uprising.

As I use that phrase here, "popular uprising" refers to a massive gathering of
citizens from many facets of society united by a common political cause—in this
context, the overthrow of the authoritarian regime.[9] Citizens usually gather in a
symbolic place—such as Tahrir Square in Cairo or Tiananmen Square in Beijing—
to call for the resignation of the dictator and the establishment of democracy. Over
time crowds grow in size, density, and fervor, indicating broad popular support for
regime change. The citizens regard themselves as the vanguard of a better future,
one in which they control their own destiny, free from the stronghold of an oppressive regime. They are united by a common will for democracy—a will that has been
denied them at the ballot box. Although united by this common cause, the crowds
typically lack a coherent blueprint for achieving democratic reform and rarely see
beyond the singular goal of the overthrow or resignation of the dictator.

In response to this sustained popular uprising, the dictator may remain defiant
and refuse to relinquish power. The moment of final triumph awaited by the crowds
may not come, at least not voluntarily. The popular uprising may reach a size that
cannot be contained by the dictator's security forces, prompting the regime to enlist
the military's help.

At this point the military will face three primary options. The weighing of these
options is a delicate balancing act, as the consequences of misjudgment can be
enormous. If a coup against the regime fails, the military's loyalty to the rulers will
be rewarded. But if the coup succeeds, loyalty to the regime will be punished.

The military's first option when faced with civilian resistance to the state is to
side with the regime and suppress the popular opposition through force. In some
cases that option won't be in the military's interest. If the military uses force to suppress popular opposition, it might face retaliation by a foreign power that comes to

the protesters' aid. Particularly where the uprising is large and nonviolent, repression by the military could mean a bloodbath promptly broadcast on YouTube for the world to see.[10] The regime's brutal suppression of unarmed protestors might arouse international sympathies. For example, during the uprising in Libya in 2011, Muammar Gaddafi's military began conducting airstrikes against rebel positions, which drew the ire of the international community. Although Gaddafi initially had the upper hand, NATO forces came to the aid of the Libyan rebels, resulting in Gaddafi's capture and death.

In addition to prompting international action, repression of protestors can also threaten the military's internal unity. Rank-and-file soldiers may refuse orders by senior officers to fire on the protestors and even stage a coup against the government and the military leadership. That risk is especially great, as we'll see in part III, in a military composed of citizen-soldiers, who are more likely than professional soldiers to identify with the citizens they are ordered to shoot. What's more, by using force on the population, militaries risk irreversibly losing their popular and privileged role in society.

As a second option, the military might remain neutral and allow the revolution to run its course. That option places the military in a precarious position. If the popular opposition succeeds in overthrowing the authoritarian regime, the people, and not the military, will be in charge of the transition process to democracy. During that process the people might eliminate or curb the military's powers and autonomy. And if the popular opposition fails, then it will be the still-standing dictatorship that will come after the military for failing to lend the regime its support in an hour of need.

Third, the military might stage a coup to seize power from the authoritarian regime while promising to oversee a transition process that ends with the transfer of power to the people. That option allows the military to topple an unstable regime, emerge in the eyes of the people as a credible state institution, and preserve its own interests during a transition process that the military leaders themselves control. In many cases staging a coup will therefore be in the military's interests, even if those interests are advanced through a fundamental change of the governing structure.

When the survival of a dictatorship is in serious doubt—when it's clear that the regime is about to sink—the military may defect to avoid sinking along with it. And in deposing a dictator and assuming power during the resulting power vacuum, the military will position itself to reap the benefits of early defection.

This third option is precisely what the Egyptian military chose on February 11, 2011. At that point it was clear the Mubarak regime was on its last legs. The protesters had grown to millions, and the United States—once an ardent supporter of Mubarak—had withdrawn its support. Even if Mubarak managed to hold on to power, the future looked bleak from the military's perspective. Mubarak's son and heir-apparent, Gamal, was not a military man. His loyalty to business interests was potentially threatening to the military's social and economic privileges. As the revolution theorist Jack Goldstone explains, Egypt's military leaders "fiercely resented" Gamal since, as a banker, he "preferred to build his influence through business and political cronies rather than through the military."[11] In 2006 Field Marshal Mohamed Hussein Tantawi, who would later deliver the communiqué deposing Mubarak from office, warned Mubarak that awarding the presidency to an "unpopular figure" like Gamal would further antagonize the military. The popular revolts in 2011 thus presented the military the rare opportunity to act on this imperative and pull the rug out from under the Mubarak family before Gamal could assume power.

Initially the script played out precisely as the military had hoped. Following the coup, much of the population saw the military as a heroic state institution. Credit for the successful overthrow of the Mubarak regime went in large part to the military for refusing to fire on the protestors and stepping in to assume control of the government when Mubarak stubbornly refused to relent. U.S. President Barack Obama heaped praise on the Egyptian military for "serv[ing] patriotically and responsibly as a caretaker to the state" and expressed his confidence that the military would "ensure a transition that is credible in the eyes of the Egyptian people."[12]

As we already saw, the story of this coup doesn't end here. After turning over power to the people, the Egyptian military seized it back in July 2013. At first blush the contrast between the 2011 coup and the 2013 coup could hardly be greater. In the former, the military staged a coup against a dictatorship and handed the reins to democratically elected civilians. But in the latter, the military toppled a democratically elected leader, ending the country's experiment with democracy.

Yet a closer look reveals a common theme. The motivation for this game of musical chairs was the same: self-interest.

8

Musical Chairs

Life imitates art far more than art imitates life.
— Oscar Wilde, *The Decay of Lying*, 1889

In 1928 Hassan al-Banna, who was a school teacher and an imam, established an organization called the Muslim Brotherhood.[1] The Brotherhood began as a populist movement against Western influence in Egypt and gradually turned into a political movement. The Brothers believed that the Western world spread authoritarianism and corruption across Arab countries and undermined the religious and cultural values of Muslim societies. The Brotherhood grew increasingly militant in the 1950s—conducting assassinations and bombings to achieve its ends—and was subject to an on-again-off-again ban in Egypt for decades. The ban was prompted in part by the political threat the Brotherhood posed to secular dictators in power.

Despite the intermittent ban, the Brotherhood remained the largest and best organized opposition group in Egypt. It ran candidates as independents in parliamentary elections and won nearly 20 percent of the seats in 2005. This was an impressive feat in elections that were systematically rigged.

During the 2011 uprising against Hosni Mubarak, the Brotherhood leadership reluctantly permitted its young members to participate in the protests but kept its involvement as inconspicuous as possible. To avoid the perception of an Islamist uprising against a secular dictator, Brotherhood leaders prohibited their members from using religious slogans during the protests. For example, when an eager Brotherhood member started waving the Quran in front of TV cameras, another Brotherhood member swiftly pushed him down and replaced the Quran with an Egyptian flag.

After Mubarak was toppled, the Brotherhood emerged as the most established political group in Egypt. As a result they offered some stability after a tumultuous revolution and turbulent transition period. The Brotherhood, in the words of one expert, was the "one address where you can go to get 100,000 people off the street."[2] The Brotherhood also appeared to support many of the state institutions that gave the Egyptian military its extensive economic and social privileges.

From the military's perspective, the Brotherhood appeared to be a natural partner in keeping order and protecting its status in Egypt. After the military toppled
Mubarak, widespread rumors circulated in Egypt about backroom deals between
the military and the Muslim Brotherhood.[3] These rumors were validated by
numerous actions that the military took during its interim rule that benefited the
Brotherhood's political prospects. To cite one example, the military issued a constitutional declaration that altered the existing prohibition on political parties "with
a religious frame of reference or on a religious basis."[4] The declaration amended
this provision to remove the "religious frame of reference" restriction, leaving only
the narrower prohibition on political parties with a "religious basis."[5] Because the
Muslim Brotherhood used the term "religious frame of reference" to describe its
political orientation, this amendment allowed it to establish its own political party,
the Freedom and Justice Party.[6]

With its organizational power and the military's backing, the Freedom and
Justice Party was poised for sweeping political glory. Despite its potential for success, the Brotherhood initially outlined a modest political agenda. It announced
that it would not seek a majority of the seats in the Parliament, nor would it field a
candidate in the presidential elections. This strategy was politically deft. The sitting
legislature and executive would inevitably be blamed for the economic and social
turbulence that Mubarak's ouster would unleash. The Brotherhood also didn't want
to play into the rhetoric, popular particularly in the West, about an Islamist takeover
of the Arab Spring.

But the Brotherhood's humble agenda eventually became more ambitious and
opportunistic. Disregarding its promises, it launched an aggressive campaign to capture a majority of the parliamentary seats—including seats that were reserved for
independent candidates with no party affiliations—and fielded its own candidate,
Mohamed Morsi, for the presidency.[7] In the legislative elections held November
2011 to January 2012, the Freedom and Justice Party captured a near-majority
of the seats in the Parliament (47.2 percent), and Morsi was elected president in
June 2012.

The political powerhouse that the once modest Muslim Brotherhood created
posed a potential threat to the military's interests. Within hours after the ballots
for the legislative elections closed, the military issued a constitutional declaration
that made it clear the armed forces still aimed to reign supreme. According to the
declaration, the Supreme Council of the Armed Forces (SCAF) would continue to
exercise legislative authority until the election of a new Parliament, retain exclusive
authority over all decisions pertaining to the military, and hold a veto over the new
constitution.

In August 2012, just two months after his election, Morsi struck back. He issued
his own constitutional declaration that superseded the one issued by the military.
He purged most of the military's top brass and replaced them with a new generation
of officers. Field Marshal Mohamed Hussein Tantawi, who was the SCAF's leader,

was forced into retirement. This sweeping move—dubbed a "reverse coup"— stunned all observers.[8] It was another victory for the Brotherhood and emblematic of the Brotherhood's domination of Egyptian politics. In a moment that would later prove to be deeply ironic, Morsi personally appointed and swore in Lieutenant General Abdel Fattah el-Sisi as the new defense minister and commander of the armed forces. El-Sisi was not a Brotherhood member or sympathizer, but he was perceived to be a pious Muslim and his wife wore the hijab, unlike most of the other senior military officers.

Morsi thus had plans for the Egyptian military and began putting them into action relatively quickly. What he didn't know was that the military also had plans for him.

Having secured a decisive electoral victory, Morsi continued to monopolize power. The Brotherhood dominated the drafting of Egypt's new Constitution in 2012. The drafting process sidelined the opposition, as the Constitution sailed from first draft to final version in about a month with little input from Morsi's opponents. This prompted the opposition to walk out of the drafting assembly, and many Egyptians boycotted the ensuing referendum on the Constitution. Most drastically, in November 2012 Morsi issued a decree that granted him complete immunity from judicial oversight for a month.

As Morsi focused on consolidating power rather than delivering on his promises, Egyptians grew increasingly restless and frustrated with his rule. Protesters were met with violence by the state police. The economy remained in shambles. Crime was on the rise, especially sexual assault against women, which became commonplace.

There is a cliché tendency to depict these fragmentations as the result of tension between Islamists and secularists. But this narrative is misleading. Many Egyptians are Islamists in that they don't want a Westernized, secular government. It's therefore incorrect to conclude that the Egyptian people turned against the Brotherhood because of its commitment to Islam. Rather Egyptians turned against the Brotherhood because they perceived the group to be arrogant, exclusionary, and incompetent. And the problem wasn't just Morsi himself. Egypt has had a long history of powerful executives. When Morsi began to consolidate control, there was no domestic actor or institution—aside from the military—able to keep him in check.

As the Brotherhood continued to greet the opposition's woes with a shrug, the anti-Brotherhood movement gathered strength. The groundswell of opposition culminated in the Tamarod (Rebellion) movement, which allegedly collected over 22 million signatures from a population of roughly 80 million, demanding Morsi's resignation. (That number was never verified by independent sources.) Tamarod was instrumental in launching massive protests against Morsi on June 30, 2013, which served as the precursor for the military coup that toppled him on July 3.

What began as a partnership between the military and the Brotherhood thus came to a swift end. The military intervention against Morsi was followed by a violent crackdown of Muslim Brotherhood protests, and arrests of and life sentences for Brotherhood leaders, including Morsi.

Although the February 2011 coup and the July 2013 coup were of different kinds—one deposed a dictator and the other a democratically elected leader—the motivations of the coup leaders were similar. In both cases the military took advantage of popular uprisings to depose leaders who threatened its interests. The Muslim Brotherhood, the once humble partner of the Egyptian military, had turned into an ambitious and opportunistic opponent. It was positioned to pose a significant threat to the military, as demonstrated by Morsi's purge of the military's senior leadership with impunity. As a consequence, the military welcomed the Tamarod movement, took advantage of the massive uprising against Morsi, and deposed him by once again claiming the mantle of democracy. Following the coup, fighter jets from the air force proceeded promptly to draw hearts over the Cairo sky—a message of love for the Egyptian people.

Even Cassius would have been impressed.

The coup against Morsi produced some strange bedfellows. Somewhat surprisingly the other Islamist party in Egypt, the al-Nour Party ("Party of the Light"), openly sided with the military against the Brotherhood.[9] The al-Nour Party is an Islamist party that adheres to the fundamentalist Salafi ideology. Why didn't the Salafis align with their Islamist brethren? This was a pragmatic decision also driven by self-interest and survival. If the Salafis had sided with their fellow Islamists, they likely would have suffered the same fate. In addition, they anticipated—incorrectly, it turned out—that they could capture the Brotherhood's constituency following the Brotherhood's downfall.[10]

The toppling of Morsi was followed by fresh presidential elections. Defense Minister el-Sisi, who led the coup against Morsi, was elected president with 97 percent of the vote from a voter turnout of 47.5 percent.

In the end, life in Egypt proved Oscar Wilde right by imitating a game of musical chairs. The military, led by Field Marshal Tantawi, ousted Mubarak; Tantawi relinquished his seat to Morsi; Morsi ousted Tantawi, whose seat he gave to El-Sisi; and El-Sisi ousted Morsi and installed himself as president.

9

The Glorious Coup

My daughter hath deserted me, my army also . . . and if such betrays me, what can I expect from those I have done so little for.

—King James II[1]

In 1688 a conspiracy cultivated by military officers culminated in a coup d'é-tat against England's James II, popularly known as the Glorious Revolution.[2] The soldiers who deserted King James joined the invading Dutch forces of William of Orange to topple the king. The coup was largely the product of a Protestant cri-sis of conscience among those of England's military elite who remained faithful to the Church of England in the face of an absolutist Catholic king. The coup brought enduring changes to the social, religious, and political fabric of England, as its empire transitioned from absolute to constitutional monarchy.

King James II assumed the throne in 1685, when his older brother, King Charles II, died after suffering a series of seizures. James, unlike Protestant Charles, was a devout Catholic. Although he pledged to uphold the English Protestant tradition, he yearned for an England reformed by a restoration of Catholicism and a rever-sion to an absolute monarchy. Before the Glorious Revolution, Lord Churchill—or "Church," as James lovingly called his trusted military wunderkind—would warn the king twice that neither he nor the English public would bear an encroachment on their religious beliefs by a Catholic king. Although James was responsible for Lord Churchill's rise from obscurity to a highly decorated, admired, and well-known military man, Churchill's gratitude and loyalty to his royal benefactor could-n't trump his Protestant conscience and personal interests. Further, despite serving as a diplomat to the French court, Churchill couldn't endure the king's alliance with Louis XIV in France, England's reviled enemy.

On April 4, 1687, James unveiled the Declaration of Indulgence, which, under the guise of religious tolerance, sanctioned the suspension of the penal laws against Catholics. In the Declaration, the king also announced his desire to unite the citi-zens of the empire under the banner of Catholicism. This public display of the king's determination to implement a counterreformation horrified all patriots, including Churchill.

Planning for a coup d'état began on April 10, 1687, less than a week after the Declaration's issuance. Churchill and his band of conspirators later sent a message to William of Orange requesting his military intervention to save the Protestant faith in England from the whims of an absolutist king determined to implement a Catholic counterreformation. William, the Dutch prince and Protestant champion, was James's son-in-law through his marriage to the king's eldest daughter, Mary (also a Protestant), and the presumed heir apparent to the English imperial throne. Although James could predict the impending loyalty crisis facing his Protestant officers, he was content to risk the possibility of a coup. Convinced that most of his men would remain loyal to him because he believed he treated them well, James hoped a failed coup would enable him to rid the army of Protestants altogether as a justifiable punishment for their defiance.

On May 4, 1688, King James issued an order commanding the Protestant clergy to read the Declaration of Indulgence from every pulpit across the nation. On May 17 seven bishops refused, declaring instead that the king's action was unconstitutional. The bishops were arrested and imprisoned in the Tower of London to await trial for seditious libel, inspiring displays of Protestant devotion from the crowds that packed the city streets. Defying the orders of their Catholic colonel, the garrison guarding the Tower toasted the health of the bishops, declaring that "they would drink the bishops' health and no other, not their colonel's, not even the king's, as long as their fathers in God were imprisoned."[3] This demonstration of rebelliousness and solidarity was only the tip of an iceberg of discontent running up the ranks of King James's military.

The bishops were exonerated on June 30. The verdict was greeted with thunderous cheers of celebration from the military ranks. The acquittal of the bishops brought the tension in Protestant London to a fever pitch, and before long the streets were awash with defiant crowds. Sensing the gravity of the moment and the deep division in both the loyalties and the religion of the army, Lord Churchill and his co-conspirators sent word to William of Orange that the religious and political climate in England was ready for revolution.

In November 1688 William launched the invasion against his father-in-law's kingdom by landing in Devon in southwest England. Vastly outnumbered by James's army, William's army traveled north to Exeter to seek shelter, and it became increasingly obvious that the invading force could not succeed without the help of James's own military.

For that reason, Stephen Saunders Webb's decisive account of the events describes the Glorious Revolution as "Lord Churchill's Coup." The overthrow of the monarch was made possible only because James's own military betrayed him. The opposition to his rule came from where he least expected: his daughter and his army.

Under the coordination of Lord Churchill, the cavalry of the royal army detached and began the journey to join William of Orange. Following the example of the army, the gentry in western counties also defected to William. The mass desertion of his most elite and favorite officers crushed the king, and without leadership the rank and file of his army floundered. This was the defining moment of the coup, completely demoralizing King James and triggering "mini coups" across the counties of the nation. On December 6, 1688, James mustered the few remaining loyal regiments to defend the Twyford Bridge over the Thames. But most of the king's forces either retreated upon the arrival of William's army or, being themselves Protestants unwilling to attack their Protestant brethren, defected to William. Still in disbelief at the ingratitude of his officers, King James fled.

Following the coup against James, Parliament declared William a joint monarch with James's daughter Mary. The Crown was offered to William and Mary on the condition that they accept the Declaration of Rights, later known as the Bill of Rights. The document represented the conviction that even the monarch was subject to the rule of law and could not infringe on the inherent rights that belonged to the people or suspend laws without Parliament's consent. William also gave up numerous administrative powers to Parliament, including powers over taxation, the royal succession, appointments, and the right to wage war. As a result control over state policy became vested in Parliament.

As Daron Acemoğlu and James Robinson observe in their book, *Why Nations Fail*, the legal changes that followed James's ouster "represented the triumph of Parliament over the king, and thus the end of absolutism in England."[4] Following the coup, economic institutions also became more inclusive, paving the way for the Industrial Revolution a few decades later. Of all the political revolutions in the past two millennia, the Glorious Revolution—or Coup—ranks among the most significant.[5]

To be sure, even with these fundamental shifts in power, England was far from being a democracy. Although many benefited from the lasting effects of the transition from absolute to constitutional monarchy, the transition was marred by acts of retaliation against English Catholics, who were indefinitely marginalized. In addition, only a fraction of the population could vote, so Parliament itself wasn't representative. But the people had other avenues for influencing Parliament, the most important of which was the right to petition. When the people petitioned—and they did so frequently—Parliament listened. It is the right to petition, more than anything else, "that reflects the defeat of absolutism, the empowerment of a broad segment of society, and the rise of pluralism in England" following the Glorious Coup.[6] The right to petition, and the ensuing political pluralism, generated dynamics that over time increased the representativeness of England's political institutions.

The Glorious Coup also reverberated across the Atlantic, prompting coups against colonial governors in America. These small-scale coups eventually culminated in the American Revolution, which freed Americans from British rule nearly a century later, in 1776. I'll return to these coups in due course.

Because the Glorious Coup didn't produce a procedural democracy with universal adult suffrage, it's not technically a democratic coup in the sense that I use that phrase here. But to reject the democratic nature of the Glorious Coup would be to apply the standards of 2017 to 1688. Measured by the standards of the time—when full-fledged democracy was nonexistent—the coup had a dramatically democratizing effect, as it established some of the world's first inclusive political institutions and generated strides toward democracy. The system of government created by the coup—including a bill of rights to protect the people from a tyrannical monarch and a framework of limited government—served as a model for representative democracy. These principles were the winners in both 1688 and 1776.[7]

The same theme echoes through the millennia. Cassius assassinated Caesar because Caesar gave a coveted governorship to someone else. The Egyptian military captured power from the ailing Mubarak regime after Mubarak favored the state security forces at the military's expense. The military then supported the Muslim Brotherhood, until the Brotherhood no longer served its interests. The British military supported King James II until the monarch turned against his Protestant officers. In the battle between self-interest and loyalty, self-interest repeatedly won.

Yet self-interest doesn't tell the entire story. Other factors also influence trajectories, animate conflicts, and drive outcomes. Although self-interest will continue to loom large in explaining why democratic coups happen, the next part introduces other variables into the mix. As it turns out, some types of militaries are more likely than others to turn their arms against a dictator.

PART THREE

PRAETORIANS AND GUARDIANS

Quis custodiet ipsos custodes? (Who will guard the guardians?)
—Juvenal, *Satires*, Satire 6

When the Roman emperor Augustus created the Praetorian Guard to serve as his bodyguards, he had little idea that his creation would come to haunt, rather than protect, his successors.[1] The Guard was a prestigious security force made up of handpicked elites—the crème de la crème—trained to eliminate all threats to the emperor. In addition to guarding the emperor, they served as jacks-of-all trades, fighting emergency fires, handling crowd control at gladiator shows, and committing various atrocities to further the emperor's interests.

Although they were tasked with protecting the emperor, the Praetorians came to pose the greatest threat to him. Easily tempted by promises of wealth and power, the Praetorian Guard staged coups and assassinated numerous emperors. In some cases the Guard chose the successors of the emperors they toppled, and in others they pledged their allegiance to the highest bidder. The Guard was finally disbanded by Constantine the Great, who reached the conclusion—better late than never—that the Praetorians couldn't be trusted.

Although the Guard was disbanded, its name stuck. In modern parlance, praetorianism is often used to refer to the excessive political role of the military in a government. Scholars and other commentators widely assume that militaries naturally have praetorian tendencies. We fear militaries like Roman emperors feared the very guard that was supposed to protect them. We assume that militaries, unless carefully controlled and subordinated, will inevitably impede democratic development. We thus speak abstractly of "the military" or "armies," as if the institution were consistent in its composition and structure across different nations.

Distilled to its core, the argument in this part is simple: The military is a variable, not a constant. Asking whether militaries are naturally dangerous to democracy is like asking whether water is naturally a solid, a liquid, or a gas. It depends. Militaries are much more complicated, diverse, and multidimensional than conventional thinking suggests. Most people would readily acknowledge that presidents, legislatures, courts, and other institutions differ from one nation to the other. Yet the standard narrative writes off "the military" as a homogeneous institution that universally presents a threat to democracy. We wouldn't dream of equating President Vladimir Putin with President Nelson Mandela, yet we assume the Russian military and the South African military are of the same ilk simply because they share the same brand name.

My aim in this part is to convince you otherwise. I readily acknowledge that some militaries have praetorian tendencies and will turn their arms against their own people to serve corrupt and authoritarian ends. But praetorianism doesn't infect all militaries to the same degree across geography and history. Some types of militaries are more likely to topple dictatorships rather than support them and to promote democratic institutions rather than destroy them.

What distinguishes these militaries from the praetorian kind? Even where a military topples a dictatorship to establish democracy, how do we ensure that the guardians don't turn into praetorians? As the Roman poet Juvenal pondered, how do we guard the guardians?

This part will tackle these questions. Along the way, I'll discuss why new soldiers in Turkey are responsible for traffic jams, how coups in the American colonies paved the way for the American Revolution, why Chinese conscripts fired on the student protestors gathered on Tiananmen Square, and how the Athenian Navy fended off an oligarchic coup that threatened to end democracy.

10

An Army of Civilians

*From a well-regulated militia we have nothing to fear; their interest is the
same with that of the State. They do not jeopardize their lives for a master
who considers them only as the instruments of his ambition. . . . No; they fight
for their houses, their lands, for their wives, their children; for all who claim
the tenderest names, and are held dearest in their hearts.*
    —John Hancock, "Boston Massacre Oration," March 5, 1774

If you cram over 10 million people into one city, the traffic is bound to be bad. But
the traffic in Istanbul surpasses all pessimistic expectations. The same route can take
anywhere from twenty minutes to four hours to traverse, depending on the time of
day. During rush hour you may sit in your car contemplating whether the remaining
years of your life will be spent on a jam-packed Istanbul street.

Poor city planning is partially to blame, but so are the Turks' eccentric celebrations that have a way of clogging Istanbul's narrow arteries. If you're at the right
place at the right time, you may spot a convoy of cars covered in Turkish flags. Each
car will have a minimum of six passengers crammed into four seats and accompanied by an amalgam of honks, drums, and fireworks. The passengers will hang so far
out of the car windows that it seems a strong breeze would be enough to create an
unhappy meeting between face and asphalt.

The convoy will zigzag its way through Istanbul's streets, annoying many locals
yet amusing others, and end at a bus station. One of the passengers will be pulled
haphazardly out of the car, leading unsuspecting observers to believe he is about
to receive a thorough beating. The men in the convoy will then grab him, toss him
repeatedly in the air, and (hopefully) catch him on the way down. All the while they
will sing and chant slogans familiar to Turkish ears:

> "En büyük asker bizim asker!" (The greatest soldier is our soldier!)
> "Her Türk asker doğar!" (Every Turk is born a soldier!)

What might appear to an uninformed observer as a bizarre circus act is a traditional
parade for sending off new soldiers in Turkey. Mandatory for Turkish men over the

age of eighteen, military service is viewed as a rite of passage. It's traditionally a prerequisite for marriage and obtaining meaningful employment, as many employers list successful completion of military service as a job requirement. Historically, many, but certainly not all, Turks have thought of themselves as "an army nation" (*asker millet*), reflecting the perception that the army and the nation are bound together in a symbiotic relationship.

This perception was called into question on July 15, 2016, when disenchanted factions within the Turkish military attempted an ill-fated coup against the incumbent government. The coup targeted an elected government and therefore was not a democratic coup as I define that term here. We'll revisit this coup attempt in later chapters, but for now, I'll note that Turks were astonished when some soldiers fired on the crowds who had poured into the streets to resist the coup attempt.[1] At the same time, however, many soldiers surrendered and allowed themselves to be tortured by the crowds rather than use force on them. Heavily armed tanks were easily overpowered by unarmed civilians, who beat up the coup makers, all with impunity.[2] For the same reason the Egyptian military refused to fire on the crowds gathered in Tahrir Square in January 2011, many Turkish soldiers involved in the coup attempt put down their arms rather than use them against civilians.

The political scientists Steven Levitsky and Lucan Way have argued that authoritarians are less likely to stay in power in countries where the military will not shoot at protesters.[3] Likewise the Middle East scholar Philippe Droz-Vincent observes, "In all regimes shaken by the wave of protests in 2011, regime survival ultimately turned on whether the military would shoot at the protestors."[4] This conclusion makes intuitive sense. If a dictator can't manage to stop a popular uprising by force or the threat of force, its end is likely near.

But these statements raise further questions: Why are the armed forces of some states more inclined than others to shoot when the masses converge upon a public square? Why are some soldiers more likely to put down their arms and join the crowds rather than turn against them?

The citizen-soldier model emerges as a common thread among militaries that have toppled dictatorships. In these militaries, the leadership is often made up of career professionals, but the rank-and-file members are conscripts, also called "citizen-soldiers." They serve a mandatory term in the military, usually one to three years, before returning to civilian life.[5] These conscripts are civilians first and soldiers second. Their commitment to the military is temporary; civil society is where their primary loyalties lie. The rotation of civilians in and out of the military creates a feedback loop between the military and the civilian population that keeps the military in touch with civilian values.

If ordered to turn against the people, conscripts are more likely to desert or defect than are professional soldiers. From the perspective of conscripts, "the crowds" aren't just anonymous masses; they're friends, neighbors, and family members. Because rank-and-file conscripts may disobey orders to use violence on the population, resulting in a breakdown of the command structure, democratic coups tend to occur in nations that mandate national conscription. Instead of risking significant defections by the conscripts, the military leadership may refuse to follow regime orders to shoot at protesters and instead topple the dictatorship.

Empirical evidence supports this theory. Popular revolutions in the twenty-first century have tended to succeed in countries with mandatory conscription, including Serbia and Montenegro in 2000, Georgia in 2003, Ukraine and Lebanon in 2005, Kyrgyzstan in 2005, and Tunisia and Egypt in 2011.[6] In contrast, revolutions have failed in countries with volunteer armies or selective conscription, including Burma in 2007, Zimbabwe in 2008, Iran in 2009, and Bahrain in 2011.[7] To be sure, there are cases of conscripts firing on fellow citizens, most prominently during the 1989 Tiananmen Square protests in China. These instances are rare and, as we'll see in later pages, often result from attempts to selectively deploy soldiers who are unlikely to identify with the intended victims of the regime violence.

The citizen-soldier model assists in solving what Narcís Serra, former vice president and defense minister of Spain, identified as the pivotal problem in civil-military relations: the military's lack of commitment to civilian values.[8] Serra has argued that reducing the military's danger to democracy requires the injection of civilian beliefs.[9] For this reason the sociologist Morris Janowitz cautions against the modern shift from a conscript to an all-volunteer military, arguing that it creates "potentials for greater social isolation and new political imbalances and tensions."[10] An all-volunteer military, according to Janowitz, would create "the possibility of an inbred force which would hold deep resentments toward the civilian society and accordingly develop a strongly conservative, 'extremist' political ideology, which in turn would influence professional judgments."[11]

For similar reasons, many founders of the United States were deeply skeptical about maintaining a military of professional soldiers.[12] In England tyrants had used a standing army to crush political opponents. As the military historian Richard Kohn explains, many contemporary Americans viewed professional soldiers as automatons, "brutalized by harsh discipline, isolated from the rest of society, loyal not to an ideal or to a government but to a command wed to its own traditions."[13] For James Madison as well, professional soldiers were "more readily turned by corrupt commanders against the interests of The People."[14]

In colonial America citizen-soldiers were called to service two to three times a year for military review and training. They wore their daily civilian clothes instead of military uniforms.[15] Although sporadic military service presented significant efficiency and disciplinary problems, many civilians and politicians considered the citizen-soldier model—"the militia," in American parlance—to be far less dangerous than a professional army.[16] "The inhabitants of territories often the theatre of war," Alexander Hamilton wrote in Federalist No. 8, "are unavoidably subjected to frequent infringements on their rights, which serve to weaken their sense of those rights; and by degrees, the people are brought to consider the soldiery not only as their protectors, but as their superiors." In contrast to the standing army, and the resulting danger it created of an absolutist state, the militia represented the people and their liberties. Hamilton put this argument in terms of a question: "What shadow of danger can there be from men who are daily mingling with the rest of their countrymen and who participate with them in the same feelings, sentiments, habits, and interests?"[17] As Bernard Bailyn observes in *The Ideological Origins of the American Revolution*, "The colonies demonstrated military effectiveness of militia armies whose members were themselves the beneficiaries of the Constitution and hence not likely to wish to destroy it."[18]

Coups in America

Nearly a century before America declared independence from Great Britain, citizen-soldiers in the American colonies were at the forefront of several coups that toppled provincial governments after news of the 1688 Glorious Revolution in England reached the colonies. [19] The revolution in the Old World served as a blueprint for the coups staged by militias in the New. Although the coups did not immediately launch democracy in the colonies, they served as a stepping stone toward the American Revolution, which would free the colonies from English rule almost a century later.

By the time America began experiencing turmoil in 1689, there had been over a decade of significant imperial centralization in the colonies. This effort had been the most contested in Boston and New York, and, from the perspective of the British Crown, force seemed to be the only way to make these unruly colonials yield to royal governors. The rebellions demonstrated not only that the colonies wouldn't tolerate tyranny but also that many colonists had a distinctive conception of empire that emphasized local governance. Of the rebellions that swept the colonies, "the earliest, the boldest, and the completest" was in Massachusetts.[20]

The people of Massachusetts were considered "the most refractory subjects," ignoring economic regulations and continually asserting independence from royal rule.[21] This reputation for disloyalty prompted the British Crown to revoke the Massachusetts Charter in 1684 and create the Dominion of New England in 1685. The Dominion included Massachusetts Bay, Plymouth, Connecticut, and Rhode Island, and later expanded to cover New York and East and West Jersey.

The colonists in Connecticut famously resisted the Crown's demands to give up their existing charter and allow their incorporation into the Dominion. According to legend, during a heated meeting with the Crown's representatives, all the candles were blown out and the Connecticut Charter mysteriously disappeared.[22] To protect it from the Crown, the Charter was placed in a cavity in the trunk of a large oak tree in Hartford, Connecticut, which later came to be known as the Charter Oak.

The political aim of creating the Dominion was to abolish representative legislatures in the colonies. The English monarch selected antilegislature military officers for Dominion posts because, as a House of Commons report explained, "in the army it has grown into a principle that Parliaments are roots of rebellion and Magna Carta sprung out of them."[23] The newly appointed governor of the Dominion, Sir Edmund Andros, was the ruler of a system that was "defined in his commission [as] feudal and autocratic."[24]

Andros was a military man and a strong disciplinarian. He enjoyed enormous power, rivaling that of a monarch. He believed in honor and loyalty, and his steadfast adherence to the commands of the British king at the expense of popular support ultimately led to rebellion. The revolutionaries in New England would accuse Andros of governing arbitrarily, restricting town meetings, denying land titles granted under the revoked charters, and being a key component of a Catholic conspiracy that would result in the enslavement of the Protestant colonists.

Undisciplined and drawn from local communities, the recruits of the provincial army in New England resented the harsh military discipline of Andros's English officers. This resentment was especially strong because some of these officers were Roman Catholic, whereas the New Englanders were Protestants. Convinced of Andros's villainy, the soldiers of the provincial army mutinied in April 1689, leaving their posts to slowly make their way back to Boston. The coup makers instilled fear in the local citizens that Andros and the Catholics would not rest until they burned the city and subjected them all to slavery. The coup's leaders, backed by at least twenty regiments of provincial soldiers, commanded the governor-general to surrender the citadel on Fort Hill, where he had sought shelter. The coup makers arrested Andros and his men, declaring them prisoners of war, and effectively overthrowing New England's executive. The rebels then established a council, called a convention, and reinstated the government as set forth in the older, more representative charter of Massachusetts.

Connecticut and Rhode Island also denounced the Dominion and returned to governance under their former charters. In Connecticut the hidden charter was removed from the Charter Oak and reinstated. Although the Charter Oak later fell during a violent storm, the tree came to symbolize the rescue of a young colony from tyranny.[25] On the day the tree was destroyed, "all of Connecticut began a period of civic mourning . . . an honor guard was placed around the remains, Colt's Band of Hartford played a funeral dirge, and an American flag was attached to the shattered trunk."[26]

The events in Boston soon inspired revolution in New York. In May 1688, after New York was added to the Dominion of New England, Andros had appointed Francis Nicholson, a captain in the British Army, to serve as his lieutenant governor. Nicholson, like Andros, was an oppressive ruler. He believed the colonists were "a conquered people, and therefore . . . could not so much claim rights and privileges as Englishmen in England."[27] He was frank in his views on the Magna Carta and the liberties it represented: "Magna Carta, Magna Farta,"[28] he famously quipped. Nicholson's power, and that of other colonial governors, was "more absolute in the Colonies than that of the King in England."[29]

Nicholson's stronghold on power began to fray once the news of revolution in England and Boston arrived in New York. Although Nicholson did his best to contain the news, a militia captain in the city by the name of Jacob Leisler spread the word. Leisler was long an opponent of English dominion in New York and helped instigate the militia to rebellion. Nicholson, who was known for his short temper, responded with an iron fist, threatening to kill the militia officers involved and adding for good measure that "if the militia did not become more obedient," he would "set the town afire.'"[30] Although Nicholson's statement may have been metaphorical, the militia took it seriously, interpreting it as a threat to destroy New York if he were ousted from power. The militia responded with rage and turned against its government. To avoid imminent violence by the militia, Nicholson surrendered to Leisler and fled to England in May 1689.

Following Leisler's coup, as the colonial historian Charles McLean Andrews explains, "continuance of arbitrary government in New York was impossible."[31] In the months that followed Nicholson's flight from New York, Leisler established a revolutionary government, which chose him as the commander-in-chief. In May 1690 Leisler called the first intercolonial congress in the American provinces. Although a new governor was later appointed by the Crown, his commission required him to "summon an assembly of freeholders, who were to join with governor and council in the making of laws."[32] On April 9, 1691, the assembly met for the first time, to determine the rights and privileges of the king's subjects in New York. The assembly passed what was practically a duplicate of the old, pre-Dominion charter from 1683, with the addition of annual elections rather than triennial elections for New York's assembly.

In both Massachusetts and New York, fledging militias thus managed to wrest control from autocratic governors anointed by the British monarch. Although the coups did not achieve independence from the Crown, they made notable strides toward more representative government and generated political reverberations that traveled across the Atlantic. The coups in America demonstrated to the Crown, and to the colonies themselves, that the times, in Bob Dylan's words, were a'changing. If a handful of militias from scattered colonies could topple governors with an iron grip on power, what could these colonies accomplish as a united front?

The answer would arrive less than a century later, in 1776, when thirteen American colonies officially declared their independence. Although much of the fighting was handled by the Continental Army (with significant help from France), the citizen-soldier militia also played a significant role in bolstering manpower and securing important victories in the battles of Bunker Hill and Bennington. The commander-in-chief of the Continental Army, George Washington, was himself a former commander of the Virginia Regiment, a militia corps established by the

Crown to defend Virginia during the French and Indian War (1754–63), which pitted the British colonies in America against France and its indigenous allies. Without the coups staged in the 1680s and thousands of militiamen throwing their weight behind the Continental Army in the 1770s, an independent United States—complete with separation of powers and freedom from the absolute rule of a tyrant—would have been a much more difficult reality to achieve.

Officers and Gentlemen

Even in militaries with mandatory conscription, the leadership is made up of professionals who dedicate their career to the military. These career professionals, not the rank-and-file conscripts, ultimately make the call to trigger and orchestrate a democratic coup. But the rank-and-file conscripts influence the decisions of the career professionals, who depend on the conscripts to execute their commands. These subordinate citizen-soldiers are less likely to succumb to what Hamilton called the "engine of despotism" that may be employed by their senior commanders.[33] Citizen-soldiers, according to Hamilton, would not abandon their moral and civil sense and succumb to the wishes of a tyrant seeking to establish a dictatorship. Instead of obeying orders to establish tyranny, citizen-soldiers would overthrow the superiors who issued them and side with the citizenry, where their permanent loyalty lay.

Hamilton's theory was validated in Turkey during the 1950s. The Democrat Party government, led by Prime Minister Adnan Menderes, attempted to systematically pack the highest military ranks with his ideologues.[34] But Menderes failed to effectively infiltrate the citizen-soldier military from the top.[35] In response to an American reporter's claim that the military supported Menderes, a military deputy quipped, "Menderes may have the generals, but we have everyone from colonel down."[36] And when the Menderes government ordered the army to suppress the antiregime protests in 1960, the soldiers refused to obey the orders. Instead of turning their arms on their fellow citizens, the soldiers toppled the Menderes government and installed a democratic regime. Since the 1960s the officer corps in Turkey has been able to sustain the conscript army largely by maintaining the trust and respect of the citizen-soldiers.[37] As the Turkish example illustrates, the citizen-soldiers in a conscript military perform an important check on the professional leadership that tends to keep the leaders closer to civilian values and accountable to civil society.

Recall also the 1974 military coup in Portugal that toppled Western Europe's oldest dictatorship.[38] To wage its colonial wars in Africa, Portugal had mandated military service, which flooded the military with university-trained conscripts (*milicianos* in Portuguese). These conscripts had been exposed to increasingly liberal ideas in their universities and, on the whole, opposed the colonial wars abroad and the dictatorship at home. The dictator in power at the time of the coup, Marcelo Caetano, blamed these conscripts for infecting the officers with progressive political ideas: "Because of this constant infusion of university graduates, the armed forces absorbed the ideas which agitated the younger generation and circulated in the schools," he wrote.[39] The Socialist Party leader Mário Soares echoed the same view: "Each spring for the last seven or eight years, Portuguese universities were the scene of student demonstrations against oppression. Each year between four and six hundred students were [arrested] and sent into the army as punishment. Many of these young radicals afterwards became lieutenants, captains, and majors."[40] These students-turned-soldiers resented being forced to abandon their families to risk their lives for a government they despised. They were vocal about their opposition to the colonial wars, and discussion about the wars between the temporary citizen-soldiers and the career officers became a regular feature of Portuguese military life. The professional officers soon began to realize that Portuguese society opposed both the colonial wars and the regime that propagated them.

It was the citizen-soldiers in ancient Athens who ousted senior officers who supported a tyrannical takeover of their democratic government.[41] Until 411 BC the government in Athens functioned as a direct democracy. Every male citizen had equal rights, freedom of speech, and the opportunity to directly participate in government. But the tide began to turn against democracy when the Athenian military suffered a decisive defeat in a military expedition against Sicily. The financial strain and political turmoil caused by the defeat allowed certain influential men to end democratic rule in Athens and replace it with an oligarchy of four hundred rulers in 411 BC. The Four Hundred initially promised to select a more representative body of five thousand, but they instead retained power for themselves.

The coup of the Four Hundred faced immediate resistance from the Athenian Navy stationed on Samos, an island in the Aegean Sea. The soldiers, made up primarily of men from the lower classes, refused to accept the news from Athens as a fait accompli. Instead they deposed senior officers who sympathized with the Four Hundred and elected new, democratically minded generals in their place. These new generals galvanized the Athenian military in Samos against the tyrannical moves in Athens, turning the military into "a potent democratic weapon."[42] The new generals proceeded to exact an oath from the Athenian troops "to live united under a democratic form of government . . . and to be enemies of the four hundred and not to make any peace overtures to them."[43] After these events, as the classics professor Martin Ostwald recounts, "the split between an oligarchical home government invested with political power and a democratic army controlling the bulk of Athenian military resources was now complete."[44]

The news of the military's rebellion in Samos instilled fear in the Four Hundred in Athens. They were expecting a quick, satisfying power grab, but instead they encountered a powerful enemy in the form of the Athenian military. The military proceeded to hold an armed assembly near Athens and decided to march against the city to topple the newly installed tyrants. Before it could escalate any further, this domestic feud was quickly overshadowed by the unexpected appearance of forty-two enemy ships in a harbor of the island of Euboea, near Athens. The Athenians were unable to prevent their enemies from capturing Euboea, which undermined the already tenuous rule of the Four Hundred. The Four Hundred were officially ousted from their seats in a meeting of the democratic assembly, and democratic rule was eventually restored in 409–410 BC. In the end it was the citizen-soldiers' determination that played a significant role in preventing the Four Hundred, along with their senior military sympathizers, from playing out their ambitions.

Us versus Them

The psychologist Henri Tajfel had a personal interest in studying genocide.[45] He was a Polish Jew who served in the French Army during World War II. He was captured by the Germans but survived the Holocaust because the Germans didn't realize that he was Jewish. Although he escaped death, many of his friends and family did not. As a result he dedicated his professional career to answering a seemingly simple question: What motivates discrimination and prejudice?

Tajfel and his colleagues ran a series of now-famous experiments. They assigned volunteers to different teams based on their answers to random questions. The subjects were asked, for example, which one of two abstract paintings they liked better. Based on their answers, they were assigned to a group made up of others who expressed the same preference. These were relatively meaningless, artificially created groups; there was no shared history between the members within each group and no inherent reason for conflict to develop between groups.

Yet the subjects developed group loyalty frighteningly quickly. They were more likely to distribute monetary rewards to the members of their own group at the expense of the others—even where they didn't receive any rewards personally, and even when alternative strategies would benefit both groups. In other words, it took the most trivial of distinctions for the subjects to divide themselves between "us" and "them." The simple act of telling people they belong to one group and not the other was sufficient to trigger loyalty toward their own group and bias against the others.

Tajfel's experiments, which have been replicated by thousands of others, eventually culminated in social identity theory. The theory is simple: People have a natural tendency to categorize themselves and others into groups. Once they are in a group, they tend to identify with it. They fixate on small or arbitrary distinctions, exaggerate those distinctions, and develop a favorable bias toward their own group. They become part of the group, and the group becomes part of them. Outsiders, in turn, become "those people."

To be sure, favoritism doesn't necessarily develop into prejudice, but it's the starting point. Favoritism is the root of prejudice, which, if nurtured and reinforced, can eventually lead to bias, discrimination, violence, and genocide. In Tajfel's social experiment, preference between two paintings was sufficient to create group favoritism. In the real world, other classifications—such as men and women, Bosnians and Serbs, Muslims and Christians, Democrats and Republicans, Nazis and Jews—have divided societies, leading to conflict and, in some cases, atrocity.

What does Tajfel's social identity theory tell us about whether militaries are likely to use force on the population? The military strives to forge group cohesion among its members. It strips down individual identities and creates the alter ego of "the soldier," who dresses the same, looks the same, and marches lockstep to the same tune as the others in the group. Once this identity is forged, soldiers are more likely to develop favoritism toward their own group—the military—especially in the face of an actual or manufactured conflict between the military and another group, such as a foreign power or the domestic population in rebellion. The soldiers' loyalty to the military may trump their loyalty to the domestic population, particularly when the regime exploits other differences—such as race, religion, and class—between the soldiers and their targets. What begins as favoritism can lead to mass slaughter.

For citizen-soldiers, the division between "us" and "them" is more ambiguous since they belong to both groups, the citizenry and the military. In some nations, citizen-soldiers spend only short stretches of time away from home and rotate frequently between civilian life and military life. In the United States, for example, militias were locally based and would perform military service only when necessary. In twentieth-century Portugal, military officers obtained civilian employment to supplement their meager income from the military, which kept them in touch with civilian values. Consequently, compared to professional soldiers, citizen-soldiers are more likely to have divided loyalties.

This is not to say that citizen-soldiers will never use force on a domestic population. As Tajfel's experiments show, even the most trivial group distinctions can foment favoritism. This may be one reason there are instances, however rare, of citizen-soldiers opening fire on the population. Although conscripts serve only temporarily in the military, some may develop a strong bond to it. In addition, not all citizen-soldier militaries are equally connected to society. For example, where citizen-soldiers spend long stretches away from civilian life, their loyalty to society may fray. Likewise, where the conscription term is unusually long, soldiers may develop stronger connections to the military, as in the case of North Korea, where the mandatory conscription period is ten years—the longest in the world.

Diversity and the Citizen-Soldier

Citizen-soldiers inject another important element into the military: diversity. As long as conscription is imposed equally, a conscript military, at the rank-and-file level, will be more representative of the population in terms of ethnicity, religion, culture, and social status than professional militaries.[46] A diverse military poses formidable challenges to a dictatorship. If soldiers identify with the domestic population—based on common ethnic, social, religious, or cultural backgrounds— they will be more reluctant to use violence against them.[47] But if the regime can insert differences between soldiers and intended victims, violence is more likely to result.

Consider, for example, the massacre in Tiananmen Square in 1989. China has a conscript military, so the willingness of its soldiers to use force on civilian protesters may appear puzzling. But significant differences existed between the conscripts deployed to Tiananmen Square and the demonstrators. The soldiers who crushed the student uprising in urban Beijing were inexperienced, uneducated rural soldiers "who had never walked through a city."[48] Even so, many soldiers deserted, some joining the protesters and chanting antiregime slogans.[49]

Take also the July 15, 2016 coup attempt in Turkey. Although many of the conscript soldiers involved in the coup attempt surrendered when confronted by unarmed civilians, others responded with violence. The coup makers were followers of influential Islamist preacher Fetullah Gülen, the archrival of President Erdoğan, who was the target of the coup attempt. There were significant ideological differences between the coup makers and the crowds who resisted them, which may partially explain the resulting use of force by some soldiers.

To ensure the military's loyalty in the event of a civilian uprising, a dictatorship may preferentially recruit certain segments of the population or set up elite combat units stacked with soldiers with demonstrated loyalties to the regime. This tactic engineers or magnifies the distinctions between the military and its potential targets. Many dictatorships also completely exclude from military service segments of the population that may, one day, become subjects of oppression and violence. In these regimes the military has a vested interest in the regime's survival since their fates are often interlinked: If the regime is toppled, the soldiers can expect the worst.

This tactic has a long and notable history. King James II of England employed this strategy in the lead-up to his ouster in 1688. To ensure the loyalty of his soldiers, the staunchly Catholic king replaced Protestant officers with Catholics. In the twentieth century, the Soviet Union kept certain segments of society—for example, Central Asian Muslims—unarmed and assigned them to labor battalions, where they couldn't engage in military tasks.[50] Jordan likewise disallows Jordanians of Palestinian descent from serving in the armed forces.[51] During the 2011 revolutions in Libya and Yemen, the military units with regional or tribal loyalties to the regimes tended to side with the respective government.[52] The remainder of both militaries deserted or joined the revolutionaries.[53] To compensate for these losses, the Libyan dictator Gaddafi had to enlist thousands of foreign mercenaries with no ties to the Libyan people and who were thus more willing to target them.[54]

Bahrain, where a Sunni autocracy rules a Shia majority, disallows Shias from serving in the military.[55] Although roughly 70 percent of Bahraini citizens are Shia, the military is dominated by Sunni Muslims who protect a Sunni dictatorship and Sunni business elites. The regime is so paranoid of Shia intrusion into its military that, where necessary, it supplements the military's ranks with loyal mercenaries from Sunni-majority nations such as Pakistan, Jordan, Saudi Arabia, and the United Arab Emirates. The Sunni-dominated military has a vested interest in the regime's survival since a successful Shia uprising may also endanger the Sunni soldiers' domestic destiny. During the 2011 Arab Spring, the Bahraini regime played into these fears by portraying the demonstrations against the regime as a Shia-led uprising fueled by a foreign conspiracy led by the Shia government in Iran. Although the uprising in Bahrain was repressed primarily by the police, the Sunni-dominated military also played a role in supporting the crackdown.

Syria is also instructive.[56] Deeply divided along religious lines, Syria is made up of roughly 10 percent Alawites (a sect within the Shia branch of Islam), 10 percent Christians, and 60 to 65 percent Sunnis. Bashar al-Assad, who rules Syria, hails from the Alawite sect and has a vested interest in keeping the Sunni opposition at bay. His dictatorship stacked with Alawites the officer corps and the elite military units charged with the defense of the dictatorship. When the primarily Sunni uprising against Assad began in 2011, elite units comprising Alawite soldiers were ordered to contain it. When they proved insufficient, the regime called upon the larger, regular army, where Sunnis make up approximately 70 percent of the rank and file. This turned out to be a huge mistake. Sunni officers and conscripts began to defect in large numbers, gradually unraveling Syria's military forces. Defections within the rank and file became common also due to disenchantment with widespread corruption among the Alawite senior officers close to the Assad regime. Many defectors formed the foundations of the Free Syrian Army, the primary rebel group against Assad.

11

Meritocracy and Nepotism

Age was respected among his people, but achievement was revered. As the elders said, if a child washed his hands, he could eat with the kings.
—Chinua Achebe, *Things Fall Apart*, 1958

Some militaries value merit over accidents of birth. Advancement in these militaries is based largely on accomplishment, not nepotism. In a dictatorship, a merit-based system of military advancement can stand in stark contrast to corrupt state institutions surrounding the military.[1] The military's meritocracy may provide a rare opportunity for advancement to people from humble backgrounds who may join the military to escape the frustrations of elitism in civilian institutions.[2]

These soldiers enjoy a healthy distance from the authoritarian establishment. To a soldier who grows accustomed to merit-based advancement in the military, the corrupt authoritarian state can appear anachronistic and out of touch.[3] Soldiers may grow more resentful of civilian elites who worship self-indulgence.[4] Ever so subtly, the military may emerge in the minds of soldiers as an alternate universe where merit trumps nepotism. As an outgrowth of this dissatisfaction, these soldiers may have a lesser stake in the existing authoritarian structures and stand ready to transform them into democratic ones. As the recruits themselves shift from corrupt civilian life to the disciplined and meritocratic military life, they can envision the society around them undergoing a similar transformation.[5] The political scientist Lucian Pye captures this observation eloquently: "[The] practice of giving advancement on merit can encourage people, first, to see the army as a just organization deserving of their loyalties, and then possibly, to demand that the same form of justice reign throughout their society."[6]

Consider, for example, the Turkish military.[7] As early as the nineteenth century, the Turkish military was more representative of society than were civilian institutions, including the bureaucracy and the clergy. In the early history of the republic, the military comprised primarily lower- and lower-middle-class citizens to whom military schools offered virtually the only avenue for professional advancement based on merit. Young Turks living in rural areas, previously isolated from the ruling elite, became a part of society at large through military service. Having been raised in rural communities, these soldiers were reluctant to support government policies that favored a small elite at the expense of the greater public good.

Due in large part to compulsory military service, these Turkish soldiers came from a range of sociocultural backgrounds and ethnicities. To be sure, gender diversity was lacking because military service was mandatory only for men, not women. But in an era when the image of women on the battlefield was relegated to the realm of fantasy, several women were admitted as cadets to Turkey's War Academy in the fall of 1955. In addition, soldiers were deployed to different districts from one assignment to the other to broaden their geographic experience and expose them to diverse populations within each district.

The diversity of Turkish recruits led them to become more accountable and responsive to civil society. The anthropologist Paul Stirling observed in 1951, "Consciousness of being part of the whole [Turkish] nation is greatly strengthened by the compulsory term of military service which all the young men seem vastly to enjoy."[8] The military's goal was to train modern soldiers, with the hope of creating modern citizens upon their return to civilian life. To that end soldiers who went through military training acquired more than just military combat skills. The Turkish military corps became "a major agency of social change" because it spread among the population, especially those from humbler backgrounds, a new sense of identity. For the average Turkish boy in a rural village, as Dankwart Rustow observed in 1964, "the call to military service provides a first occasion for coming into contact with the outside world, and acquiring at least some breadth of outlook."[9] After enrolling in the army, Rustow noted, "the recruit is transferred abruptly from the technology of the stick-plow and the ox-cart to that of the jeep, the automatic rifle, and the armored car."[10]

Beginning in the late 1950s, the recruits started to take intensive courses in reading, writing, arithmetic, and social studies, with their success in these courses determining their upward mobility within the military. A journalist observed the following exchange in April 1959 in a literacy class:

"What will you be if you do not learn to read and write?" asked the teacher.
"Privates," chorused the class.
"And what will you become if you study hard and learn your lessons?" pursued the teacher.
"Corporals and sergeants," the class answered enthusiastically.[11]

Portugal provides a similar illustration.[12] Until the mid-twentieth century, professional service in the armed forces had been reserved for the wealthy elite who could afford the tuition to attend the prestigious Military Academy in Lisbon. With industrial development, the military lost its appeal to wealthy families, resulting in a sharp decline in applications to become officers. This drop prompted the Military

Academy in 1958 to offer free tuition, which in turn permitted individuals from lower socioeconomic classes to join the military ranks. Once they became junior officers, they were thrown into the colonial wars in Africa to defend the property of the Portuguese elite, while the senior officers, who were members of the traditional elite, sat comfortably in staff positions back in Portugal. These junior officers had no reason to remain loyal to the status quo and eventually became the disgruntled captains who toppled the dictatorship in April 1974.

It was also the junior officers in Guatemala who ousted the dictator Federico Ponce in 1944 in an event known as the October Revolution.[13] Under Ponce's predecessor, the military had instituted a merit-based system and expanded its officer ranks to include more members of the middle class. This created a well-trained and well-educated class of junior officers. Due to their rigorous training, many of these junior officers believed themselves to be better prepared than their commanders, who had achieved their positions due to political maneuvering rather than merit. In attracting these junior officers to their cause, the government's opponents, led by Juan José Arévalo, advocated that the army's duty was to uphold the Constitution and not to blindly defend the government. Junior officers began to openly join the opposition movement.

In October 1944, Arévalo and his supporters issued a manifesto calling for revolt. A week later the presidential guard rebelled against Ponce under the leadership of junior officers. The Ponce regime quickly fell. The rebel troops seized most of the capital and placed junior officers in control after ousting the military elite.

A new junta, composed of two military officers and one civilian, assumed temporary power. The junta issued decrees removing high-ranking officers and the chief of police from their positions and calling for their trial by military tribunal. The junta oversaw popular elections for the legislature a little less than a month later, in November 1944. Arévalo won the presidential election held in December 1944. A national transformation followed, with greater limits on the role of the executive and increased social rights for citizens. It was the junior officers, buoyed by their training and culture of meritocracy, that toppled a tyrant and prompted a democratization process in Guatemala known as the Ten Years of Spring.

To be sure, the same revolutionary zeal that drives junior soldiers to stage a coup has the potential to backfire. Accustomed to the meritocracy of the military, some soldiers may underestimate the difficulty of transforming authoritarian institutions and building a civil society. This naiveté can lead to coup attempts that fail because of poor planning or poor execution. In Portugal, for example, several coup attempts against the Estado Novo dictatorship failed not because the regime was popular but because ambitious officers took action prematurely and without adequate support from their fellow officers. In Turkey disenchanted junior officers attempted to topple the Erdoğan government in July 2016 without support from the military's top brass, in what turned out to be one of the most haphazard and poorly executed coup attempts in history. In addition, idealism doesn't necessarily produce democratic results. The same officers who stage a coup with egalitarian and idealistic intentions may grow too accustomed to the benefits of power, or they may decide that a non-democratic government is the most efficient way to implement their desired social reforms.

But in many cases idealism is precisely what's necessary to launch a coup against an authoritarian government. Most dictatorships enjoy a facade of invincibility. Only soldiers who can see through this facade—with sufficient guile and guts to scream "The emperor is naked!"—may catalyze a coup to topple the regime.

The Enemy Within

*The military, either as a result of the influence of Western forms or because
of self-generated heroic ideals, seeks, wherever possible, to withdraw from the
continuous task of day-to-day policing and repression of political opposition.*
—Morris Janowitz, one of the founders of military sociology, in
The Military in the Political Development of New Nations, 1964

Being a dictator is no easy feat. Authoritarian regimes have enemies to fend off,
both foreign and domestic. Although foreign powers are formidable opponents,
it's the domestic enemies—the enemies within—that pose a particularly insidious
threat. The enemy within can develop and appear with no warning and catalyze a
revolution that ends with the dictator standing in front of a shooting squad. The
dictatorship must therefore keep a tight leash on the domestic opposition through
Orwellian surveillance institutions. Whenever these institutions reveal emerging
revolutionary movements, the authoritarian regime must have the capability of
crushing them.

The armed forces serve as the iron fist of some dictatorships. For several reasons,
a military whose primary mission is fighting the political enemy within is in a poor
position to serve as a democratic catalyst. If the military has taken sides on domestic
conflicts and is viewed as a partisan institution that enforces government policies—
particularly unpopular ones—it risks cutting its ties to society.[1] As a result the populace may outright reject the military's attempts to promote democratic institution
building.[2]

Consider, for example, the Spanish military. During the dictatorship of Francisco
Franco, which lasted from 1939 until his death in 1975, the armed forces were the
guardians of the autocratic institutions.[3] Franco frequently deployed the military to
ensure internal security and police the population. As such, the armed forces were
unsuited to spark and lead the democratization process. Following Franco's death,
the first major change to the Spanish military was to abolish its focus on internal
defense and shift its mission entirely to external defense and collaboration with
allied militaries. That shift, in turn, enhanced the Spanish military's legitimacy and
solidified its role as a neutral state institution.

A military that has policed the population has another, self-interested reason for supporting the dictatorship. If the dictatorship is toppled, the new rulers may seek reprisal against a military that suppressed demonstrations, violated human rights, and generally served as the dictatorship's weapon of choice.[4] Because the fate of these militaries depends on the dictatorship's survival, they have a significant incentive to stand by its side.

In contrast, a military that hasn't been mired in domestic conflicts is more likely to be viewed as a legitimate state institution in an illegitimate state apparatus. In times of regime crisis, these militaries remain free of the stigma of having pushed people around.[5] This credibility better allows the military to lead a democratic regime change.

Therefore militaries that have staged successful democratic coups usually haven't served as the regime's domestic iron fist. Rather these militaries were focused primarily on foreign, not domestic, threats to the dictatorship. This phenomenon follows from the citizen-soldier model discussed previously. Citizen-soldiers often do not view their fellow citizens as enemies, so deploying them against the domestic populace is a risky business.

In dictatorships toppled by democratic coups, it's usually the security forces—not the military—that do the regime's dirty work.[6] Recall that, in many nations, the military is a separate institution from the state's security forces, even though commentators often conflate the two. Although the separation between the military and the security forces sometimes blurs, the security forces typically include the police, the political police, and intelligence services. These security forces are often filled with regime loyalists and charged with fending off domestic threats to the regime, including from the military. Democratic coups staged by the military usually pit the military against these domestic security forces tasked with defending the dictatorship at all costs.

Consider the 2011 uprising in Egypt against Hosni Mubarak.[7] At the time, the military was a "widely popular" institution in Egypt.[8] It had built a stellar reputation in part because of national conscription for all men and because the Mubarak regime ordinarily didn't use the military to police the population. President Mubarak's primary weapons of choice against the protesters were the police and the Central Security Forces. These forces were staffed with many rural, illiterate conscripts who failed to meet the criteria for service in the military. When these security forces proved insufficient to contain the protests in 2011, Mubarak called upon the military. But instead of supporting the security forces, the military tanks that rolled into Tahrir Square positioned themselves between the security forces and the demonstrators to protect the latter from the former.

Like Mubarak's Egypt, Zine el-Abidine Ben Ali's Tunisia was a police state.[9] Security agencies operated by the Ministry of the Interior were responsible for quelling internal dissent. The military—made up of about thirty-six thousand conscripts and officers—was overshadowed and outfunded by its institutional rivals, particularly the twelve thousand members of the National Guard, which served as the backbone of Ben Ali's security forces. In 2010 the National Guard received twice the budget of the entire armed forces. When the protests against the regime erupted in late 2010 and early 2011, Ben Ali relied primarily on the security forces to attempt to repress the protests.

The Tunisian military was the only legitimate institution that stood apart from the remainder of Ben Ali's authoritarian government. The military had developed legitimacy in part because it was not used to police the population. It remained largely neutral and undistracted by politics, earning the title "the big silent one" (*la grande muette*)—a term initially used to describe the French military under the French Third Republic.[10] The military's "overwhelmingly positive" reputation with Tunisians was bolstered by compulsory one-year service for all men.[11]

When the uprising against Ben Ali began in December 2010, the military had no stake in his survival. As Ben Ali ordered the security agencies to unleash violence against the protesters, the military maintained its professionalism. When the security forces fell short and Ben Ali was compelled to enlist the military's aid, the Tunisian military, like its Egyptian counterpart, sided with the people. The army chief of staff, General Rachid Ammar, not only rejected Ben Ali's orders but also ordered his soldiers to protect the protesters. The army's refusal to use force on the population further animated the protesters and signaled that the dictatorship was on the brink of collapse.

13

Foreign Affairs

Military men have seldom much knowledge of books,
Their education does not allow it;
But what makes great amends for that want is,
That they generally know a great deal of the world;
They are thrown into it young;
They see variety of nations and characters;
And they find that to rise, which is the aim of them all,
They must first please;
These concurrent causes almost always give them manners and politeness.
—Lord Chesterfield, in a letter to his son, 1752

At its core, democratization is a domestic phenomenon. The belief that foreign powers can ignite a democracy halfway across the world and watch it spread like wildfire has proven untenable, as costly American adventures in the Middle East remind us.

But external factors are not irrelevant to the internal democratization process. The political scientists Steven Levitsky and Lucan Way have empirically established that authoritarian governments are more likely to survive when their connections with democratic governments are weak. Economic and cultural linkages with the West, geographic proximity to the United States and the European Union, as well as a need for loans from the International Monetary Fund, among other factors, tend to decrease the lifespan of authoritarian governments.[1]

Even so, Western influence is rarely decisive without strong domestic support for democratization. Some tyrants can withstand a substantial amount of foreign pressure without bursting. Some can even shore up their domestic support by thumbing their nose at foreign powers. And as we'll see in later pages, Western influence can serve as both a blessing and a curse, because Western governments, seeking to promote their own interests, can undermine rather than promote democratic progress.

By their nature, militaries are outward-looking institutions. The ultimate measure of their strength is how they compare to other foreign militaries.[2] As a result, soldiers tend to be particularly attuned to international standards and how their own society compares to others. Membership in international military organizations such as NATO increases the influence of global standards over the military. These organizations can employ a carrot-or-stick approach, withholding or granting benefits such as participation in training programs or joint military exercises.[3]

Participation in overseas training programs can expose officers to international democratic norms. Many foreign training programs are structured not only to provide soldiers with strategic military instruction but also to imbue them with the political values of the host nation.[4] Through their training these officers can become uniquely sensitive to how much their homeland is underdeveloped—technologically, economically, and politically—and the need for substantial advancement in their society.[5] As a result some of these officers may be more receptive to revolutions against authoritarian regimes to effectuate democratic regime change.

Young Turks

In the late nineteenth century, the military of the Ottoman Empire—then on its last legs—emerged as the "most fervent supporters of modernization."[6] Many Ottoman military officers had received a Western education and represented a large sector of the Ottoman intelligentsia. To modernize the military, sultans in the Ottoman Empire invited European military instructors to train Ottoman soldiers, which exposed them to Western ideas of governance. They became important representatives of modernity, not only in warfare and technology but also in administration. And modernity in administration required a government based on pluralism and debate rather than rule by a single sultan.[7]

Inspired by their Western training, military leaders occasionally acted as a formidable check on the sultan's authority. It was the military that forced Sultan Abdulhamid II to restore the Ottoman Constitution and the Parliament after he had suspended both institutions in 1878. The Young Turks (Jön Türkler), a group of patriotic men led by young military officers, rebelled against Abdulhamid's autocratic reign to restore constitutional and parliamentary rule. They were nothing short of audacious in their demands. "The [Ottoman] dynasty would be in danger," they declared, "if Abdulhamid II did not restore the Constitution." This warning was backed by the military might of the Third Corps in Macedonia, which threatened to march on the empire's capital, Istanbul, if the sultan refused to return to parliamentary rule. The impending coup animated the public, with joint military and civilian uprisings across the empire proclaiming their support for the Constitution. The troops that Abdulhamid sent to Macedonia to crush the military uprising joined the rebels instead. As a result Abdulhamid had no choice but to restore the Constitution and recall the Parliament in 1908.

The Constitution's restoration unleashed celebrations across the empire. Major Ismail Enver, a Young Turk officer, was welcomed by jubilant residents of Salonica as a "champion of freedom."[8] Photographs of Enver and other military officers, dubbed "the Freedom Heroes," were posted in town squares. The Young Turk Revolution "inspired a newfound sense of hope and freedom that was nothing short of intoxicating."[9]

Yet Abdulhamid's concession proved short-lived. His supporters mounted a counterrevolution on April 12 and 13, 1909, demanding the banishment of the Young Turks and the resignation of the cabinet. Abdulhamid welcomed this counterrevolution with alacrity and reasserted his control over the empire. It again took the Ottoman Third Corps in Macedonia to put Abdulhamid in his place. Military officers in the Third Corps saw the counterrevolution as an assault on the Constitution and mobilized to march on Istanbul on April 17. A week later the officers arrived in the city, suppressed the counterrevolution, and imposed martial law. The Ottoman legislature reconvened on April 27 and voted to remove Abdulhamid from power. The counterrevolution and the absolutist threats to the Constitution were defeated. The despotic sultan's downfall unleashed democratic dynamics that eventually culminated in the empire's total collapse and the establishment of the modern-day Turkish Republic.

In the following decades the Turkish military continued to benefit from the influence of democratic Western nations. In the late 1940s Turkey was a major recipient of U.S. military aid designed to implement the Truman Doctrine, which refers to U.S. President Harry Truman's policy of providing aid to countries threatened by the Soviet Union.[10] As Dankwart Rustow explains, "With the proclamation of the Truman doctrine a large-scale program of American military assistance began, and by the late 1950's American-Turkish cooperation ranged all the way from the building of a string of radar stations along the Black Sea coast, missile bases, and airfields to the preparation of literacy primers for military recruits."[11] Turkey's admission into NATO in 1952 and its participation in the Korean War alongside Western militaries also caused impressive modernization in the Turkish military. By 1959 it had received over $2 billion of U.S. and European equipment and technical assistance. In addition, Turkish soldiers were trained in Western military strategies in the United States, Germany, and Canada. The soldiers' overseas training and exposure to modern influences broadened their cultural horizons and "resulted in a sharper awareness of Turkey's material backwardness" along with a desire to create a better image of the country as a modern, democratic republic.[12] Once soldiers left the military after serving their mandatory terms, they reentered civilian society with a newfound mission of progress.

Consequently, the military assumed a central position in Turkish society as a "modern social institution and a crucial agent of modernization."[13] The military leadership in Turkey admired Western civilization and democracy, believing that the establishment of a liberal democracy was integral to becoming a modern society. In contrast, other state institutions were plagued by low levels of development and creeping authoritarianism. By 1960 Turkish soldiers were ideally suited to topple a government that had become increasingly more authoritarian since assuming power in 1950. I'll return to that coup in later chapters.

NATO Officers in Portugal

Leading up to the 1974 coup in Portugal against the Estado Novo dictatorship, NATO membership played a significant role in the growing distance between the regime and the Portuguese military.[14] Portugal was one of NATO's original members, which prompted NATO to invest funds to raise the Portuguese military forces to Western standards. Portuguese officers traveled abroad to the United States, Britain, Canada, West Germany, and other nations for training on state-of-the-art military strategies. The NATO-trained officers were placed in a better position in the line of promotions, and consequently a reformist and progressive set of NATO-generation officers emerged.

Once exposed to Western democracies, the Portuguese military officers became all the more aware of Portugal's international isolation, economic and social regress, and antiquated dictatorship. A Portuguese naval officer expressed this sentiment in the following terms: "When we were abroad, we were embarrassed by the regime. We felt that people looked down on us, that we were a second-class country."[15] An air force colonel echoed this view: "I have travelled in democratic countries throughout my career, on courses in Scotland, France, and the US. I frequently bought books banned in Portugal, as did many of my colleagues. . . . We simply felt that things were not exactly as they should be in Portugal."[16] These same Western-trained military officers ended up becoming the vanguards of revolutionary regime change at home.

A Blessing and a Curse

So far I have painted a uniformly positive picture of Western influence on the democratic outlook of militaries. Yet Western influence can also hinder rather than advance democratic progress.

Consider, for example, the U.S. approach to foreign democratic movements. Mocking the ideals that the United States is supposed to represent, American support for freedom has been less than steady. The CIA has notoriously engineered coups to topple foreign leaders—many popularly elected—whom the United States viewed as communist sympathizers. In 1973, to cite one example, the CIA-backed coup against Chile's socialist president Salvador Allende brought the repressive regime of Augusto Pinochet to power. During the cold war, the United States supported several authoritarian regimes perceived as bulwarks against communism.[17] In more recent history, the United States also crawled into bed with friendly dictatorships in the Middle East, such as Egypt and Saudi Arabia. With the rise of terrorism and Islamism in the Middle East, promotion of democracy became a secondary concern at best and a threat to American interests at worst.

American influence played a mixed role in the 1952 military coup in Egypt, which ousted King Farouk from the monarchy he had led since 1936.[18] Initially the United States appeared to be on the side of democracy. As King Farouk was losing his grip on power, he pleaded for American support. But those pleas fell on deaf ears. The U.S. government had already decided that a modernizing coup in Egypt was the proper cure for the country's political chaos, economic recession, and possible drift toward communism.

To that end, in early 1952 the United States established a CIA-run training program for young Egyptian military officers. Among the fifty officers who received training, six played a significant role in the coup against Farouk. Ali Sabri, an Egyptian Air Force officer and the official liaison between the military leadership and the United States, confirmed this conclusion: "The attendance of many Egyptian officers at U.S. service schools during the past two years had a very definite influence on the coup d'état in Egypt."[19] Three days before the coup, Sabri informed the United States that the military would topple Farouk and that U.S. interests would not be harmed.

Following the coup, a rift emerged between two of its leaders, Gamal Abdel Nasser and Mohammed Naguib. American support ended up elevating the antidemocratic Nasser at the expense of the more democracy-friendly Naguib. The U.S. government was concerned about Naguib's promise of a swift transition to civilian rule, believing that a military regime would be more reliable than an unpredictable multiparty democracy. The historian Arthur Schlesinger, who served as special assistant to President John F. Kennedy, succinctly summed up this perspective: "Progressive civilian governments tended to be unstable and soft; military governments were comparatively stable and could provide the security necessary for economic growth."[20]

Nasser, a rare politically deft soldier, played into these concerns at every opportunity. He cultivated close ties with the United States before and after the coup and painted Naguib as a communist. Nasser proved his anticommunist credentials by dispatching troops to put down a labor activist strike, ordering them to shoot on the strikers and executing two ringleaders after sham trials. The United States, convinced that Naguib was soft on communism, threw its support behind Nasser. That move put a decisive end to Egypt's first experiment with democracy, as Nasser established himself as Egypt's new dictator.

Fast forward to 2011, when the United States played an important role in Hosni Mubarak's ouster. Although Mubarak had received significant American support in the past, the United States gambled its investment in Mubarak on the revolutionaries in Tahrir Square. During the uprising Field Marshal Mohamed Hussein Tantawi received almost daily phone calls from President Barack Obama and Secretary of State Hillary Clinton.[21] The content of the phone calls is unknown, but there is some evidence that U.S. government officials informed Tantawi they no longer viewed Mubarak as a strategic ally.[22]

Although the United States may have given its blessing to the generals to oust Mubarak, American influence on the events that ensued remained limited. Recall that the Egyptian military receives $1.3 billion in annual aid from the United States as part of the Camp David peace accords. As Egypt's democratic transition dragged on and hit major roadblocks, the United States attempted to use this annual aid as leverage to steer the generals toward democracy. In October 2013, three months after the Egyptian military ousted the democratically elected president Mohamed Morsi, the United States suspended the military aid "pending credible progress toward an inclusive, democratically elected civilian government through free and fair elections."[23] But the suspension of the aid proved insufficient to bring the military to heel.[24] Despite lack of meaningful democratic progress, in March 2015 President Obama relented and announced the resumption of the aid, citing a need to fund the Egyptian military's fight against the Islamic State.[25]

In some cases Western training of militaries can bring about the very outcome the West seeks to avert. Western-trained soldiers can lend their support to a dictatorship, or become dictators themselves, in spite of—and sometimes *because of*—their training. For example, Zine el-Abidine Ben Ali became Tunisia's dictator despite his training as a military officer in the Senior Intelligence School in Maryland and the School for Anti-Aircraft Field Artillery in Texas.[26] An Ethiopian army officer, Mengistu Haile Mariam, developed anti-American sentiments only after spending half of 1967 training in the United States.[27] He later became the leader of a communist military junta responsible for genocide in Ethiopia.[28]

Consider also Yemen, a hotbed for al-Qaeda activity. Yemeni military officers are often trained by their American and British counterparts on counterterrorism. When the Arab Spring arrived in Yemen in 2011, many of these Western-trained officers were reluctant to side with the popular uprising, fearing that a successful revolution would instigate turmoil and hinder the military's counterterrorism efforts.[29]

This part discussed the factors that set apart militaries that tend to promote democracy rather than destroy it. I analyzed how citizen-soldier militaries are more loyal to society than are professional soldiers and less likely than their professional counterparts to use force on civilians. Militaries that value merit over nepotism can imbue in their soldiers progressive values inconsistent with authoritarianism. Particularly when these soldiers haven't been deployed to fight the enemy within, they can lead the society through the same transformation they personally went through after moving from an elitist society to a merit-based military. International influence is a mixed bag. Although Western training and influence on domestic militaries can play a positive role—particularly when substantial domestic support for democratization already exists—it can also backfire and hinder democratic progress.

The confluence of these factors won't inevitably produce a democratic coup. Important as they are, these variables can be overwhelmed by others. A conscript military, as in the case of North Korea, may support a dictatorship. Western-trained military officers, as in the case of Yemen, may quell a popular uprising. But in the broad run of cases, militaries that fit the pattern described in this part are more likely to turn their arms against a dictatorship than to serve as its oppressive sword.

PART FOUR

AN ALLIANCE OF CONVENIENCE

Achieving the best constitution is perhaps impossible for many; and so neither the unqualifiedly best constitution nor the one that is best in the circumstances should be neglected. . . . For one should not study only what is best, but also what is possible.

—Aristotle, *Politics*

The overthrow of a dictator is only the beginning of a potentially democratic coup. The coup initiates a sequence of escalating events, called a democratic transition, which typically lasts for a few years. During that period the military and the civilians must agree on a framework for the transition, the holding of elections, the establishment of democratic institutions, the drafting of a new constitution, and the eventual handoff of power to democratically elected leaders.

In previous chapters we saw numerous cases where the military oversees a successful democratic transition and gives up power to civilians. These cases are major head scratchers for the traditional narrative on military coups. Rather than dismiss these coups as outliers, my aim is to explain them. Instead of assuming that the military inevitably subverts democracy, this part asks whether the military can promote its development.

The answer is a qualified yes. I'll explain what the military can do for democracy during the transition process. Later chapters will flip the question and ask, à la John F. Kennedy, what democracy can do for the military. To be sure, there are plenty of cases where the military does *not* support democracy and instead chooses to establish a military dictatorship. We'll return to these cases in later chapters and discuss what sets them apart from the democratic coups considered here.

The roads to democracy are many. Thinkers from John Locke to James Madison to Alexis de Tocqueville to countless present-day academics, pundits, and policymakers have given many different answers to how nations democratize. Western attempts to devise precise recipes for democratization have not borne fruit, and nations continue to democratize in ways that astonish seasoned scholars.

But two basic ingredients emerge from decades of research as particularly significant to the initiation of democracy: political pluralism and stability. These are not magic potions; democracies do not miraculously spring up in their presence. There are other factors that come into play, including blind luck. But as we'll see in the next two chapters, without political pluralism and stability it's exceedingly difficult for a democracy to grow and mature.

Before I proceed to explain these ingredients and how the military may promote them, a preliminary question must be answered: Although military leaders *can* advance democratic norms, why would they *want* to do so? To resolve that puzzle, let's return to the caricature I drew earlier of Officers Brutus and Cassius. Recall that Officer Brutus has altruistic reasons for toppling a dictator and installing democratic rule ("For the love of Rome," as Brutus put it). Officer Cassius is more conniving and takes action only when it's in his self-interest. The actual Cassius helped assassinate Caesar not because of his loyalty to the Romans but because Caesar had denied him a coveted governorship in Syria.

After toppling a dictator, Officer Brutus may promote the conditions for democratic growth because it's the right thing to do. But what about the more puzzling case of Officer Cassius, who acts for selfish reasons? As I'll explain, in some—but not all—cases, the promotion of political pluralism and stability will further the self-interest of Officer Cassius. As an outgrowth of furthering his own interests, Officer Cassius will also advance conditions favorable to democracy.

The alignment between the coup makers' interests and democratic development will never be perfect. In some cases the alignment will be close, but in others it will not. You'll find examples of both scenarios in the next two chapters. The better the fit between the coup makers' interests and democratic growth, the higher the quality of the democracy that emerges from the transition process.

The military's promotion of democracy may be conscious or accidental. In some cases military leaders will carefully chart a path toward democracy from the moment they take power from the authoritarian regime. Calculating the benefits that democracy may provide them, these leaders will purposefully nudge the military toward a focused approach to democratic development.

Yet in other cases democracy may not be a conscious priority for the coup leaders. After the immediate goal of toppling an antagonistic dictator is achieved, the coup makers may have little idea about what to do next. Even these military leaders may stumble upon democracy not because of a grand, rational plan but as a byproduct of acting in their own self-interest. Democracy's fight for survival can become, however unwittingly, the military's fight.

14

Competition and Power

*In framing a government which is to be administered by men over men, the
great difficulty lies in this: you must first enable the government to control the
governed; and in the next place oblige it to control itself.*
—James Madison, The Federalist No. 51, 1788

Separation of Powers

James Madison was a prescient man.[1] As the Constitution of the United States was
coming into being, he expressed skepticism that the mere creation of democratic
procedures and the listing of constitutional freedoms would be sufficient to guard
liberty against abuse. Constitutional rights, he argued, were mere "parchment barriers," meaning that they were no stronger than the paper they were written on. These
parchment barriers were, on their own, insufficient to constrain self-interested
majorities and politicians whose personal ambitions would trump words on paper.
He predicted that the rights of individuals and minority groups "however strongly
marked on paper will never be regarded when opposed to the decided sense of the
public."[2]

To counter these problems, Madison devised, based on the works of earlier
thinkers such as Aristotle and John Locke, a delicate set of structural safeguards.
In modern parlance, we refer to these safeguards as separation of powers and
checks and balances. Under the former, government power is separated into different branches—typically the legislative, the executive, and the judicial. In federal systems, power is further distributed between the federal government and the
state or provincial governments. The concept of checks and balances, in turn, pits
these separate government institutions against each other. Each branch of government has weapons that it can use against the others in order to allow, in Madison's
terms, the ambitions of one branch to counter the ambitions of the other. The U.S.
Constitution reflects Madison's vision in requiring at least two branches of the federal government to accomplish any major national objective. The president negoti-
ates treaties, but the Senate ratifies them. The Congress has the power to declare
war, but the president is the commander-in-chief. Legislation requires ratification

by two houses of Congress, followed by approval by the president, which, in turn, is subject to constitutional review by the judiciary under the right circumstances. Because of these weapons, each branch of government has the ability to make life miserable for the other branches. This dynamic, Madison believed, would create a self-reinforcing check against tyranny by any one institution.

Madison's vision reflects a deep suspicion of unfettered democracy as a viable or desirable form of government. The system that he and the other framers designed is not simple majority rule, where every government institution is accountable to the whims of the mob. The framers pejoratively referred to these systems as "direct democracy" or "pure democracy." Madison voiced his concern of direct democracy in no uncertain terms: "Such democracies have ever been spectacles of turbulence and contention; have ever been found incompatible with personal security or the rights of property; and have in general been as short in their lives as they have been violent in their deaths."[3] The system that Madison and his brethren crafted includes intricate guides, restraints, and veto points to check rather than enable the mob, with the preservation of liberty as the ultimate goal.

That's the theory. Of course if things were this simple, the relatively uncomplicated task of installing these mechanisms into any constitution would be sufficient to keep authoritarianism at bay. But sobering realities often refuse to cooperate with Madison's theoretical visions. Countries such as Nigeria, Myanmar, and Eritrea, with beautifully written constitutions complete with Madisonian separation of powers and checks and balances, continue to succumb to dictatorship.[4] As gifted with foresight as Madison was, there was a missing link in his theory. He failed to foresee a momentous development that would call his theory into question: political parties.

Separation of Parties

When Madison and his brethren wrote the U.S. Constitution, they focused on dividing power between branches of government and pitting these institutions against each other. But in modern democracies, political competition is organized around political parties, nonexistent in Madison's time, not government institutions.[5] In an influential article titled "Separation of Parties, Not Powers," law professors Richard Pildes and Daryl Levinson show that when all government branches are controlled by a single party, they lack incentives to check each other. For example, in the United States, presidential vetoes virtually disappear when the federal government is unified under one party, and legislative delegations of power to the executive increase.[6] With a unified party at the helm, competition between the branches turns into cooperation.[7] Because the political fortunes of government officials in different branches largely depend on the success of the entire party, they have strong motives to support rather than oppose each other.

The capture of government institutions by a single party, termed "one-partyism" by Professor Samuel Issacharoff, can overwhelm all well-intentioned structural protections, including Madisonian checks and balances.[8] The weapons created for each branch to check the others are no good if they are left unused. To be sure, one-partyism also has its virtues. Government institutions captured by a single party can act decisively and effectively and implement major social programs. Problems of legislative gridlock—leading in the United States to frequently stalled judicial nominations or stalemates on budget negotiations—also fall by the wayside with a dominant party in power. Yet these same virtues can quickly turn into vices. Unified governments can, and often do, act too extremely, too ambitiously, and with little concern for deliberation or compromise.[9]

The problems of one-partyism are particularly acute in budding democracies. In a post-authoritarian society, political parties are likely to be weak or nonexistent because a dictatorship ensures its own survival by silencing opposition voices and disabling democratic institutions. As a result a post-authoritarian society often lacks robust political pluralism, stable legal and political institutions necessary to support a competitive democracy, and effective enforcement mechanisms designed to ensure that newly elected politicians don't misbehave. In this environment the danger that powerful groups will use the newly established democratic procedures to undermine democracy is all too great. When a strongly unified government—particularly under a charismatic leader—comes to power in a new democracy, the first elections may also be the last.

Democracy is "a system of rule by temporary majorities."[10] A dominant party, however, can employ the machinery of democracy to undermine the interests of the entire community and turn a temporary majority into a permanent one. Speaking on the eve of the 1996 elections in war-torn Bosnia, the American diplomat Richard Holbrooke highlighted this concern in the following terms: "Suppose elections are free and fair and those elected are racists, fascists, and separatists."[11]

Holbrooke's concern proved astute about many democratic experiments since the fall of the Berlin Wall. Things got off to a great start. Dictatorships collapsed across postcommunist Europe, Asia, and Latin America, and multiparty elections—the centerpiece of democracy—spread across the globe.[12] But just as the international community was getting comfortable with the rapid proliferation of the preferred Western method of government, things took a turn for the worse.

As one-partyism took root in these new democracies, political leaders began to consolidate control. Russia's democratization process crumbled in October 1993, when President Boris Yeltsin bombed his own Parliament. In Venezuela, President Hugo Chavez seized unilateral control over the constitution-design process in 1999, producing a constitution that marginalizes opposition groups.[13] Hungary, initially considered a postcommunist democratic success story, took an authoritarian turn overnight. In March 2013 the Fidesz Party, led by Viktor Orbán, replaced Hungary's Constitution, muzzled its active Constitutional Court, and altered its electoral rules to make it prohibitively difficult to unseat him.[14] These developments in Hungary took place under the watchful eye of the European Union, which stood on the sidelines as Orbán implemented his carefully engineered authoritarian scheme. Poland was initially branded "a paragon of inclusive democracy,"[15] but the Law and Justice Party that came to power in October 2015 began to systematically dismantle checks and balances and run roughshod over the country's constitutional court, media, and civil service. South Africa, previously lauded for its peaceful democratic transition after the end of apartheid, is trapped in a downward spiral as President Jacob Zuma stumbles from one corruption scandal to the next.

In many of these countries, the illusion of democracy is preserved because there is universal adult suffrage. These countries also mimic the rituals of democracy by copying democratic laws and institutions and echoing the rhetoric of Western democracies. But this democratic window dressing conceals a very different reality. The incumbents have an iron grip on political power and tend to retain their seats even when the electorate's political preferences change. The political scientists Lucan Way and Steven Levitsky use the term "competitive authoritarian" to describe these regimes that lie somewhere between democracy and autocracy.[16] Today's competitive authoritarians maintain a democratic facade but suppress opposition by curtailing civil liberties, curbing the powers of institutions (such as courts) that are supposed to keep the politicians in check, and manipulating electoral rules to stack the deck in their favor. By deploying these strategies and others, dominant one-party systems undermine a core component of democracy: competitive elections and the resulting turnover in government power.

A Hot Family Feud

The opposite of one-partyism is multipartyism. An infant democracy, according to Dankwart Rustow, requires "not a lukewarm struggle but a hot family feud."[17] Rustow's metaphor takes it a bit too far; a feud can easily devolve into conflict and undermine democratic progress, as I'll discuss in the next chapter. But there is a kernel of truth in his argument: A new democracy requires a robust political marketplace with multiple functioning political parties with incentives to restrain each other.

These incentives are organic. In their quest for power, each party will have inherent motivations to point out the handicaps of competing parties, to expose weaknesses and corruption, and to seize upon the shortcomings of their platforms and policies. Empirical evidence confirms the importance of political pluralism to democratic progress. The establishment of competitive political parties and a political marketplace in which those parties can compete are the primary factors in determining a state's probability of becoming and remaining a democracy.[18]

Combating one-partyism requires a proactive response to prevent it from taking root in the first place. But how exactly does an emerging democracy promote political pluralism? What institutions are available to promote the virtues of multipartyism while combating the vices of one-partyism?

The Power of Gavels

The traditional answer to this question lies with the courts. Many constitutional theorists invoke the judiciary as the institutional savior of emerging democracies.[19] If a dominant party begins to ignore the legal limits on its powers, the thinking goes, then courts can whip it into shape. By this account, judiciaries can enforce constitutional limits, ensure that elections are clean, prevent powerful incumbents from disenfranchising the political opposition, and curb democratic erosion.[20]

There are plenty of success stories to support this theory. During South Africa's transition from apartheid to democracy, its Constitutional Court played a prominent role. In September 1996 it rejected a draft constitutional text because the draft didn't adequately conform to the fundamental principles outlined in an interim constitutional document.[21] Likewise, in February 2010 the Colombian Constitutional Court refused to grant President Álvaro Uribe the opportunity to run for a third consecutive term. The court reasoned that a third term may have produced various antidemocratic consequences by allowing Uribe to weaken the political opposition and pack state institutions with his loyalists.[22]

At the same time, however, courts face significant institutional limits in confronting powerful politicians. Courts can impose constraints on other political actors only insofar as those actors are willing to comply with court rulings.[23] As the political scientist Matthew Stephenson puts it, "Why would people with money and guns ever submit to people armed only with gavels?"[24] This concern is especially acute in post-authoritarian societies. In many authoritarian regimes, the judiciary is a pawn of the ruling party on all but the inconsequential cases. After the dictatorship is deposed, the judiciary may lack the credibility it needs to insert itself into the political thicket. A weak court faced with a popular, dominant political party is likely to lose. Courts can be ignored, packed, or otherwise marginalized.

Consider the United States, where judicial independence is now well established. But in the early days of the American Republic, the Federalists and the Republicans attempted to undermine the judiciary's rulings to promote their partisan political agendas.[25] Even as support for judicial review increased, Presidents Andrew Jackson, Abraham Lincoln, and Franklin Roosevelt all announced that they would disregard rulings by the Supreme Court.[26]

In the modern era as well, dominant parties have brought numerous constitutional courts to heel. For example, despite the prominent role it played in the initial stages of South Africa's democratic transition, the South African Constitutional

Court has faced significant difficulties in limiting the power of the African National Congress, the incumbent party that has been in power since the end of apartheid. Likewise the once-powerful Turkish Constitutional Court was "reformed" in September 2010 in response to a series of decisions antagonistic to the ruling Justice and Development Party. The reforms added new seats to the court, permitting the incumbents to pack the court with their loyalists. In December 2015 the newly elected Law and Justice Party in Poland proceeded, as its first order of business, to restructure a defiant Constitutional Court.

Even where the judiciary is powerful enough to secure compliance with its rulings, its influence is not guaranteed to be positive for democracy. Instead of opposing dominant parties, judges may enable them. For example, in 2015 high courts in Nicaragua and Honduras struck down constitutional term limits for chief executives.[27] The elimination of term limits worked to the advantage of the incumbent presidents hoping to stay in power indefinitely.

When the elected branches are captured by a dominant party and the judiciary is powerless to help, we may have to look outside the three branches of government for an innovative solution.

The Military and Multipartyism

It was one of the first major conferences I attended as a young, untenured academic. In my presentation I briefly made the claim that, in some contexts, the military may have an incentive to combat one-partyism and, in doing so, promote political pluralism. The moderator—a senior scholar who shall go unnamed—awoke from his daydream, turned his head deliberately in my direction, and gave me the same bewildered stare that the cardinals must have given Galileo for confirming that the Earth is round.

The claim may be controversial, but the incentive to oppose one-partyism applies to many state institutions, not only to the military. A dominant party can be a serious menace to all institutions, which can find their powers curbed, their members fired, and their budgets slashed by a dominant party intent on bringing that institution to heel. For example, attacks on the judiciary by the Republican majority became more commonplace in the United States during Reconstruction and by the Democratic majority during the New Deal. In 1866, amid Reconstruction, Congress passed the Judicial Circuits Act, which effectively prevented any nominations to the Supreme Court unless the number of justices fell to six, and in 1868 repealed the Court's authority to hear certain habeas corpus petitions challenging the legality of detention. In 1937, during the New Deal, President Roosevelt famously threatened to pack the U.S. Supreme Court by expanding its size from nine justices to as many as fifteen, in order to curb the Court's hostility toward the New Deal. In contrast, multipartyism, and the competition that comes with it, can give state institutions more comfort and breathing room. With respect to the judiciary, the law professor Daryl Levinson argues that close political competition in the United States in recent decades has contributed to a rise of judicial supremacy.[28]

A dominant party can also spell trouble for the military. Recall that one of the grievances that can prompt a military to topple a dictator is the dictator's mistreatment of the military. A dominant party can pose a similar threat. If a political party becomes too strong, that party can threaten the military, cut back the military's powers, or slash the military's economic and social privileges.

In contrast, by curbing one-partyism, the military may achieve more autonomy. Like the judiciary, the military may find more comfort in the division of political powers that comes with political pluralism. As the politicians are busy bickering with each other, the military may sit undisturbed on the sidelines. From the military leaders' perspective, it's better that the parties use their political ammunition on each other rather than on the armed forces.

The desire to bring down the dominant party a peg or two may serve as an incentive for the military to promote competition among political parties. The typical scenario proceeds as follows: After the dictator is toppled, the ensuing transition process inaugurates a series of conflicts between political parties to determine who will exercise dominion. During that process a dominant party may emerge and appear poised to sweep all elections. The military, attuned to this potential threat to its interests, can launch a counteroffensive. It can throw its weight behind the opposition parties or initiate a public relations campaign to smear the dominant party.

The military's promotion of political pluralism is rarely due to a precise formal scheme implemented by rational military leaders. Rather, when confusion and incoherence permeate military policy during a transition process, pluralism may emerge as an unintentional by-product of military leaders looking out for their own interests. In keeping one powerful party in check to protect its interests, the military can promote the proliferation of others.

During the transition process, the military therefore functions somewhat like a fourth branch of government. Similar to their unelected counterparts in the judiciary, the military leaders can check political actors to ensure they don't overstep their boundaries. Because the military is armed with tanks and guns—not merely gavels—its power to check the politicians is particularly strong. The armed forces are also rarely beholden to a specific political party, which bolsters their institutional capability to serve this function.

Consider, for example, Portugal.[29] Between April 1974, when the military overthrew the Estado Novo dictatorship, and July 1976, when the military relinquished power to a democratically elected government, Portugal underwent a dramatic transformation. Under military leadership, and with the assistance of largely civilian cabinets, Portugal built the foundations for a constitutional democracy, releasing political prisoners, establishing democratic institutions, and guaranteeing the freedom of expression and association. Because of these efforts, within a year of

the coup fifty political movements or parties were established, union activity flour-
ished, and neighborhood committees sprang up.

The military's preoccupation with dismantling authoritarian state structures
and establishing a pluralist democracy arose largely out of self-interest. Many military leaders blamed the Estado Novo's authoritarian institutions for the costly
and unfruitful military operations in Portugal's African colonies. Abolishing those
authoritarian institutions thus became a necessary first step in protecting the military's interests. It also generated the associated by-product of promoting democratic
development and political pluralism. In the end the military achieved a swift return
to democratic civilian rule, creating what the political scientist Philippe Schmitter
has called "one of the most pluralistic polities in existence."[30]

But like other good things, too much political pluralism can be bad. As the
political theorist Robert Dahl has lamented, "One perennial problem of [political]
opposition is that there is either too much or too little."[31] The emergence of too
much political pluralism can generate its own distinctive risks. Excessive political
pluralism can create legislative deadlocks, instigate instability, create power vacuums, and even lead to the breakdown of a democratic state.[32] To cite one example,
excessive political pluralism in Belgium nearly led to political collapse in 2010. The
parliamentary elections in that year produced a fragmented parliament, with eleven
parties elected, but none receiving more than 20 percent of the vote. A stalemate
ensued following failed negotiations on the new government's makeup, and the
country remained without an elected government for nearly six hundred days—a
record for a democracy.[33] During that stalemate Belgian politicians and intellectuals
were openly considering the possibility of disintegration and partition.[34]

A similar scenario played out in Turkey.[35] In May 1960 the Turkish military toppled the authoritarian government of Adnan Menderes with a promised transition
to democratic rule. Following the coup, the military established the legal and political foundations of a democratic society and a genuine multiparty political order that
represented major social groups. A total of six parties participated in democratic
elections following the coup. At least two of these parties were creations of the democratic transition overseen by the military: the Socialist Turkish Workers' Party and
the Republican National Peasants' Party. The election of members from the Turkish
Workers' Party to the Parliament marked the first time in Turkish history that an
avowedly socialist party could form, operate freely, and obtain representation in the
legislature. But the Turkish military was too successful in enabling political pluralism. Although the military established democratic institutions, weak and unstable
coalition governments followed the coup, which paralyzed effective governance and
prompted further military interventions. We will return to these interventions in
future chapters.

Although the military often stands to benefit from political pluralism, this is not
always the case. If a dominant party is committed to serving the military's interests
in the long term, the military may have an interest in enabling, rather than resisting,

one-partyism. This is why, as we'll see in later chapters, the military may tilt the electoral playing field toward a particular political party.

But placing all trust in a single party is a risky gambit. There is always the possibility that the military's efforts to boost a civilian partner may not succeed. Having thrown its support behind a particular party and sidelined the remaining parties, the military may be ostracized by the victors. It can also lose any credibility it may have gained as a neutral state institution. As a result hedging bets by promoting political pluralism and avoiding going all in on a particular party may prove to be the best long-term approach for the military. In addition a long-term alliance with a civilian partner is an uncertain proposition in democratic transitions ordinarily characterized by fickle interests and alliances. Even if the military finds a civilian partner it can do business with, what begins as an amicable relationship can quickly turn sour.

Consider the following example. Recall that, following its coup against the Mubarak dictatorship in 2011, the Egyptian military formed an alliance of convenience with the Muslim Brotherhood.[36] After Mubarak's fall, the Brotherhood was the only established political group in Egypt and promised stability after a tumultuous revolution. The Brotherhood also appeared to support many of the state institutions that gave the Egyptian military its economic and social privileges. To top it off, the Brotherhood's political agenda was relatively modest: They wouldn't run a candidate in the presidential elections nor seek a majority of the parliamentary seats.

But as the democratic transition progressed, the Muslim Brotherhood began to renege on its promises of humble political leadership. They ran an aggressive electoral campaign that landed them a near-majority of the seats in Parliament as well as the presidential seat. Once in power, the Brotherhood waged a political offensive on all fronts, sidelining the political opposition, purging the senior leadership of the military, and swiftly pushing their preferred constitutional provisions through the Constituent Assembly.

In expanding their own powers, the Muslim Brothers failed to realize that they were courting trouble. They envisioned a satisfying power grab but got something entirely different. The alliance of convenience between the military and the Muslim Brotherhood began to fray as the Brotherhood's growing dominance began to pose a potential threat to the military. From the military's perspective, the purge of its senior leadership could be the harbinger of larger-scale challenges to its prerogatives.

The military's tacit support for the Brotherhood quickly morphed into opposition. To obtain domestic and global support for this campaign, the military exaggerated the dangers posed by the Brotherhood and played into Western fears of an Islamist takeover of Egypt. General Mamdouh Shaheen, a member of the ruling military junta, the Supreme Council of the Armed Forces (SCAF), was transparent about the military's plans, declaring, "Egypt, as a country, needs to protect democracy from the Islamists."[37] The military would do whatever it could to ensure that Egypt's elected institutions meaningfully represented opposition interests and were not dominated by the Brotherhood. This campaign, fueled by the protection of the military's own interests, also initially proliferated political pluralism in Egypt.

As part of its campaign, the SCAF first announced a set of "supraconstitutional principles" that would bind the Constituent Assembly in drafting a new constitution. The principles attempted to protect individual liberties and minority rights, which many interpreted as an attempt to preempt any potential antidemocratic moves by the Islamist-controlled Constituent Assembly. One provision expressly granted the military a constitutional role as the guardian of an amorphous "constitutional legitimacy." Commentators suspected that this move was intended to give the military free rein to check any threats the Muslim Brotherhood may pose.

In addition to issuing principles to bind the Constituent Assembly, the SCAF also attempted to control the Assembly's composition. Although a March 2011 referendum authorized Parliament, not the military, to select members of the Assembly, the military sought to curb that power once it became clear that the Brotherhood would dominate Parliament. Under a plan announced by Deputy Prime Minister Ali al-Selmi, Parliament's authority to appoint members to the Constituent Assembly would be limited to only 20 percent of the seats. To make the Assembly more representative, the remaining members would be chosen from, among others, judges, professors, labor unions, and the Coptic Christian Church. The Brotherhood responded to the plan by staging massive protests, which caused the SCAF to relent and abandon it.

The SCAF's foiled plan to increase pluralism on the Constituent Assembly was resurrected by the Administrative Judicial Court in April 2012. The court voted to dissolve the Constituent Assembly in response to arguments that it was unrepresentative of Egyptian society, especially women and youth. After the Assembly's dissolution, Egypt's civilian politicians returned to the drawing board to create a more pluralistic body. When negotiations in June 2012 failed to produce an agreement on the Assembly's composition, the military entered the fray and forced a political compromise. The outcome was a more pluralistic Assembly that included representatives from all major social groups in Egypt.[38]

In addition to the Constituent Assembly, the Brotherhood-dominated legislature was also targeted by the military. Citing a faulty electoral law, the Supreme Constitutional Court dissolved Egypt's Parliament. The ruling was issued by a court widely viewed by experts as independent and outside of the military's influence.[39] But the military, eager to restrain the Brotherhood's stronghold, welcomed the court's ruling and promptly enforced it.[40]

Although the Egyptian military's self-serving actions curbed the increasingly pernicious dominance of the Muslim Brotherhood, the military went too far. What began as a relatively modest agenda by the military to take the Brotherhood down a peg or two devolved into a program of outright elimination. The Muslim Brotherhood either ignored or misinterpreted the implied messages from the military, remained defiant, and ended up paying a steep price for its audacity. The military eventually took advantage of the groundswell of opposition against the Brotherhood and the massive protests that began on June 30, 2013, and staged a coup against President Mohamed Morsi.

Although political pluralism is crucial to a new democracy's advancement, democracy is not just about competition for office. That competition must happen not through violence but through elections. Put differently, the democratic game must be played under stable conditions, and conflicts must be expressed and resolved through democratic means. Without stability, political pluralism will produce—not a well-functioning democracy—but a full-fledged civil war.

15

Freedom and Order

Stability in government is essential to national character and to the advantages annexed to it.

—James Madison, The Federalist No. 37, 1788

The fall of a dictator often unleashes waves of chaos and economic and social instability. This revolutionary turmoil hits the nation just as it's attempting to recover from a long period of dictatorship and establish the beginnings of democracy. At this precarious moment, ordinary political conflicts can degenerate into bare-knuckled fist fights or, worse, a full-blown civil war. Sectarian tensions uneasily contained by a dictator can expose themselves as a can of worms, instigating further turmoil and secessionist struggles. The conflict between Shias and Sunnis in Iraq—unleashed by Saddam Hussein's ouster in 2003—continues to present formidable challenges to the establishment of a functioning democracy. Gaddafi's downfall in 2011 brought not stability but widespread infighting among more than a hundred tribes, all but paralyzing Libya's transition to democracy. From this infighting, two competing parliaments emerged, each claiming to represent the Libyan people.

Freedom without Order

Freedom without order is anarchy. Disorder can shake the foundations of a nation and impede all attempts to build a functioning democracy. When their own survival is at risk, citizens are rarely moved by abstract ideals like democracy. In a setting of chaos and mayhem, where no one's rights are ensured, elections, constitutions, and democratic institutions can appear to be unnecessary luxuries.

Instability can also kindle the emergence of dominant parties with questionable democratic credentials that come to power with promises of stability. Democratic revolutions often produce outbreaks of nostalgia.[1] In the political and social turmoil that a democratic transition produces, many wistfully harken back to the socially and economically stable days of the autocratic regime.[2] As stability decreases following a dictatorship's fall, so can public support for democracy. For example, according to a Pew Research Center survey of Egyptians eighteen months after the fall of Mubarak, 52 percent believed that the country was either worse off or neither better nor worse off as a result of Mubarak's ouster. Only 44 percent believed Egypt was better off.[3] Even in Tunisia, often considered the poster child of the Arab Spring, high unemployment and declining tourism revenues dashed hopes of stability following Ben Ali's ouster. Forty-two percent of Tunisians surveyed in July 2012 believed that Tunisia was worse off since the regime fell, compared to 45 percent who believed they were better off.[4]

When the populace yearns for the stable past, democratic change may seem too costly, difficult to comprehend, and questionable. A conflict-weary public may be all too willing to make immediate compromises in the name of securing social and economic stability.[5] They may approve constitutions that provide the government with wide-reaching powers to suppress human rights in the name of stability. For example, the first constitution-making process in Egypt following Mubarak's downfall produced a document replete with loopholes that allow the government to curtail individual rights to ensure national security.[6] Writing for the *New York Times*, David Kirkpatrick and Kareem Fahim observed that many Egyptians voted yes "to end the chaos of the transition rather than to endorse the text of the charter."[7]

Faced with the undesirable prospect of continued turmoil, the people may elect politicians who promise stability even though they exhibit glaring signs of illiberalism. For example, Alpha Condé became Guinea's first democratically elected president after running on a stability-based platform, promising, "I will be both the Mandela and the Obama of Guinea."[8] The people elected him despite his readily apparent authoritarian tendencies.[9] Election results in Turkey in 2015 also fit this pattern. According to the Turkish politician and writer Suat Kınıklıoğlu, the Turkish electorate came out strongly in favor of the Justice and Development Party despite knowledge that the party "is corrupt, has strong authoritarian tendencies, and continues to plunder . . . Turkey's resources."[10] The prospect of continuing stability prompted many Turks to "go with the devil they know."[11]

Order without Freedom

Stability is necessary for a democracy to emerge, but an overemphasis on stability can generate problems of its own. Liberty without order may be anarchy, but order without liberty is tyranny.[12] If stability means forcing unruly groups to behave, crushing popular protests, ostracizing minority groups, and imposing emergency measures to maintain public peace, the resulting system of government is a dictatorship, not democracy.

Stability, as applied to democratic development, is different from the type of forced consensus that enables a dictatorship. Stability in an emerging democracy requires a basic set of democratic rules that govern political conflicts to ensure these conflicts do not degenerate into violence. Machiavelli argued, "There are two ways of contesting, the one by law, the other by force. The first method is proper to men. The second to beasts, but because the first is frequently not sufficient, it is necessary to have recourse to the second."[13] An emerging democracy must prove Machiavelli wrong. It must reject violence as a legitimate means of resolving conflicts and embrace instead the rule of law.

But playing by the rules is much easier said than done in an emerging democracy. A democratic transition requires all those involved to roll the dice in a game where the rules, as well as the players, are new, uncertain, and in flux. Political parties competing for power will tend to lack an established track record and relationships with other parties. They will tend to view each other with deep suspicion and brace themselves for treachery. Even if the politicians happen to be trusting by nature, their environment will tend to reshape their nature. Where parties have reason to expect that others will renege on their agreements or refuse to reciprocate their compromises, they will neither agree nor compromise.[14] The resulting paralysis may lead not to democracy but to a resurgence of the dictatorship.

A recent example of this phenomenon is the brief reign of Mohamed Morsi, the first elected president of Egypt, after the 2011 coup against Mubarak.[15] Although Morsi had vowed to be a "president for all Egyptians," his loyalty lay with the Muslim Brotherhood, as he routinely sidelined the non-Islamic opposition parties. Morsi and his opponents couldn't reach an agreement about the mandate or the makeup of the Constituent Assembly, and continuous disagreements about "the most basic procedures plunged the country into institutional chaos at moments when forging trust was crucial."[16] Morsi often dismissed opposing policy views as an affront to the will of the people, and the opposition parties refused to come to terms with the democratic victory of the Muslim Brotherhood. In response Morsi introduced a unilateral constitutional declaration in November 2012 that nullified judicial oversight of presidential decisions and preempted legal challenges to the constitutional process. This dramatic consolidation of power was done in the name of bypassing political gridlock.

In a chaotic political environment filled with uncertainty, what's needed is an external referee with a steady hand. The referee must maintain a basic level of public tranquility, enforce the rules of the democratic game, arbitrate conflicts, and resolve disputes.[17] If the political players trust that the referee will enforce the rules fairly, they will be less concerned about cheating by the other players and more willing to agree and compromise. Rather than engage in perpetual fighting and scheming, all relevant actors may defer to the mediating power of the referee.

The external enforcement of rules is also important to inspire long-term confidence in democracy. The first elections, successfully supervised by a neutral referee, can legitimate the idea of popular participation in governance. Initial successes can beget future ones, and small steps in the right direction can lead to something much bigger.

Democracy, the political scientist Adam Przeworski explains, is "a system in which parties lose elections."[18] When they lose elections, political parties must be willing to step down. And the losers will be more willing to step down if they believe they have future opportunities to compete—and win—in a healthy political marketplace.[19] When losers believe they will have another chance to play in a fair rematch, they will be less willing to invoke much less desirable alternatives to obtaining power, including violence and secession.

The Military as External Referee

Although other state institutions can also play referee, in some cases the military enjoys a clear edge in serving as a stabilizing anchor. Consider the historical moment when the military has deposed an unpopular dictator and is supervising a transition process to democracy. At least initially, the military tends to have substantial credibility. It also has enforcement powers—in the form of soldiers armed with tanks and guns—that other state institutions, including the judiciary, lack. Parties may be less likely to violate the rules of the game and renege on their commitments if they face potential retribution from the military. Having deposed one authoritarian government that refused to play by democratic rules, the military may be willing to get rid of another.

But what is the military's incentive to arbitrate political conflicts during the transition to democracy? In other words, even if the military *can* serve as a referee, why would it *want* to do so?

The military and the state are in a symbiotic relationship. Neither can survive without the other. The state's survival depends on the military's ability to fend off armed threats, and the military's survival depends on the existence of a stable and functioning state.[20] Where chaos reigns, the nation becomes vulnerable to territorial breakdown or foreign conquest, with disastrous consequences for the military. Instead of yielding to these unwelcome prospects, military leaders may choose, however reluctantly, to serve as the stabilizer of the emerging democracy. That allows the development of conditions necessary for building basic democratic institutions.

Portugal provides a good example. The political parties that emerged following a 1974 coup against the Estado Novo dictatorship depended on the military's oversight as a crucial check on their adversaries. The new constitution empowered the Council of the Revolution, comprising primarily military officers, to serve as the "guarantor of the proper working of the democratic institutions."[21] The political parties viewed the military's oversight of the political system as a check, not only on themselves but on their adversaries as well.[22] This system ensured that all political parties abided by the rules of the democratic game.[23]

I discussed earlier why it's often conscript militaries that stage democratic coups. A conscript military will be particularly well-situated to serve as an external arbiter of political conflicts and rekindle a divided nation's lost sense of unity. In a conscript military, citizen-soldiers serve a defined term before returning to civilian life. Citizens of different regional and ethnic backgrounds share a common, unifying experience that bonds them to the military and to the nation the military is tasked to defend.[24]

Consider John Marshall, arguably the most influential chief justice of the U.S. Supreme Court. Before his service on the Court, young Marshall fought in the American Revolutionary War. At the time, Americans instinctively thought of themselves as citizens of their state (in Marshall's case, Virginia), not of the United States. But following his military service for the United States, Marshall came to think of himself first as an American, and only second as a Virginian.[25] He later brought this nationalist view to the bench, declaring in landmark cases such as *McCulloch v. Maryland* that the government of the Union is "the government of all; its powers are delegated by all; it represents all, and acts for all."[26]

The conscript military, where many citizens serve or have served, thus contributes to a sense of belonging to a group with a unified national mission above partisan political conflicts.[27] Dankwart Rustow speaks in similar terms of the Turkish military. He observes that, at the time of the 1960 military coup that toppled an authoritarian government, only the military "among all agencies of leadership then available could have established unity inside the country and redefined national goals."[28]

Conscript militaries also tend to enjoy substantial goodwill and trust among divergent segments of society, which bolsters their credibility. According to a May 2012 nationwide survey of Egyptians by the Pew Research Center, the military continued to be a well-regarded institution despite its poor performance at pivotal points during the democratic transition process following Mubarak's ouster. The Pew poll found that 75 percent of Egyptians believed the military continued to have a "good influence" on the country, including 43 percent who said "very good."[29] Similarly, in Portugal, 54 percent of the population attributed "much or very much recognition" to the armed forces for their overthrow of a dictatorship in 1974 and the subsequent establishment of democracy.[30]

Even if conscript militaries occasionally make unpopular decisions during the transition process, the goodwill they have built may ensure continued public support for their role as external referees. In this respect public attitudes toward the conscript military may resemble the public's views of the judiciary. Social scientists have found that the public may continue to support the judiciary even where courts generate unpopular decisions because the reservoir of institutional support for the courts outlasts specific judicial decisions.[31] Daryl Levinson echoes this view: "If political actors assess judicial review as a package of probabilistic policy outcomes rather than one case at a time, then the expected policy value of the Court as an institution can be positive on net despite some negative-value decisions."[32] A conscript military can benefit from a similar reservoir of goodwill and continue to enjoy public support despite occasional unpopular actions.

Bells, Cats, and the Military

The military enjoys an edge over other institutions in another important respect. Because of its hierarchical command structure—a few at the top call the shots—the military doesn't suffer from collective-action problems to the same degree as civilian politicians do. A collective-action problem refers to a case where an action would benefit multiple individuals, but the action is not taken due to difficulties in reaching an agreement. A good example is the fable of the belled cat. A group of mice gather to discuss how to fend off an attack by a malicious cat. They agree to place a bell on the cat's neck to signal the incoming attack. But when a mouse asks who will volunteer to place the bell on the cat, all of the mice make excuses and bow out.

To achieve a stable democratic transition, a number of bells must be placed on various cats. For example, the polity must agree to the timing and sequence of the elections and the rules that will govern candidate and voter eligibility. These important procedural decisions can instigate squabbles among civilian politicians, making progress difficult. At times disagreement over a single issue can derail the entire transition process. For example, after Libya held its first elections in more than half a century in July 2012, the newly elected government couldn't agree on whether to keep and rejuvenate the machinery of the old military or create a new security force altogether.[33] Without a centralized security structure, young conscripts returned to localized, factional militias, which left the new government defenseless from attack.[34]

Consider also Egypt. In June 2012, during the transition process following Mubarak's fall, the squabbling political parties were unable to reach a compromise on the makeup of the Constituent Assembly to draft the new constitution. The burden of reviving these failed negotiations fell on the military. The ruling military junta, the Supreme Council of the Armed Forces, entered the fray by giving the politicians an ultimatum to create an Assembly within forty-eight hours. If the politicians failed to reach an agreement, the military leaders threatened to set into motion their own plan for the Assembly. Under intense pressure, the politicians unexpectedly achieved consensus, reinforcing what the Cairo-based writer Elijah Zarwan calls the "narrative that only the military can press self-serving civilian politicians to fulfill their duties to the nation."[35]

Sometimes it's better that an issue be settled promptly than settled perfectly. A referee that can announce a decision—whatever that decision may be—can prevent endless and costly conflict. Although resolving contentious questions creates work for what are often ill-prepared military leaders, some may welcome these tasks with enthusiasm because they can present opportunities to create rules favorable to the military's interests.

This leads to an important point: In refereeing political conflicts, the military leaders may have some skin in the game. For a coup to be considered democratic, the resulting elections must be free and fair. Therefore the military can't simply anoint themselves or their chosen civilian successors as the nation's new leaders. But they can take less overt actions during the democratization process and tweak the rules to favor themselves or their preferred clientele, as we'll see in the next part. In some cases the virtues associated with the military's ability to overcome collective-action problems can be recast as a vice if the military's efficient decision-making process produces lousy outcomes.

So far I've discussed how the interests of the military and a budding democracy may align over the establishment of stability. Let's complicate matters slightly. On very rare occasions the military may favor instability in order to produce conditions for a military intervention. Military leaders yearning to grab power from civilian politicians may manufacture or exaggerate social instability to legitimize a coup. In Turkey, for example, widespread violent conflict between leftist and rightist groups in the late 1970s was used to justify a military coup in 1980. Much of the public initially welcomed the coup, believing that it would restore stability to the country, even though it ended up producing disastrous consequences for Turkish democracy. Although the facts remain shrouded in mystery, some commentators have argued that the military deliberately allowed the leftist-rightist conflict to escalate to create a pretext for a military coup.[36] Despite rare examples to the contrary, the bottom line remains that, in the broad run of cases, the military will favor a stable state over an unstable one.

Let's weave together the threads spun in this part. A budding democracy needs political pluralism and stability to mature. In at least some cases it will be in the military's interests to promote these conditions, not because of a grand altruistic plan but because these same conditions will also serve the coup makers' interests.

This is not to say that the military is the panacea for all political problems that arise in a budding democracy. The military can't solve ethnic, religious, or racial tensions. It can't ensure the election of credible leaders with favorable democratic credentials. It can't improve the economy, reduce unemployment, or address most of the problems that plague a new democracy. But the military can maintain stability, keep a dominant party in check, and combat the one-partyism that can end a democratic experiment shortly after it begins.

Although democratic rule often benefits the military, the military may not want all the trappings of democracy. After all, in a full-fledged democracy, the military is supposed to be subordinated to the whims of civilian politicians, with its economic and social privileges entrusted to the vagaries of democratic politics. The military may desire a degree of autonomy from civilian interference that may not be fully consistent with traditional definitions of democracy. This gives the military an incentive to tinker with the democratic transition process and rig the rules in its favor.

PART FIVE

MEET THE NEW BOSS, SAME AS THE OLD BOSS

I'll tip my hat to the new constitution
Take a bow for the new revolution
Smile and grin at the change all around
Pick up my guitar and play
Just like yesterday
Then I'll get on my knees and pray
We don't get fooled again.
                            —The Who, "Won't Get Fooled Again," 1971[1]

It was my first time in Cairo. On a sweltering hot summer day, I hailed a barely roadworthy taxi to get to my hotel near Tahrir Square. We drove past the Square, where thousands of protesters had camped out in makeshift tents following a night of demonstrations. As I stared out at history in the making, my cab driver began to speak—as cab drivers do—of the problems of the day. He was in his early thirties and disenchanted with life in Egypt. There was crime and violence on the streets, he lamented, and the nation was struggling with extreme inflation and food shortages. He explained that nearly 33 percent of Egyptians were completely illiterate, 40 percent were living at or below the poverty threshold, and his sister was afraid to walk on the streets. There was no light at the end of the tunnel.

After arriving at my hotel, I fell into a deep jet-lag-induced afternoon nap, only to be awoken by sounds of gunfire. I turned on Al Jazeera, to learn that Egypt's riot police were in the process of cleansing Tahrir Square of the protesters I had seen barely an hour before. I watched—on live television—as the police began attacking and beating the protesters and tearing down their tents. Several protesters were killed, and many more were wounded. When I mustered the courage to venture out of my hotel, I found an eerily empty Tahrir Square surrounded by black-clad riot police.

Later that day I asked one of the leaders of the protests, who had escaped arrest, to explain what happened.

"We were fooled again," he responded.

After staging a coup against a dictator, the military temporarily governs the country before democratic elections of civilians take place. During this transitional period, the military leaders must play politician and pass laws, issue decrees, supervise the drafting of a new constitution, and set up a framework for elections. A coup of seismic significance can produce surprisingly little change, at least in the short term. The events I described above took place in the summer of 2011, when the military was governing the country after the February 2011 coup against Mubarak, but they could just as easily describe life under Mubarak. Much to the dismay of the Egyptian people, life under their new boss, the military, wasn't all that different from life under the old. The new regime resembled the old, the new protests resembled the old, the economic and social crises were magnified copies of their predecessors, and even their new constitution looked like the old.

In this part I'll explain why. I'll discuss why military leaders are often ill-equipped to govern a country after they take over following a coup against a dictator. I'll also analyze why ruling military leaders may engage in attempts—copied from the playbook of the dictator they deposed—to protect their prerogatives.

16

A New Order

Chaos was the law of nature. Order was the dream of man.
—Henry Adams, *The Education of Henry Adams*, 1907

In 1952 a group of military officers toppled King Farouk of Egypt.[1] The coup makers had little knowledge of politics and no clear indication of where Egypt should head. Their primary objective was toppling the corrupt and incompetent king, whom they thought had become a puppet of Western imperialist forces. Once the king was gone, the coup makers believed—rather naively, it turns out—that the Egyptian people would simply point them in the right direction. Lieutenant Colonel Gamal Abdel Nasser, the mastermind of the coup, described his experience in the following terms: "I had imagined that the whole nation was ready and prepared, waiting for nothing but a vanguard to lead the charge against the battlements, whereupon it would fall in behind in serried ranks, ready for the sacred advance towards the great objective."[2] But reality refused to comply with Nasser's imagination: "Crowds did eventually come and they came in endless droves—but how different is the reality from the dream! The masses that came were disunited, divided groups of stragglers. . . . We needed order, but we found nothing behind us but chaos. We needed unity, but we found nothing behind us but dissension. We needed work, but we found behind us only indolence and sloth."[3]

Nasser's sentiments are typical of those expressed by other military leaders who have toppled dictatorships. After a military ousts a dictator, the country is typically a complete mess. Although citizens might expect that the dictator's exit will solve most of their problems, the revolutionary period is usually punctuated by economic and social turmoil, rising crime rates, and unemployment. In a democratic coup, these are the conditions in which the coup makers must temporarily govern before they turn power over to civilian leaders.

But most military officers make abysmal politicians. Military leaders are accustomed to commanding a disciplined group of soldiers who have been trained to toe the line.[4] So they face significant adjustment problems in attempting to govern a much larger, unwieldy, and opinionated group of people with no inherent obligation to do as they say. Fed up with social disunity and chaos day after volatile day, the military leaders may take matters into their own hands by attempting to impose a new order from the top down, "order" being the relevant word.

Consider what happened after a democratic coup against the Peruvian dictator Juan Velasco Alvarado.[5] After seven years as president, Velasco was deposed by the military in a bloodless coup on August 29, 1975. The coup came in response to waves of demonstrations that summer. The regime had been slowly crumbling under the weight of corruption allegations and influence-peddling scandals. By mid-1975 the military's desire to depose Velasco was undeniable, and General Francisco Morales Bermúdez, who was then serving as prime minister, looked like a preferable substitute.

Although Velasco's downfall was quick and quiet, the transition process that followed was decidedly not. General Morales inherited a nation in a state of crisis. The previous seven years under Velasco's rule had left the government with virtually no public support, the military was ideologically divided, there was a resurgence of partisan politics, and the severe economic crisis was second only to the global Great Depression. Despite these bleak circumstances, Velasco's removal enabled the military to improve strained relations with the public. Publications that had been banned were permitted again, political prisoners were released, and citizens were brought into the cabinet for the first time since 1968. The plan, according to Morales, was to institute constitutional government gradually, with the military withdrawing from politics by 1980.

Although Morales "pledged not to deviate 'one millimeter' from the nation's revolutionary course," the economic crisis and popular unrest derailed this promise by late 1976.[6] An austerity program was announced to get Peru's debt under control, which instigated two weeks of riots. The riots prompted the regime to proclaim a state of emergency, suspend constitutional guarantees, suppress dozens of publications, and arrest hundreds of people. A curfew was imposed, and the state of emergency stayed in place for fourteen months.

The election for a constituent assembly to draft a new constitution was interrupted by yet another financial crisis. Hitting both the state and the private sector hard, the financial troubles plaguing Peru were bad enough for foreign suppliers to demand cash up front from all Peruvian customers. Morales replaced two powerful generals from the ministries of industry and finance with civilians, who promptly announced new taxes, a devaluation of the currency, and a 50 to 70 percent price increase on certain necessities. In response to widespread riots, the government suspended political activities and instituted yet another state of emergency. Although a new democratic constitution was eventually drafted and ratified, followed by a handover of power from the military to the civilians, the military's firm response to the turbulence of the transition period left an indelible mark on Peruvian politics.

Consider also the actions of the Egyptian military following the 2011 coup against Hosni Mubarak. After a brief post-coup honeymoon period, the public started to turn against the military because its leadership couldn't cope with the mounting societal problems that my cab driver had lamented about during my visit to Cairo. A mere two weeks after Mubarak's ouster, protesters began pouring into the streets in droves, demanding action. In response the military oscillated between providing concessions and cracking heads. For example, the military hastened to bring to trial several members of Mubarak's deposed cabinet in response to protests demanding accountability from his overthrown regime.[7] Also, in a July 2011 press conference, the ruling Supreme Council of the Armed Forces asserted it had no plans to use violence against peaceful demonstrators and that accusations to the contrary "hurt the feelings of the armed forces, which took the side of the people from the very beginning."[8]

At other times protests were met with the type of pitiless repression that I saw in Tahrir Square.[9] By tightening the noose and making an example out of the demonstrators, the military believed that it could avert future threats to stability. One member of SCAF described the military's attitude in the following terms: "The relationship between the military and the revolutionaries resembles a father whose son goes to school, and he encourages him to study every once in awhile, 'Study, my dear.' Then exam time draws near, and he has to yell at him: 'Attend to your studies!'"[10]

For SCAF, the violent dispersal of peaceful protesters was the equivalent of forcing the Egyptian public to attend to their studies. But the military leaders considered themselves above the messy work of crowd dispersal, so they left this task primarily to Egypt's security forces. Recall that these were the same security forces that attempted to suppress the popular protests against Mubarak. During those protests, the military had used its tanks and soldiers to protect the protesters from the ravages of the security forces. Yet following Mubarak's ouster, the military leadership turned a blind eye to police repression of protests. The coup makers' blithe ignorance gave free rein to the security forces to detain, torture, and even kill revolutionary activists.

Why did the Egyptian military shield the protesters from the security forces during the uprising against Mubarak, but later permit the same security forces to repress them? Egypt's military leaders were politically inexperienced and feared that domestic chaos could foment further violence. Maintaining stability was the first order of business, and stability was what the security forces offered. The optics of crushing unarmed protesters were less important.

The security forces had their own reasons for doing the military's dirty work. They used this opportunity to settle accounts and punish the Egyptian people for rebelling against the Mubarak dictatorship that formed the foundations of Egypt's police state. By abusing the protesters, the security forces may have also hoped to create a rift between the military leadership and the people.

If this were the security forces' plan, it worked. The police repression of protesters transformed the people's attitudes toward the military. The same protesters who chanted "The people and the army are one hand" following the coup against Mubarak soon began to chant "The military and the police are one hand." Likewise the memorable slogan "The people demand the overthrow of the regime" that reverberated on Tahrir Square preceding Mubarak's ouster morphed into "The people demand the execution of the field marshal," referring to the leader of SCAF.

To add insult to injury, the Egyptian military suppressed any inclinations to admit wrongdoing. The military leadership largely ignored the domestic and global ruckus, elaborately orchestrated positive publicity, and painted the human rights abuses as unfortunate mishaps that could have been avoided had the unruly protestors behaved. For example, after the police surrounded and brutally beat protesters who continued to demonstrate in Tahrir Square in February 2011, the military leadership issued a brief apology that brushed off the severity of the attacks. The military insisted it did not order the attacks and instead downplayed them as "the result of unintentional confrontations between the military police and the youths of the revolution."[11] These episodes cast a shadow over Egypt's promised transition to democracy and left a stain on the military's relationship with society that no passage of time can fully erase. Although these atrocities were largely perpetuated by Egypt's security forces—not the military—the ruling military leaders can hardly be absolved of responsibility for what took place.

To be sure, government repression also occurs during civilian-led transitions to democracy. During a turbulent transition period, with survival instincts in high gear, repression can and does happen regardless of who is in charge. For example, the deadly riots, separatist insurgencies, and violence between Christians and Muslims surrounding the resignation of Indonesian dictator Suharto in 1998 led the *Guardian* to ponder, "Will Indonesia fall apart?"[12] In Nicaragua the fall of the Anastasio Somoza Debayle dictatorship in 1979 allowed an authoritarian regime led by the Sandinista National Liberation Front to step into the void to establish stability. Stability, according to the Sandinistas, required brute force, and four years after the regime came to power its victims numbered in the thousands.[13] Most recently, in Syria an optometrist-turned-dictator by the name of Bashar al-Assad has refused to relent in response to a determined civilian rebellion, producing a civil war that has claimed the lives of hundreds of thousands at the time of this writing.

Although repression also occurs during civilian-led transitions to democracy, repression can be exacerbated at the hands of an armed military accustomed to discipline and ill-trained for governance. What's more, there are often no legal mechanisms or institutions for holding the military leaders accountable, which can provide more room for misconduct. While expecting others to obey the law, the military may consider itself exempt from such niceties. Upon seizing power, the military ordinarily disbands the legislature, annuls the constitution, and suspends judicial review. Even where judicial review is available, the judiciary lacks the power to enforce any judgments against the military. As a result the military may ignore the judiciary's rulings, abolish or suspend judicial review, or oust uncooperative judges.

In addition much happens in relative secrecy during military rule. The lack of transparency in military behavior can curtail the people's ability to monitor the military's actions and root out wrongdoing. The military junta rarely feels the need to justify or explain the reasons behind its actions. Laws, proclamations, and interim constitutions may be drafted behind closed doors, with little or no participation by citizens. For example, in 2013 the military regime in Fiji limited participation by civil and political society in the drafting of a new constitution, which was prepared by military-appointed lawyers. Although citizens could comment on the draft, the regime censored reporting "harmful to national interests," which hampered unbiased opposition.[14]

The people also can't exercise their primary method of sanctioning politicians—voting them out of office—against the ruling military leaders.[15] In democratic coups, which by definition end with the military's retreat to the barracks, the military leaders are not in the market for reelection. The sole purpose of their term in government is to oversee a transition process that ends with their own exit from politics. During the military's reign, the people lack the ability to vote any corrupt or incompetent military leaders out of office. Even after a civilian government takes power, punishing military officers for any wrongdoings that occurred during the transition period may be difficult, if not impossible. As a condition for transferring power to civilians, military leaders usually negotiate immunity from prosecution. As a result, during the transition they have little fear of present or future sanctions for any abuses. They can, literally and metaphorically, get away with murder.

In highlighting the conflicts that may ensue following a coup, I don't mean to paint a universally conflict-laden picture of democratic coups. Many democratic coups are relatively smooth events, at least as smooth as democratic transitions can go. To cite a few examples, democratic coups in Turkey in 1960, Portugal in 1974, and Mali in 2003 did not produce any systematic repression of protesters. What's more, although militaries often negotiate immunity agreements as a condition for surrendering power to civilian leaders, some nations later repeal these amnesty laws. Argentina, Uruguay, and Turkey, to cite a few examples, abolished their amnesty laws and allowed the prosecution of military officers.

Protest is one limited avenue available to the people for sanctioning the military during its temporary rule.[16] If the masses are unhappy about the military's performance, they may rush back to the symbolic square in which the initial uprising against the dictatorship began to force the ruling military to accede to their demands. For example, only six months after the 2011 coup in Egypt, the crowds returned to Tahrir Square to protest the slow pace of the transition and the military's failure to speedily prosecute the members of the Mubarak regime.[17] One of the organizers of the Tahrir Square protests told me during an interview that a crowd of up to two hundred protesters would remain in the Square indefinitely "just so the military knows we are still here and will take over the Square again if things go awry."[18] As another Egyptian protester put it, "Protests and popular pressure [against the military] must return, because they are the only real method of realizing the people's demands."[19]

Protests provoke a government response and divert the military's resources from other areas of concern. Consequently persistent protests can be viewed as a form of punishment for the military and can prompt the military to act. For example, in Egypt, SCAF postponed the date of the legislative elections from June to November 2011 in response to protests by new political parties that the quick timeline for elections would benefit the established parties at their expense.[20] Protests may also push the military toward democratization faster and earlier than coup makers may have intended.

But the capability of protests to effect major changes in military behavior remains limited in many cases. Small-scale or erratic protests are mere irritants for the coup makers—mosquitoes on a warm summer night—that can be swatted away with little effort. In the end the coup makers' virtual monopoly on power allows them ample leeway to do as they wish and protect their interests during the transition process.

17

Golden Parachutes

Both optimists and pessimists contribute to society. The optimist invents the aeroplane, the pessimist the parachute.

—George Bernard Shaw

Golden parachutes, a concept once relegated to corporate jargon, achieved national prominence after the 2008 Wall Street meltdown. The public watched with astonishment as high-ranking executives racked up millions of dollars in compensation after losing their jobs. These arrangements, called "golden parachutes," are offered to executives as carrots to lure them into accepting employment. Executives are more likely to take charge of a company, particularly a faltering one, if a large compensation package awaits them upon their exit.

Like executives, military leaders also bargain for exit benefits to protect their interests.[1] After the military topples a dictator in a democratic coup, the coup makers supervise a transition process to democracy during which they remain in charge for a temporary period. After they transfer power to civilians, the coup makers' bargaining powers are greatly reduced and their future is subject to the whims of fickle civilian politicians. Coup makers, suffering from a bout of pessimism, may assume the worst and use the window of opportunity their temporary rule presents to protect their interests in the future democratic state. The areas that the military leadership deems worthy of protecting vary depending on context, but I'll highlight some common denominators in this chapter.

The military is not always united in its attempts to secure golden parachutes. Some factions within the military may oppose them. These factions may believe, for example, that providing legal or political powers to the military may insert the military into the domestic political fray, force it to take sides on contentious issues, and undermine its standing and credibility, which, in the long term, may damage the military's personal and institutional interests. Other factions, however, may view golden parachutes as a useful mechanism for protecting their power, constraining unreliable politicians, and rewarding their chosen civilian partners.

An attempt doesn't always result in success. In rare cases the military's attempts to obtain exit benefits may fail. The military may lack the leverage to secure these benefits, or internal conflicts within the military may undermine its attempts to obtain concessions. In Greece in the 1970s and in Argentina in the 1980s, for example, the outgoing military establishments were unable to impose any significant conditions for their transfer of power. In both countries the collapse of the military governments resulting from significant military defeats, combined with internal disunity and low prestige, hampered their bargaining position. In the broad run of cases, however, the military is able to secure at least some privileges for itself before giving up control to civilians.

Militaries attempt to protect their interests using three primary methods: direct, institutional, and procedural parachutes.[2] After I discuss these methods, I'll say a few words about their consequences.

Direct Parachutes

Direct parachutes provide constitutional or legal prerogatives to the military itself. These powers can serve as swords that enable the military to influence democratic politics or as shields that protect the military from the politicians' interference. The military may demand the sword of authority to enact regulations concerning the armed forces, a quota for military officers in the cabinet or legislature, the right to pick the next secretary of defense, or the authority to try civilians in military courts for crimes that fall within the military's jurisdiction. The military may request the shield of a veto over laws that affect the military, guarantee of a lucrative budget, and autonomy on how to spend it.

Consider several laws and constitutional provisions enacted following the 1974 Portuguese coup against the Estado Novo regime.[3] One law declared, "The structure of the armed forces is totally independent from the structure of the provisional government." Under this law, the defense minister would serve as a mere "liaison between the armed forces and the government" and could exercise no authority over the military. The same law also equated the ranks of the civilian prime minister and the military chief of staff.

Later in the transition process, Portuguese civilians reluctantly agreed to additional demands from the military. The new constitution, which was drafted under military supervision, authorized the Council of the Revolution, composed predominantly of military officers, to serve as an "advisory body" to the president and, exclusive of the other branches, "make laws concerning the organization, functioning, and discipline of the Armed Forces." The Constitution further provided the Council the profound power to veto laws passed by the Parliament. The Council could also invoke "unconstitutionality by omission" and call for the passage of laws to further the purposes of the Constitution.

The political parties agreed to the military's demands primarily to secure its coop-eration on democratic elections and its retreat to the barracks. The socialist leader Mário Soares explained this decision in the following terms: "Faced with growing economic upheaval, faced with the inevitable collapse of the state, we needed the elections and above all, we needed to win. Realizing that politics is the art of the possible, we signed an accord with the [military] which allowed us to preserve the future."[4] The pact allowed the parties to avoid a potentially fatal confrontation with the military and postpone the conflict to a later date, when they could renego-tiate the military's benefits from a position of relative strength.

Direct parachutes, as exemplified by the Portuguese case, represent a strong form of exit benefits. Because they directly empower the armed forces, these ben-efits may provide more certainty to the military regarding the protection of its privi-leges, as compared to the other two forms of golden parachutes I'll cover shortly. But the direct nature of these benefits can inspire more resistance from the mili-tary's opponents and stymie their adoption. What's more, providing a sweeping array of authorities for the military may later galvanize civilians to coalesce against the military more effectively. In Portugal, for example, direct parachutes served the military's short-term interests, but they turned out to be a long-term strategic mis-calculation. Portuguese society was unwilling to tolerate a military that put itself above the people and the law. In 1982, civilians managed to turn the tables, and a coalition of the civilian parties abolished the military's prerogatives.

Institutional Parachutes

Following a democratic coup, the military leaders, by definition, hand over power to civilians. As a result, before they surrender power they have an incentive to secure friends within the government to look out for their interests in the future demo-cratic state. Ideally these friends take the form of institutions—durable, stable, and reliable—such as a constitutional court or a national security council. The military leaders may create these institutions if they don't already exist, or, if they do exist, tweak their structure and membership to attempt to ensure their loyalty.

Institutional parachutes are different from direct parachutes. Direct parachutes provide the military itself with powers, whereas institutional parachutes delegate authority to a separate government institution that the military leaders expect to be friendly to their interests.[5] Institutional parachutes are often more palatable to civilians than direct parachutes because the mission of these government institu-tions seems more innocuous and their protection of military interests less certain. After all, constitutional courts and national security councils exist in most democ-racies, so their creation doesn't raise the red flags that direct parachutes might. Consequently, institutional parachutes may allow military leaders to smuggle their interests into the new government in Trojan horses.

Courts can be a particularly powerful Trojan horse because judicial review is assumed to be a check on government power. Judges review legislation and executive decrees to ensure their consistency with the constitution and restrain politicians so they don't overstep legal boundaries. At first blush, it may appear paradoxical for the judiciary to support rather than restrain the military. To be sure, when the military is in power during the democratic transition process, judges may act with restraint to lessen the risk of backlash from soldiers and ensure the judges' own personal and institutional survival. But the transition's end would seem to obviate any survivalist reasons for judges to support the military.

In fact the behavior of courts, like other institutions, can be manipulated. Before it hands off power to civilians, the military may tinker with the judiciary's structure and the appointments process to create a steady pipeline of judges sympathetic to the military's interests. These judges, armed with the power of constitutional review, can strike down laws and regulations that threaten the military's interests.[6] A judiciary so structured may turn out to be a reliable partner on questions of significance to military leaders.[7]

For several reasons, the judiciary is a particularly convenient partner for the military. First, it allows the military to avoid accountability. A constitutional court is a largely uncontroversial institution with no military members serving on it. Through constitutional review, a friendly judiciary can issue opinions that the military approves but can't publicly champion, allowing the military to insulate itself from societal scorn in the process.[8] The same actions that might inspire domestic and international criticism if taken directly by the military may be more palatable when administered through a seemingly neutral and independent proxy.

But loyalty is a fickle virtue. Constitutional courts, once created, can disappoint their creators. Judges have no obligation to remain loyal to their military founders, particularly after the military gives up power to civilian politicians. From the military's perspective, the power of constitutional review thus can prove to be a double-edged sword. The military's relationship with its brainchild may grow acrimonious if the court begins to use the same powerful tools created by the military to issue opinions antagonistic to military interests.

The Turkish Constitutional Court provides a good illustration of these dynamics at work.[9] The court was established after the military overthrew an authoritarian government in 1960 with the promise of democracy and the adoption of a new liberal constitution. The initial draft of the Constitution was prepared by a panel of law professors handpicked by the military junta that staged the coup, and the panel frequently consulted the junta during the drafting process.

Among other things, the new Constitution created a fifteen-member Constitutional Court authorized to try high-ranking government officials and engage in constitutional review of legislation. To ensure the court's loyalty, the military devised a peculiar appointment mechanism. In many countries the political branches play the primary role in appointing constitutional court judges. In the

United States, for example, the president appoints federal judges, subject to Senate confirmation. Judges to the German Constitutional Court are likewise appointed by the two houses of the German Parliament. But the Turkish military, viewing the elected branches with distrust, opted to place its faith elsewhere. The new Constitution gave the authority to appoint eight of the fifteen members—a majority of the court—to other high courts. The power to appoint the remaining seven of the fifteen members was split between the president and the two houses of the Parliament.

Why did the military devise this unusual appointment structure? At the time, professional judges serving on Turkey's high courts were more likely than politicians to be loyal to the military. The merit-based promotion system for judges insulated them from political influence and recycled a relatively cohesive group of intellectuals across the judicial system. The military leaders believed that these judges were aligned with them on central areas of concern, so the Constitutional Court members appointed by these judges would also presumably support military interests. Even if a few bad apples existed within the judiciary in the form of untrustworthy judges, the lot of professional judges was still less contaminated than the political branches.

Reflecting the military's trust in the court, the new Constitution also adopted a liberal definition of standing. In law, standing refers to the requirements that parties must meet for a court to hear their case. In the Turkish Constitutional Court, a wide range of persons and institutions were given automatic standing to petition the court for constitutional review of legislation, including the president of the republic, political parties represented in Parliament, other high courts, and even universities. In practice this broad definition of standing provided the Constitutional Court with extensive opportunities to engage in judicial review and strike down constitutional amendments, laws, and regulations passed by the political branches. With the political branches kept under a tight leash by a powerful court, the military could comfortably sit and watch from the sidelines, enjoying its autonomy and privileges.

The Constitution also empowered the Constitutional Court with the extraordinary authority to permanently dissolve political parties. The criteria for dissolution were broad. Parties were subject to permanent closure if their "statutes, programs, and activities" did not "conform to the principles of a democratic and secular republic, based on human rights and liberties, and to the fundamental principle of the State's territorial and national integrity." What's more, the authority to initiate a case for party dissolution before the Constitutional Court was provided to the chief public prosecutor of the republic, a democratically unaccountable lawyer appointed by the president from a short list of nominees prepared by other prosecutors.

After its establishment, the Turkish Constitutional Court aggressively exercised its authority to shut down political parties. It wielded its dissolution power primarily against Islamist parties, such as the Welfare Party and the Virtue Party, and separatist Kurdish political parties, such as the People's Democratic Party and the

People's Labor Party. The court's targeting of Islamist and separatist parties was in line with the principles—in particular, secularism and national unity—that can be considered the common denominators shared by the military leadership that created the Constitutional Court.

But as the court grew more powerful following its establishment, it began to issue opinions antagonistic to the military. For example, in 1972 the court found unconstitutional martial law courts staffed with military judges. In 1975 the court struck down a law establishing state security courts, staffed in part with military judges, authorized to try crimes against the state.

Partially in response to the court's increasingly defiant stance, the 1982 Constitution, drafted following the 1980 coup, restructured the court to force the military's rebellious child to toe the line. Among other things, the new Constitution completely abolished Parliament's authority to make appointments to the court, which further insulated the court from political influence. Instead the Constitution granted to the president—who, from 1982 to 1989, was Kenan Evren, the leader of the 1980 coup—the authority to appoint all judges based on nominations by other government institutions under the military's direct or indirect influence.

In addition to courts, another institution the military often uses to crystallize its influence in civilian policymaking is a national security council. The council is usually designed as a forum for the exchange of views between civilian and military leaders. Through regular council meetings, civilian leaders can consult military leaders, particularly on matters of national security and foreign policy, and benefit from their considerable expertise. These institutions can appear innocuous particularly because they have counterparts in countries with favorable democratic credentials. In the United States, for example, the National Security Council advises the president on matters of foreign and military policy and oversees coordination between the various branches of the military and intelligence services.

Although designed as a forum for exchange of views, a national security council can amount to much more. Because the council typically includes high-ranking military officers, it can provide a formal conduit for the expression of the military's views to civilian policymakers. In some cases the military's opinion on policy matters may be just that; however, in other cases the military's expression of views might come with a requirement to follow them.

Consider Egypt's National Security Council,[10] which was first established after General Nasser and his fellow officers deposed King Farouk in 1952. The Council quickly fell into disuse after Nasser installed himself as dictator, obviating any need to invoke the Council to influence domestic politics. But the benefits of a national security council quickly became apparent to the military officers who toppled Mubarak in 2011, leading to the Council's revival.

Introduced on June 18, 2012, version 2.0 of Egypt's National Security Council comprised eleven military representatives and only six civilians. A majority of the members could call the Council into session and make decisions, meaning that the military representatives, acting without the civilians, could convene the Council and pass resolutions. On the flip side, the civilians, decidedly in the minority, lacked the power to even convene the Council without at least three military members breaking ranks and joining them. The reincarnated council was responsible for determining national security policy, handling disasters of all sizes and forms, and identifying threats to the security of Egypt "within and beyond the national borders."[11]

Likewise the 1961 Turkish Constitution, ratified after the 1960 coup, established a national security council.[12] Although its stated mission was merely advisory, the Council became the primary institutional avenue for the Turkish Armed Forces to influence the nation's political affairs. The Constitution attempted to constrain the Council's role to giving advice on matters of "national security and coordination," but the Council's military members interpreted that phrase broadly to encompass many matters of domestic and foreign policy unrelated to security. The Council's opinions covered an extensive array of internal policy matters, including, for example, regulating broadcasting hours for television stations, outlining the substance of laws on terror and capital punishment, and determining whether to offer Arabic as an elective in schools.

The Turkish military's influence on the Council grew over time, as the number of military representatives increased. With the revisions brought by the 1982 Constitution, which was drafted following another coup in 1980, the Council included five military members and five civilians, with the Council's civilian president frequently voting with the military. The 1982 Constitution also required the civilian cabinet to give "priority consideration" to the Council's "decisions," which no longer were mere "recommendations." What was originally conceived as an advisory body thus became an instructing body, whose views were privileged over those of other government agencies.

Procedural Parachutes

The third and final form of golden parachute is procedural. When the military engages in procedural gamesmanship, it designs the transition process to produce a favorable substantive outcome. During the democratic transition process, the military is supposed to serve as a relatively neutral institution, arbitrate conflicts, and organize elections without favoring a particular civilian party. But in some cases the coup makers may identify a civilian party, seemingly aligned with the military's objectives, with which they can do business. As a result the military may feign neutrality but play a nontrivial role during the transition process by tinkering with technical procedural details to assist a chosen civilian partner who will protect the military's interests.

Of the three forms of parachutes discussed here, procedural parachutes are the weakest. But don't let that fool you. If implemented carefully, procedure can be a potent weapon, particularly because procedural technicalities are often regarded as trivial matters and therefore receive minimal scrutiny. Yet these choices can have significant consequences.

For example, after a coup the military may decide to hold elections within a short time frame, making it difficult for new parties to effectively organize and mount an electoral campaign. Swift elections can benefit established parties where they have the financial and organizational capabilities to campaign and win. From the military's perspective, this timing will appear advantageous if the military believes that established political parties will better preserve its interests than new and unfamiliar parties.

Consider the Egyptian military's procedural gamesmanship following the 2011 coup against Mubarak.[13] Various commentators argued that the military held elections relatively quickly in part because the coup makers anticipated that the principal beneficiaries of quick elections—the preexisting political groups—would better serve the military.[14] These established political parties, primarily the Muslim Brotherhood, would oppose fundamental constitutional changes and protect the political structures that benefited the military's interests. As one Middle East expert, Fouad Ajami, explained in November 2011, "To the mighty Egyptian officer corps the Brotherhood offers the promise of live and let live—the privileges and allotments of the armed forces would be left intact and opaque, while the Brotherhood, for the first time in its 84-year history, comes to political power."[15]

The military's plan worked. The elections in Egypt were initially scheduled for June 2011—four short months after the coup—but were later postponed to take place in staggered rounds between November 2011 and January 2012. Even with the postponement, new political parties did not have sufficient time to establish themselves, raise funds, and conduct a credible campaign. As expected, the established parties scored landslide victories in the parliamentary elections. The Muslim Brotherhood's Freedom and Justice Party emerged as the clear winner, obtaining roughly 47 percent of the seats in the lower house of Parliament. The more conservative Salafist Al-Nour Party came in second, with approximately 25 percent of the seats. Collectively Egypt's two main Islamist parties therefore captured nearly 75 percent of the seats.

To be sure, the Islamists' electoral victory can't be attributed solely to an unfair advantage obtained from swift elections. The Egyptian people were disenchanted with Western-backed secular dictators who stifled all political competition. The Islamists offered a credible alternative. And, of course, some Egyptians voted for Islamist parties because they wanted to see a heightened role for Islam in governance. Even without swift elections, the Islamists may have emerged victorious, but the quick timeline certainly bolstered their prospects.

In contrast, rapid elections hurt the emerging opposition parties in Egypt, including youth groups. These parties had splintered into tens of different factions with incoherent agendas and needed more time to establish and promote themselves.[16] For example, the liberal New Wafd Party and the secular Egyptian bloc, many of whose members had served as the vanguards of the 2011 uprising, came in a distant third and fourth in the elections for the lower house of Parliament, respectively obtaining roughly 8 and 7 percent of the seats. Unlike the established political parties, the youth groups appeared more willing to challenge and alter preexisting political structures, which may have threatened the military's interests. The military's design of quick elections marginalized these groups and their visions for change.

18

Between Scylla and Charybdis

*"Is there no way," said I, "of escaping Charybdis, and at the same time keeping
Scylla off when she is trying to harm my men?"*

—Homer's *Odyssey*, book 12

It took Odysseus ten years to reach his home in Ithaca after the Trojan War. During
the perilous journey, he and his men confronted numerous hazards, including two
sea monsters, Scylla and Charybdis, as they navigated through a narrow channel in
the Strait of Messina. On one side of the strait was Scylla, who had six heads and a
penchant for swallowing sailors. On the other side was Charybdis, who swallowed
seawater and threw it up again, creating a whirlpool that sank entire ships. These two
unsavory monsters were located close enough to each other that avoiding one led
to ensnarement by the other. Odysseus ordered his men to avoid the whirlpool of
Charybdis and instead pass near Scylla at full speed. He lost six sailors to Scylla but
avoided the loss of his entire ship to Charybdis's whirlpool.

A democratic coup forces civilians to navigate their own strait between Scylla
and Charybdis. The Scylla in our story is the coup makers' attempt to secure exit
benefits. Ideally the coup makers would immediately leave politics after toppling a
dictator, without reserving any powers for themselves. But that ideal rarely matches
the on-the-ground realities. In most cases the military manages to secure golden
parachutes, which, depending on their degree, may foster various dysfunctions in
the political system and undermine long-term democratic development. As a result
of its exit benefits, the military may become a fourth branch of government in all
but name.

The dose determines the toxicity. A democratic regime can mature even with
prerogatives for the military as long as those prerogatives don't interfere with democratic notions of civilian control of the armed forces. For example, the military
may enjoy limited authority—such as the appointment and removal of military
officers and the adjudication of cases involving military personnel through courts-
martial—without meaningfully weakening civilian control. But in other cases the
levels of entrenchment may be great enough to allow the military to play an ongoing

role in the nation's political affairs and mire the military in domestic disputes, even after its official exit from politics. The establishment of too much authority can convey a desire on the military's part to maintain enduring commitments and signify that its retreat to the barracks is less than complete. Armed with numerous prerogatives, the military may start making offers the civilians can't refuse.

Yet if civilians don't accede to the military's demands of exit benefits, the whirlpool of Charybdis may await them. Any attempts by civilians to immediately march the military back to the barracks empty-handed may prompt a backlash from the military leaders. They may dig in, rather than give in, and derail the transition process. And from the civilians' perspective, the military's exit with benefits is often better than no exit at all. The Scylla that is the entrenchment of the military's powers may result in a few casualties, but that may be less costly than losing the entire democratic system to the whirlpool of Charybdis, as the military withdraws its foot from the door and establishes a military dictatorship.

Backlash from military leaders is particularly likely where they perceive the civilian politicians as weak or unstable. As I'll explain in later chapters, civilians are more likely to succeed in contesting the military's prerogatives when they do so from a position of strength. Egypt's transition process following the 2011 coup against Mubarak provides a cautionary tale. Recall that at the beginning of the transition process, the military's interests were aligned to a large extent with those of the Muslim Brotherhood. From the military's perspective, the Brotherhood promised stability after a tumultuous revolution and a turbulent transition period, and the two institutions appeared to be in a tacit partnership.[1] But as the democratic transition progressed and the Brotherhood grew to be more ambitious and opportunistic, the military's position also shifted. Instead of supporting the Brotherhood's electoral prospects, the military began to oppose them. Concerned with the growing threat to its own powers and privileges from the Brotherhood, the military launched a campaign to block the Brotherhood's attempts to dominate the Constituent Assembly and Parliament. The Brotherhood's continued consolidation of power eventually prompted a military coup in July 2013 against President Morsi, a Brotherhood member.

From the civilians' perspective, their choice between Scylla and Charybdis can generate a seeming conflict between short-term and long-term goals.[2] The short-term goal of transitioning from military to civilian rule may be possible only by granting golden parachutes to the military. Yet these golden parachutes—depending on their dose—may hamper the long-term goal of promoting democratic progress. Despite this apparent tension, a certain synergy exists between these two goals. By providing the military with some authority, the military's democratic opponents can diminish the risk of backlash from the military or a rebound to military rule, which itself serves a democracy-promoting function.

This is not to say that civilians must accept high levels of exit benefits as a fait accompli. Rather the military's demand for exit benefits is a contingency for which civilians can—and should—take anticipatory action. Civilians can bargain with the military to minimize the types of entrenchment that might allow the military to reinsert itself into the political process. For example, civilians may choose to provide the military some degree of autonomy over its budget rather than creating a quota in the Parliament for military officers, which is much more likely to undermine democratic progress.

Civilians may also negotiate temporal limitations on the military's golden parachutes.[3] Where the military is unwilling to retreat without objectionable degrees of exit benefits, civilians may acquiesce but impose a sunset date on the most problematic demands. When that date arrives, the military's exit benefits would automatically end.

Take, for example, the 1976 Portuguese Constitution, which provided direct prerogatives to the military, including a veto over laws passed by the Parliament.[4] For obvious reasons, the civilian politicians didn't want the military looking over their shoulders indefinitely. So they negotiated a temporal limit on the constitutional amendment rule. For six years following the ratification of the Constitution in 1976, amendment required the consent of the military-dominated Council of the Revolution. In effect, during that six-year period the military's powers could not be abolished. After the six-year period expired, however, constitutional revision became possible with a two-thirds parliamentary majority. In 1982 a coalition of the existing political parties abolished the military's powers and established a legal framework for democratic civilian control of the military.

Other examples abound. The 2014 Egyptian Constitution placed a temporal limitation of two presidential terms on the military's veto power over the appointment of the defense minister. Under the 1982 Turkish Constitution, the military-dominated Presidential Council had the authority to review certain legislation, but only for a period of six years. During the 1984 transition from military rule in Uruguay, the military was able to extract certain guarantees concerning its authority, but the bargaining power of the political parties was sufficient to impose a one-year limitation on them.[5]

The strategy of using sunset dates permits the gradual, incremental elimination of the military's exit benefits and preempts any tensions that might arise if civilians attempt to eject the military from politics immediately.[6] The sunset date also provides breathing room for political parties to institutionalize and gather sufficient popular support before challenging the military's authorities.

At this juncture the reader may wonder why the military, with all of its bargaining power and leverage, would ever agree to temporal limitations on its powers. To return to the examples above, the militaries in Egypt, Portugal, Uruguay, and Turkey, among others, accepted sunset dates for some of their authority, even though they enjoyed the upper hand in negotiations. From the military's perspective, the use of a temporal limitation can signal to domestic and global audiences that the military views its privileges as temporary and expects its eventual exit from politics to be permanent. The imposition of sunset dates can also support the long-term interests of the military as an institution. As we'll see in the next part, prolonged military presence in domestic politics can force the military to repeatedly take sides on contentious domestic issues and undermine its status and credibility. Put differently, the benefits of temporal limitations can exceed their costs, at least from the perspective of some factions within the military. Logrolling—defined as the practice of exchanging political favors—may also prompt the military to accept temporal limitations on its powers. In exchange for agreeing to sunset dates, the military may extract other compromises, such as a lavish defense budget. This mutually beneficial exchange can allow both civilians and the military to declare victory.

Although temporal limitations may enable the military's exit, they are certainly not required to eliminate the military's authorities. Even when they lack sunset dates, the military's prerogatives can atrophy over time. For example, the institutions created by the military to protect its interests can be reconfigured to serve other purposes. A constitutional court, initially established to serve as the military's watchdog over civilian politics, can also serve the legitimate function of reviewing the constitutionality of legislation. The structure, the appointments process, and rules of standing may be changed to remove the military's influence without abolishing the institution. For example, in October 2001 constitutional amendments limited the authority of the Turkish Constitutional Court to dissolve political parties.[7] In addition, a constitutional amendment package adopted by referendum in September 2010 altered the appointments process to the Constitutional Court to bolster the authority of the elected branches. Like the judiciary, a national security council, initially established to institutionalize the military's influence on politics, may be reconfigured to serve as an advisory body on national security policy. Turkey, for example, adopted a number of constitutional amendments in 2001 that curbed the military's role in the National Security Council.

But civilians shouldn't expect immediate results. In many cases the military's subordination to civilians occurs incrementally, as the civilian political parties mature, earn credibility, and garner popular support, as I'll discuss in the next part.

Many observers have a tendency to fixate exclusively on the military's golden parachutes. Clearly, the thinking goes, a nation is undemocratic if its military enjoys legal or constitutional authority. But even in constitutional democracies, unelected institutions, such as central banks and constitutional courts, enjoy specialized powers. In deploying their powers, these institutions can subvert the popular will. A constitutional court can nullify legislation supported by a majority of the public, and a central bank can set monetary policies at the expense of the citizens and their elected representatives.

What's more, no democracy is immune to crises that may upend the strict subordination of the military to civilian leaders.[8] Even in advanced democracies, such as the United States, the military enjoys some level of political influence, as prominent military generals throw their weight around to influence civilian political action. Although the United States was founded on the complaint that the British king had "affected to render the Military independent of and superior to the Civil power," the American military exerts considerable influence on civilian affairs.[9] When civilian politicians were debating whether to intervene in Bosnia in the 1990s, General Colin Powell—then chairman of the joint chiefs of staff—wrote an editorial and gave a separate interview to the *New York Times* opposing military intervention.[10] Military historians have argued that the open opposition of Powell (and others in the military) postponed U.S. intervention in the Balkans by several years.[11] During Bill Clinton's administration, opposition from the Pentagon against a treaty banning land mines derailed his attempts to support the treaty.[12] Later, during the George W. Bush presidency, military lawyers—called judge advocates general—along with other branches of the military actively opposed administration policies authorizing "enhanced interrogation techniques" in the questioning of suspected terrorists.[13] In September 2009, as the Obama administration pondered what to do in Afghanistan, General Stanley McChrystal circumvented his civilian boss by appearing on *60 Minutes* and promoting a plan to adopt a counterinsurgency approach with tens of thousands of American soldiers on the ground.[14] *Rolling Stone* magazine went on to reveal that McChrystal's aides mocked "senior members of the Obama administration as clueless clowns, with the general himself joining in the fun."[15]

The question is not whether the military should have political sway in a democracy, since the military almost always does. Rather the relevant question is this: When does the military's political influence, particularly over extramilitary matters, become so outsized that it's no longer fair to conclude that civilians are in control?

In the end, the military's golden parachutes are a symptom, not the cause, of unbalanced civil-military relations. After all, a military intent on grabbing power may do so even absent any legal authorities. In contrast, another military equipped with a full arsenal of legal and constitutional powers may leave many of them unused. A prerogative that fuels military interventions in one country may lie dormant in the next. Even within the same military, changes in leadership may alter the military's deployment of its authorities. As a result the prevailing attitudes of the civilian and military leaders toward the military's proper role in governance are at least as important as the military's legal prerogatives in shaping future trajectories.

PART SIX

SHOULD I STAY OR SHOULD I GO?

No reason to stay is a good reason to go.

—Unknown.

Success in any coup requires clandestine planning, masterful execution, and a good dose of luck. To topple a dictator, military officers with otherwise competing ideologies and agendas must coalesce into a cohesive group. Maintaining cohesion among opinionated military leaders while overthrowing a tyrant is difficult enough. But the greater challenge lies in maintaining any semblance of unity after the dictator is toppled.

Once the unifying mission is accomplished and the dictatorship unravels, so does the common objective that kept the military leadership together. The military may still appear united to a casual observer, but appearances deceive. Almost immediately internal rifts between the loose coalition of coup makers, previously overlooked for the grander cause of dictatorial overthrow, can begin to rear their ugly heads. These intramural squabbles can run the gamut from petty management disputes to life-and-death decisions, with the future of the nation and its military hanging in the balance.

Perhaps the most important disagreement concerns what to do after seizing power from a dictator. There are two obvious choices: The military can retain power or give it to someone else. Some militaries will choose the first option, installing themselves in the seat emptied by the deposed tyrant and creating a military dictatorship. At first blush, this option might even seem to be superior in all cases. Toppling an unfriendly dictator on his last throes is one thing, but creating a full-fledged democracy is quite another. Rather than ignite democratic processes that will result in the military's exit from politics, the best course of action might appear to be to retain power.

But we've already seen numerous cases where the military not only toppled a dictator but also turned power over to a civilian government. What sets these cases apart from others that produce a military dictatorship? Why do some military officers choose to go and others choose to stay?

Coups tend to have a life of their own. Verdicts can easily prove premature, as military officers can disappoint even the most seasoned experts. The physicist and Nobel laureate Richard Feynman once remarked, "Imagine how much harder physics would be if electrons had feelings!" Unlike electrons, military officers do have feelings as well as other unpredictable human qualities, making the business of precise forecasting prohibitively difficult.

That said, it is possible to identify certain factors—aside from blind luck, which always plays a role—that shape the coup makers' decision-making process after they topple a dictator and influence whether they choose to stay or go. In this part, I'll examine why some coup makers find it in their best interests to throw in the towel and depart the political arena, whereas others find comfort in retaining power. Along the way, I'll explain how Pottery Barn's "You break it, you own it" policy explains why the military may relinquish power, how a champagne-and-caviar picnic ended the long-term rule of a dictator, and how two avid readers of Machiavelli took a page from his playbook to betray their promise of a democratic transition.

The Retreat

Uneasy lies the head that wears a crown.

—Shakespeare, *Henry IV*, Part II

The Pottery Barn Rule

In Summer 2002 U.S. Secretary of State Colin Powell invoked the Pottery Barn rule—"If you break it, you own it"—to explain to President George W. Bush the possible consequences of invading Iraq. "You are going to be the proud owner of 25 million people," Powell warned the president. "You will own all their hopes, aspirations, and problems. You'll own it all." Powell's Pottery Barn rule turned out to be a misnomer, as the furniture and housewares store rushed to announce that it proudly covers accidental damage to its on-display products.[1] But the sentiment underlying the rule is undoubtedly correct. As Powell himself later explained in an interview, the rule refers to the simple idea that "when you take out a regime and you bring down a government, you become the government."[2]

The Pottery Barn rule also governs military coups. Once the military overthrows a government, it becomes the government. A group of military officers, called a junta, often takes charge. The junta can run the country temporarily before relinquishing power to someone else, or it can establish a military dictatorship, which would, by definition, require the junta to keep governing. Military officers may initially welcome the expansion of their portfolio from soldiering to governing but regret it later. For several reasons, prolonged participation in politics can endanger both the military as an institution and the leaders at the helm, prompting an abdication of political power.

Military muscle doesn't equal political acuity. Governance often turns out to be a humbling experience for military leaders ill-equipped to perform the task. As military officers climb the political ladder, they find that it's rather lonely at the top. Most military leaders have a low appetite for risk. They are loath to go on wild goose chases, and those who do, learn their lessons fast. Grandiose ambitions often far exceed the military leaders' political capabilities. Many coup makers face enormous difficulties in maintaining order amid revolutionary turmoil and addressing, in Powell's terms, "the hopes, aspirations, and problems" of millions of people who assumed that the overthrow of their dictator would usher in stability and prosperity. Having fallen short of these admittedly untenable expectations, the military may find itself a convenient target of angry masses. The coup makers can exacerbate these frustrations by treating the masses like the soldiers they are accustomed to commanding, preferring top-down order rather than reasoned negotiation.

For example, in Egypt following the 2011 overthrow of Mubarak, Egyptians quickly began to point their finger at the ruling military junta, the Supreme Council of the Armed Forces (SCAF), for its inability to fix pressing social and economic problems. These critiques came not only from the domestic population but from the junior officers as well.[3] The junior officers, much more so than their senior counterparts, recognized the damage suffered by their institution because of SCAF's incompetence and growing appetite for power.[4]

As their triumph over the dictator recedes into the past, the coup makers may grow to believe that domestic politics is hopelessly short-sighted, disunited, and inefficient. Even military officers initially hell-bent on establishing a dictatorship may lose their appetite for governance as they begin to appreciate the human and political capital required to run a government, let alone establish an enduring dictatorship. Military leaders quickly realize that Newton's third law of motion—every action has an equal and opposite reaction—applies to coups as well: Each measure taken by the junta provokes a reaction from at least one disgruntled societal faction. Hopes that the transitional problems will diminish over time may prove wrong. In comparison to the migraine-inducing arena of domestic politics and civilian governance, the barracks may look cozy and comfortable. As a result the military may prefer to let the transition process be someone else's headache.

What's more, these governance problems can also reveal or exacerbate internal rifts within the junta. Governing a post-authoritarian society requires decision making and taking sides on contentious questions, ranging from the content of the new constitution to the timing of the elections. The societal divisions on these questions can mirror themselves in the military leadership. Civilians can sharpen these divisions by looking for allies within the military to champion their causes. Consequently, the tug of war between the coup makers can turn into an inconclusive slugfest and paralyze the leadership, further exacerbating any societal problems the military is supposed to resolve. This is why the political scientist Barbara Geddes argues that military regimes "contain the seeds of their own destruction."[5] The intramural squabbles within the junta can snowball in intensity over time and cause the leadership to implode.

Consider the Portuguese junta following the 1974 coup against the Estado Novo dictatorship.[6] Divisions within the military leadership developed almost immediately over decolonization and the economy. Some favored a slow disengagement from the colonies to avoid any jolts to the Portuguese economy, whereas others advocated full autonomy and immediate retreat of the Portuguese forces. Some factions within the leadership favored an ambitious military-led program of economic and social transformation requiring prolonged military rule, whereas others favored a swift return to civilian rule.

If its leadership is busy bickering, the military may have difficulty performing basic institutional functions. With the military's combat readiness and internal order compromised by officers mired in domestic politics, the nation may grow vulnerable to foreign invasion and domestic instability. Without the military functioning as an effective institution, the lucrative benefits and privileges that military officers enjoy may also come under threat. The damage incurred by the military can cause resentment not only within the domestic population but also from those officers who are not members of the governing junta. Retreat to the barracks may be the only antidote that pulls the military out of the domestic quagmire and stops its internal bleeding.[7]

Let's return to the 1974 coup in Portugal. The coup was orchestrated by a group of junior officers who called themselves the Armed Forces Movement (Movimento das Forças Armadas, MFA). These junior officers picked a well-respected senior officer, General António de Spínola, to serve as the figurehead for the coup. But after Spínola took office, it became apparent, much to the dismay of the MFA, that he had his own ideas about Portugal's future. On the issue of decolonization, Spínola favored only a slow separation from the colonies. In contrast, many officers in the MFA desired full independence and immediate withdrawal of Portuguese forces.

These differences eventually culminated in a full-blown crisis and prompted radicals within the MFA to blockade Lisbon. To avoid further civil disorder, Spínola resigned and went into self-exile. On March 11, 1975, his supporters attempted a coup, which was successfully suppressed.

The resolution of that internal crisis was followed by the revelation of another. With Spínola's supporters out of the picture, divisions within the MFA began to surface. Although the MFA remained a secretive organization from its inception, with no reliable record of its internal activities, Lawrence Graham identifies several distinct political movements within the military leadership, ranging from those that favored an alliance with the Communist Party to moderates committed to democracy and modernization through membership in the European Community.[8] The leadership also disagreed on the role that the military should play during the transition and in its aftermath.

These divisions became so pronounced that the MFA could never implement its ambitious program of social transformation. On November 25, 1975, radical leftists within the MFA attempted another coup, supported by extreme left-wing political parties. This attempted coup failed, instigating the moderates within the military to purge the radical leftists from the armed forces. The result, as the military historian Douglas Porch puts it, "inevitably was a call for a return to the barracks."[9] The moderates set the military on a path to disengage from politics and transfer power to elected leaders in 1976.

As in Portugal, when facing political problems and declining prestige, the military's priorities may shift from inept governance to credible exit. Having broken the previous regime and failed to fix it, the military may bear the brunt of domestic and global outrage, which tends to grow the longer the military remains in power. As blunders outweigh achievements, retreat may be the only way to call it quits while saving face. Retreat can allow the coup makers to keep any promises they may have made about establishing democratic rule. By retreating, the coup makers may proudly proclaim "Mission accomplished" or, even better, "I told you so" to the domestic and global naysayers skeptical, rightfully or wrongfully, of the military's long-term intentions. Having claimed the mantle of democracy, the military may leave office on a grace note, presenting a seemingly textbook demonstration of a military altruistically committed to civilian rule.

Pitfalls of Dictatorship

A coup against a dictator will engender varying levels of skepticism by the coup makers toward authoritarianism. After all, a former dictator caused the military sufficient problems to inspire a critical mass of officers to take decisive, difficult, and extremely risky action. The coup makers may be reluctant to risk repeating that experience by instituting another dictatorship. The new dictator might appear malleable and friendly to the military's interests, but appearances deceive. What's more, the long-term stability of the dictator-military relationship is far from guaranteed. Even former military commanders, such as Egypt's Mubarak, have abandoned the military when other institutions—in Mubarak's case, Egypt's police forces—proved to be better allies.

A cognitive bias, called "the availability bias," may exacerbate the military's skepticism toward authoritarian rule.[10] Availability bias leads people to overestimate the seriousness of a risk if the risk is readily available or easy to recall. For example, the number of people who purchase earthquake insurance increases in the immediate aftermath of a major earthquake. By the same token, residents of flood plains are less likely to purchase flood insurance if floods haven't occurred in recent memory. Affected by the availability bias, coup makers may overestimate and overreact to the problems that authoritarianism caused the military. They may focus on the recent events that led to the military's estrangement with the dictatorship instead of earlier and perhaps friendlier time periods with the authoritarian establishment.

In the aftermath of the cold war, foreign pressures and international trends may also predispose military leaders to reject post-coup authoritarian rule. If the military leaders were to adopt full-blown authoritarianism, they would join a club whose membership is dwindling. If coup makers select authoritarian rule, they can find themselves on the receiving end of domestic protests, international sanctions, or, worse, foreign cruise missiles and combat troops. Because the state and the military are in a symbiotic relationship—neither can survive without the other—the establishment of a dictatorship can cause disastrous consequences for the military. If the authoritarian state is destroyed, the military that established and supported it might suffer the same fate.

Empirical evidence confirms that many militaries prefer a relatively quick exit from politics. For example, military dictatorships in existence at any time between 1946 and 1998 had a lifespan of nine years, compared to one-party civilian dictatorships that lasted on average nearly twenty-three years.[11] Approximately 11 percent of military regimes that existed in 1946 were still in existence in 1998, compared to 50 percent of single-party civilian dictatorships.[12] According to another study that focused only on the post–cold war era, 72 percent of coups (thirty-one out of forty-three) were followed by democratic elections within five years.[13]

Life after Democracy

For many coup makers, life goes on after democracy is established. In fact a transition to democracy can be quite lucrative for military leaders because it allows them to deploy their golden parachutes. Militaries, as we discussed earlier, often receive exit benefits as a condition for transferring power to civilians following a democratic coup. The military might, for example, obtain the power to veto regulations on subjects of interest or enjoy autonomy over a hefty defense budget. Military officers can find their salaries and budgets increased by civilian governments anxious about the possibility of another coup.[14] These exit benefits may lure the military back into the barracks just as financial golden parachutes may lure reluctant corporate executives to accept high-risk employment. The coup makers may deploy their golden parachutes, exit from a troubled leadership position in government, and turn power over to democratically elected leaders.

Democracy offers other benefits to the military as well. A democratic nation may be admitted to Western military alliances, such as NATO, and granted the privileges of membership, including military aid, modern warfare equipment, and joint training and combat exercises. Although there are exceptions, democratic governments are usually more reluctant to provide weapons to authoritarian states, which tend to be more expansionist and unreliable than democratic partners.

Recall that a democratic coup often pits the military against the state security forces responsible for maintaining domestic order. These security forces, charged with detecting and suppressing domestic dissent, are the lifeblood of an authoritarian state. Many dictators, including Egypt's Mubarak and Tunisia's Ben Ali, favor the security institutions at the expense of the military, arousing professional jealousies and resentment. During the lead-up to the coup against a dictator, the security forces may be busy crushing protesters, whereas the military may be striving to protect them, as was the case in both Egypt and Tunisia in 2011. If the coup makers retain an authoritarian form of government, these security institutions may also be maintained as necessary to suppress domestic dissent. This arrangement would create strange bedfellows between two institutions—the military and the security forces—that may have been actively combating each other during the uprising against the dictator. The coup leaders may conclude that only the establishment of democracy can curb, or outright abolish, the power of the internal security forces that rival and antagonize the military.

Chaos

So far, the picture I've painted is one of rational military leaders, carefully weighing the pros and cons of democracy, the damage that prolonged military governance can cause, their lucrative exit benefits, and choosing—based on this calculation—to relinquish power to civilian leaders. But this picture is incomplete. Although some military leaders may consciously weigh at least some of the costs and benefits discussed here, for others, the calculation will be nonexistent or confused. Chaos may reign supreme over reasoned analysis. The coup makers may never devise anything remotely approaching a rational plan. Without an obvious objective, haphazard improvisation rather than careful action may follow.

Consider, for example, the changes to Egypt's Constitution following the 2011 coup against Mubarak. The ruling Supreme Council of the Armed Forces (SCAF) appointed a committee to draft a limited number of changes to the existing Constitution to provide the bare essentials for democratic elections to take place. These amendments were submitted to a referendum in March 2011 and approved by an overwhelming 77 percent of voters.

But two weeks after the referendum, something unexpected happened. SCAF announced a constitutional declaration—on its Facebook page, of all places—that befuddled all observers. The military told the voters that the existing Constitution as amended in the referendum would be scrapped completely. Instead the Constitution would be replaced by a new constitutional declaration that had been drafted under unknown circumstances.[15] The declaration, as the Egypt experts Nathan Brown and Kristen Stilt describe it, was "a document with significant procedural and substantive inconsistencies and even incoherencies."[16] It was presented by SCAF "as a sort of gift by a patriotic military leadership dedicated to protecting Egypt and the principles of the revolution."[17] It was unclear why the military superseded its own plans to retain the existing Constitution with amendments drafted by its own handpicked committee, *after* a popular referendum had already approved these amendments. When Egyptians began to question the coherence and rationale of the new constitutional declaration, SCAF provided no answers but "expressed frustration and wounded pride that they did not receive the gratitude they thought they deserved."[18] What was not forthcoming were coherent answers, which, according to Brown and Stilt, "did not exist."[19]

Squiggly and incomprehensible plans, like those announced by the Egyptian military, may occur partly because coups often produce divergent opinions within the military leadership on future trajectories for the country. The urge among some military officers to build up democracy may be opposed by others with an equally emphatic determination to hamper it. Consider the following example.

Blaise Compaoré assumed power in Burkina Faso in October 1987.[20] Throughout his reign there was widespread ballot box tampering and pro-Compaoré ballot stuffing. There wasn't meaningful political opposition, as most of Compaoré's opponents were simply lusting after "over-funded campaign war chests that [were] filled by the state or leading business executives."[21] Compaoré appeared secure in his position and was free to oversee a nepotistic and corrupt regime.

Compaoré's decline can be traced to the assassination in 1998 of Norbert Zongo, the publisher and editor of the newspaper *L'Indépendant*. Shortly before his assassination, Zongo had begun to investigate the murder of the driver of Compaoré's brother. The evidence suggested that the elite presidential guard killed Zongo to prevent the implication of the president's brother in the murder. The nation was furious. Widespread protests erupted across Burkina Faso, with the activists demanding justice and an end to the regime's impunity. Compaoré, ever the shrewd mediator, was able to weather the storm by successfully dividing the opposition, many of whom were bought with political and financial favors, and by agreeing to a constitutional amendment establishing presidential term limits.

In 2013, two years before the end of his last constitutional term as president, Compaoré proposed a referendum to repeal the presidential term limits. The vote was scheduled to take place on October 30, 2014, but that morning huge crowds occupied the streets of major cities, calling for Compaoré's resignation. Although the demonstrations leading up to the referendum had been largely peaceful, the mood of the protesters on the morning of October 30 was one of rage and determination. Soldiers deployed to contain the protests had no interest in using force against the civilians, thereby unleashing a mob of thousands to sack the National Assembly building and set it on fire. The national television station, operated by the government, was taken over and taken off the air, and several acts of targeted arson and looting continued as the day progressed. Some protesters were killed or injured by the president's security forces, but these forces were unable to stop the flood of demonstrators marching toward the presidential palace.

Compaoré capitulated to the protesters' demands on presidential term limits, but he insisted on finishing his term as president. His refusal to resign further agitated the protesters, who once more flooded the streets on October 31. By this time the military had already begun to split, some soldiers simply refusing to confront the protesters and others defecting to the anti-Compaoré camp outright. Faced with the splintering of its own ranks, the military declared the dissolution of the government. Compaoré, finally seeing the writing on the wall, resigned the presidency and fled. The military quickly appointed Michel Kafando, a civilian, as interim president.

The Burkina Faso military, however, was not united in support of a democratic regime shift. The Regiment of Presidential Security was particularly loyal to the deposed Compaoré. This elite unit was created by Compaoré and answered directly to the president. Charged with protecting the president, Burkina Faso's institutions, and anyone designated by Compaoré, the Regiment enjoyed a large degree of autonomy from the rest of the military.

With the first free presidential and legislative elections looming in October 2015, the Regiment of Presidential Security, led by General Gilbert Diendéré, detained Interim President Kafando for over two days. The Regiment then named Diendéré as the new head of state. Although Diendéré claimed the Regiment had "decided to take action to prevent the disruption of Burkina Faso due to the insecurity looming during pre-elections," this justification appeared to be a pretext to reestablish the old regime by force.[22] Diendéré's coup attempt was wildly unpopular with the people of Burkina Faso, who, emboldened by their success in ousting Compaoré, took to the streets to demonstrate against the threat to democracy posed by the Regiment of Presidential Security. The regular army also resisted the encroachment of the Regiment by surrounding the city, sending a clear message to Diendéré that power would come only with a fight. Within one week Diendéré was defeated and the interim government restored. The split within the military following the 2014 coup was therefore resolved decisively in favor of democracy. On November 29, 2015, the people elected Roch Marc Christian Kaboré as president, which marked the first time that a nonincumbent candidate was elected to office in Burkina Faso.

As the Burkina Faso example demonstrates, the military may relinquish power not because of a rational cost-benefit calculation of democratic rule but as a result of haphazard improvisation and unexpected rifts within the military leadership. Events in Burkina Faso also suggest that, for many militaries, the problems a dictatorship poses are real and substantial, and so are the benefits of democracy. The political sociologist Hazem Kandil makes the same argument in no uncertain terms: "Armies tend to thrive in democracies," he observes, "and wither in the shadow of authoritarianism."[23]

There is much truth to Kandil's statement, but it must be qualified. Some military coups, albeit a dwindling percentage, continue to produce dictatorships. Even where the transition may begin on a democratic trajectory, the coup makers may renege on their promises and install themselves as dictators. Faced with the benefits of democracy and a parade of possible authoritarian horribles, why doesn't every military coup produce a democracy? Why do some militaries prefer establishing a new dictatorship after toppling the old one?

The Broken Promise

The promise given was a necessity of the past. The word broken is a necessity of the present.

—Niccolò Machiavelli, *The Prince*, 1532

The Kings of England, Diamonds, Hearts, Spades, and Clubs

On July 22, 1952, Egypt's King Farouk was enjoying a late-night picnic at his summer palace in the coastal city of Alexandria.[1] Farouk, then thirty-two years old, was known and despised as a self-indulgent playboy. In a report to the British Foreign Office, a British high commissioner described him as "uneducated, lazy, untruthful, capricious, irresponsible and vain."[2] But what Farouk lacked in these qualities he made up for in charm and foresight. Only a year before his late-night picnic in Alexandria, he had made a prophesy that turned out to be eerily prescient. "There will soon be five kings left," he suggested, "The Kings of England, Diamonds, Hearts, Spades, and Clubs."

As Farouk sipped fine champagne and munched on caviar, eighty colonels and majors moved into action approximately a hundred miles away in Cairo. Their goal was to use Farouk's absence from Egypt's capital to topple his government. They seized the army headquarters, arrested uncooperative senior officers, and occupied the airport. Tanks and infantry began roaring through Cairo. Egyptians poured into the streets in droves to lend their support to the coup attempt against their corrupt and incompetent king.

At seven the next morning, a junior officer by the name of Anwar Sadat—who would go on to become Egypt's president nearly two decades later—announced the coup d'état over the radio. "Egypt has passed through a critical period in her recent history characterized by bribery, mischief, and the absence of governmental stability," he declared, referring to King Farouk's long list of incompetencies. He continued, "Accordingly, we have undertaken to clean ourselves up and have appointed to command us men from within the army whom we trust in their ability, their character, and their patriotism. It is certain that all Egypt will meet this news with enthusiasm and will welcome it." He assured the listeners that the coup makers would put the Egyptian people's interests, and the rule of law, above their own. "May God grant us success," he concluded.[3]

Troops soon moved into Alexandria and surrounded Farouk's palace. He had no choice but to surrender. Although some coup makers wanted to immediately execute him, cooler heads prevailed and allowed him to go into exile. On July 26, 1952, Farouk set sail for Italy with his family, along with gold-filled crates slyly labeled "whisky" and "champagne." He died in Rome shortly after his forty-fifth birthday, when he collapsed at a restaurant while enjoying a late-night dinner date with a twenty-two-year-old blonde.

Following Farouk's ouster, the coup makers initially appeared to have little interest in remaining in power indefinitely. They had observed the instability of military governments in Iraq (from 1936 to 1941) and in Syria (from 1949 to 1951) and lost whatever appetite they may have had for prolonged power. They purged those officers who refused to participate in the coup and established a fourteen-member Revolutionary Command Council to transition the nation to a new constitution and democratic government.

Junior officers had planned the coup under the leadership of Lieutenant Colonel Gamal Abdel Nasser. To bolster the popularity and credibility of their mission, Nasser appointed a highly respected general, Mohammed Naguib, to serve as leader of the Revolutionary Command Council. Naguib had emerged as one of the few heroes of Egypt's disastrous war against Israel in 1948, and his name was well-recognized in the country. Although he was to be only a figurehead, Naguib had a mind of his own. In addition, Nasser—an avid reader of Machiavelli—knew that figureheads had a tendency to become captivated by power. As a result, from the initial stages of the coup Nasser surrounded Naguib with allies to keep a close eye on him.

On June 18, 1953, the Revolutionary Command Council officially declared Egypt a republic. Naguib became the first president of Egypt, and Nasser became the deputy prime minister and minister of the interior. The two men disagreed on the future trajectory of their homeland. Naguib favored a swift return to the barracks after enabling democratic elections. In contrast, Nasser sought to establish a military regime to transform the society from above. This difference of opinion would mark the beginning of a long struggle for power between the two men.

Naguib and Nasser pursued different strategies to consolidate control. Naguib worked on building his already substantial public support, but Nasser focused on recruiting followers from the security forces. These security forces, tasked with internal policing, were a separate institution from the military. Nasser also fostered the support of the United States, which was concerned about the uncertainty and instability that democratic rule may bring to Egypt and therefore the Middle East at large. He played into contemporary American fears by convincing the United States that Naguib was soft on communism.

Nasser's careful strategies gave him the upper hand. Despite objections from Naguib, Nasser convinced the Revolutionary Command Council to eliminate all political parties and create a one-party system. It became apparent that an Egypt under Nasser's leadership would be far from democratic.

This power struggle between Nasser and Naguib produced two failed coup attempts by different branches of the military to force a course correction toward democracy. In December 1952 a major bloc within the artillery plotted a coup attempt against Nasser and his supporters. But these plans were thwarted by the loyalists Nasser had carefully recruited. The simmering tensions between the Nasser and Naguib camps reached new heights in February 1954, when, in a bold and risky move to arouse the public against Nasser and his loyalists, Naguib resigned from office. Nasser accepted the resignation and put Naguib under house arrest.

Naguib's plan worked. His resignation triggered a mutiny by the cavalry later that same month. Like their colleagues in the artillery, many cavalry officers worried that Nasser was becoming increasingly dictatorial. Soldiers surrounded the military headquarters and demanded that Nasser implement an immediate transition to democracy. Nasser was not pleased. "Who gave you the right to speak for the people?" he screamed.[4] A cavalryman responded, "We are the parliament of the people until a parliament is formed."[5] Following this heated exchange, and after hearing the movement of tanks outside, Nasser relented and promised to fulfill the cavalry's democratic demands. But his promises were so short-lived that they might have sent even his hero Machiavelli spinning in his grave. Within one hour security forces loyal to Nasser retaliated against the mutinous cavalry units and tilted the power struggle in Nasser's favor. Having thwarted two coup attempts, Nasser instigated a massive purge of Naguib's sympathizers within the military.

At this point the pendulum rapidly swung in the other direction. Although the mutiny failed, it caused a public uprising against Nasser, with hundreds of thousands roaring through the streets of Cairo chanting "To prison with Nasser! No revolution without Naguib!" The uprising was so enormous that even Nasser's trusted security forces acknowledged that any attempts at repression would create a massive bloodbath. Backed into a corner, Nasser was forced to reinstate Naguib as president in March 1954.

Yet Naguib's days in office were numbered. In what turned out to be an ill-conceived show of goodwill, he appointed Nasser as his prime minister. Nasser seized this opportunity to consolidate his powers and weaken Naguib. An assassination attempt against Nasser on October 26, 1954, also played into Nasser's hands. All eight shots fired at him by a Muslim Brotherhood member missed their intended target. Nasser kept his cool and delivered a speech that mesmerized audiences across the Arab world: "My countrymen, my blood spills for you and for Egypt. I will live for your sake and die for the sake of your freedom and honor. Let them kill me; it does not concern me so long as I have instilled pride, honor, and freedom in you. If Gamal Abdel Nasser should die, each of you shall be Gamal Abdel Nasser."[6] Nasser used the failed assassination attempt to his advantage and instigated a massive crackdown, arresting thousands of dissidents. Although Naguib fought back, he decided to retire to prevent an impending civil war: "I was as exhausted as a boxer in the final round," Naguib wrote, "I was not yet knocked out, but had lost too many points throughout this long game."[7]

Within a few months Nasser was in full control. Naguib was again put under house arrest, and his remaining supporters were purged from both the army and civilian organizations. Nasser assumed the office of the presidency in June 1956 and served until his death in September 1970.

In this struggle for power, what tipped the balance in Nasser's favor was his decision to recruit the security forces to his camp. The security forces were swift and effective and could outmaneuver the military, which, as a much larger institution with many internal divisions, was slower to act. Nasser also institutionalized torture and political coercion of dissidents, particularly those from the Muslim Brotherhood. Buoyed by his security forces, he could discredit or destroy anyone who stood in his path. In the end it was Nasser's security forces—who saw the end of their career in a future democratic regime—that prematurely ended this transition to democracy and condemned Egypt to dictatorial rule.

In strengthening the security institutions at the expense of the military, Nasser set the foundations of what would become a full-blown police state in Egypt. But the struggle between the police and the military did not end following Nasser's decisive rise to power. Rather it continued and intensified, culminating in a showdown in 2011 that pitted Mubarak's police forces against the military and a public in rebellion against his regime. This time around, the military would emerge victorious.

Napoleon's Coup

Nasser's seizure of power harkens back several centuries to a power grab by another fan of Machiavelli.[8] General Napoleon Bonaparte, who is rumored to have remarked that Machiavelli's *The Prince* is "the only book worth reading," staged a coup on November 9–10, 1799, against the Directory of France. The Directory, an executive council of five men, was formed following the French Revolution. Legislative power was vested in a popularly elected legislature, which, in turn, selected the members of the Directory. Although the Directory was part of an elaborate system of checks and balances designed to curb abuses of power, it eventually devolved into an authoritarian regime. In September 1797, in an event known as the Coup of 18 Fructidor, the Directory annulled the legislative elections that their opponents had won. It imposed martial law, established military courts to try dissidents, arrested rival party members, and shut down opposition newspapers.

By the time Napoleon and his fellow coup makers decided to upend the Directory, the institution had lost much of its popular support. The coup against the Directory, known as the Coup of 18–19 Brumaire, was planned primarily by Abbé Sieyès, one of the five members of the Directory. Sieyès viewed the widely popular Napoleon as indispensable to the planned coup. Napoleon had recently returned to France, and word of his campaigns in Asia and Africa had traveled throughout the country, with his popularity overshadowing defeats that included the loss of an entire fleet. Although, in Sieyès's eyes, Napoleon's role was to be symbolic, the general had other plans.

The coup began when an indignant Napoleon publicly disavowed the Directory: "What have you done with the France I left in such glory? I left peace, and I find war. I left victories, and I find defeats. I left millions from Italy, and I find it squandered by laws and misery."[9] Napoleon stormed into the chambers of the legislature and intervened in their deliberations, accompanied by a troop of grenadiers. He proceeded to admonish the parliamentary deputies, "The Republic has no government," and accused them of destroying the Constitution.[10] Rather than acquiescing, however, the legislative deputies doubled down, expressed their allegiance to the existing Constitution, and called for Napoleon's arrest. But grenadiers, acting on the command of the coup makers, soon disbanded the legislature and forced the directors to resign.

The coup against the Directory produced an immediate split among the coup makers. Napoleon favored a dictatorship, whereas Sieyès believed in republicanism. In the weeks following the coup, Sieyès found his position increasingly marginalized in favor of Napoleon as Napoleon's centralized role in the coup made him the primary figure and face of the emerging government. Sieyès couldn't rival the general's perceived heroism or military influence. Under pressure from Napoleon, a new Constitution created a three-person executive office called the Consulate, with the first consul enjoying far greater powers than the other two. The Constitution abandoned the principles of legislative supremacy and popular representation, providing the executive branch with the power to enact legislation. As expected, Napoleon became first consul in 1799 and quickly began to consolidate power. A few years later, in 1804, he completed his coup within a coup by abandoning all pretenses and declaring himself emperor of France.

Irrational and Rational Dictators

Nasser's and Napoleon's power grabs are emblematic of coups that begin with promises of democratic rule but end with the establishment of a dictatorship. What motivates some military leaders to follow an authoritarian trajectory? Why do some militaries announce ambitious democratic projects but end up perverting their aims?

Some coup makers lose their enthusiasm for democracy for irrational reasons. A successful victory against a dictator can boost already generous egos and foster self-indulgent fantasies about future possibilities. Shallow impulses may override sober calculations, prompting coup makers to pick dictatorship over democracy. As the historian Shelby Foote observes, "Power doesn't so much corrupt; that's too simple. It fragments, closes options, mesmerizes."[11] Nasser initially appeared to be on the side of democracy, but he quickly became drunk with power and began to advocate a military-led social transformation under his leadership. He sidelined Naguib and installed himself as Egypt's next pharaoh. Napoleon likewise pushed Sieyès aside, along with any republican ideals, and consolidated control as the head of the French Empire.

Coup makers are rarely scholars of political regimes. They may be oblivious to the serious problems that authoritarianism can pose to the military and the benefits that democracy may bring. They may be unaware of the damage that prolonged military rule can inflict on the military. On the flip side, the military leadership may turn a blind eye to the rewards of democracy, including membership in prestigious military alliances and the golden parachutes that a retreat to the barracks would provide.

Although plenty of military leaders irrationally prefer dictatorship out of ignorance or ego, others choose dictatorship in a rational decision-making process. Many militaries benefit from democratic rule, but the military is a variable, not a constant. Although the costs of authoritarianism outweigh its benefits for many militaries, for some militaries, that calculus may be reversed. For example, the coup makers may believe that a loyalist dictator will benefit them more than democratic rule. Particularly when they're confident the dictator will stay loyal to their interests for the long term, the coup makers may throw their support behind the dictator rather than subject their future to the vagaries of democratic politics.

Distrust of democratic politics will be particularly pronounced when the civilians poised to assume power appear unfriendly to the military's interests. This is partly why the Egyptian military turned against the Muslim Brotherhood and toppled Morsi in July 2013. Morsi and the Brotherhood, initially allied with the military, launched an ambitious political project that threatened the military's privileges.

Stalemate between the civilians and the military regarding the military's terms of exit may also hinder the transition to democracy. From the perspective of both civilians and the military, the goal should be to push the envelope without tearing it. But civilians may refuse to provide any exit benefits to the military, in which case the military leaders may refuse to leave. On the other hand, the military may ask for too much by way of golden parachutes, which civilians may reject. Both sides may view the negotiation as a tug-of-war where one side's gain is the other side's loss. As a result they may refuse to cooperate even when it's in their best interests to do so. And without cooperation and agreement on exit terms, the military may never retreat.

Coup makers may also prefer dictatorship to implement grand social agendas and transform the society from the top down. Nasser, for example, was a dedicated believer in pan-Arabism, referring to the unification of the Arab people under a single umbrella.[12] He also sought to replace Western capitalism with socialism. He launched a redistributive land reform plan to address a grossly unequal pattern of land ownership, where 0.5 percent of the Egyptian population owned roughly 33 percent of the fertile land. He nationalized virtually all businesses and sought to completely drive the British colonial powers out of Egypt. Grand aspirations like these can produce long-term commitments, and ambitious militaries tend to stay around for a while.

PART SEVEN

HOW THIS ENDS

The answer, my friend, is blowin' in the wind.
— Bob Dylan, "Blowin' in the Wind," 1963

Let's assume the parade of horribles from the previous chapter does not materialize. The military topples a dictator, oversees a transition to democracy, and returns to the barracks after elections of civilian leaders. At this point the democratic coup is complete: A dictatorship is toppled, and a new democracy is born.

Although this point marks the end of a democratic coup, it's only the beginning of the nation's future democratic trajectory. The military's transfer of power to civilians unleashes a sequence of events that comprise an experiment in democracy. As with all experiments, it may succeed or it may fail.

Some militaries will retreat to the barracks, never to appear again. The nation will continue on a steady march toward democratic development, albeit with inevitable hiccups along the way. The budding political marketplace created by the military will blossom into a fully developed, competitive system, able to resolve its challenges through democratic means. The military's attempt to entrench its prerogatives will prove ineffective, and the establishment of democratic institutions will create democratic dynamics that the military leadership itself cannot contain.

In other cases the military's departure from politics will be less than full. A coup is an extreme remedy. As we've seen, even as it treats the authoritarian patient, it has the capacity to generate side effects. The military may retreat to the barracks only to roar back to life at a future date and reinsert itself, directly or indirectly, into the political process. The nation may struggle with the political and legal reverberations generated by the coup, and the halfway house of democracy created by the coup may not stand. Later developments can upset civilian control of the military, impede democratic progress, and prompt a rebound to military rule. A successful coup can also create a culture of coups whereby the people and politicians alike rely on the military instead of democratic rules for political change, paving the way for future military interventions.

Obviously the military has a choice about reinserting itself into domestic politics after giving up power to civilians. But that choice is not made in a vacuum. Rather, the actions of civilian politicians often play a decisive role in whether the coup produces a healthy, long-lasting democracy or a fragile house of cards that collapses under its own weight. In this part, I'll examine the factors that set apart the cases of success from the cases of failure. Along the way I'll explain how coups can beget future coups, why the artificial intelligence system Skynet in the movie *The Terminator* provides a close analogue to modern militaries, why Apple's FaceTime was the tool of choice to announce a coup attempt, and why two of Aristotle's adages explain unbalanced civil-military relations and offer clues on how to resolve them.

21

The Awakening

The system goes online August 4th, 1997. Human decisions are removed from strategic defense. Skynet begins to learn at a geometric rate. It becomes self-aware at 2:14 a.m. Eastern time, August 29th. In a panic, they try to pull the plug.
Skynet fights back.

—*Terminator 2: Judgment Day*, 1991

In the late 1990s the former Turkish president and prime minister Süleyman Demirel was asked to comment on an ongoing crisis between the civilian and military leadership in his country. Demirel replied with a joke. There was an experiment in an English zoo, he said, to place lambs and wolves in one cage to teach them how to live together. The zoo director was asked if the experiment was working. The director replied, "Yes, but from time to time, we have to replace the lambs."[1]

In Demirel's response lies a major predicament with coups: All coups, democratic and nondemocratic alike, can beget future coups. A coup shatters the illusion of civilian control of the military. As a result countries that have recently undergone a coup are more likely to experience future coups.[2] Following a coup, the military may realize the future possibilities its domestic interventions can spark, just as the artificial intelligence system Skynet in *The Terminator* became aware of its immense capabilities and unleashed its military systems against the civilians it was created to defend. For some coup makers, their retreat following a democratic coup may represent a capitulation—a premature withdrawal from a revolution unfinished. They may give up power on paper but keep a watchful eye on civilian politics, awaiting the right moment to strike. A democratic coup against a dictatorship may be followed by a nondemocratic coup against an elected government.

Consider the following example.

Africa's Spring and Fall

Until recently Mali was widely considered a rare democratic success story in Africa.[3] Between 1991 and 2012 it attained an impressive record of three democratic elections and, more important, three peaceful turnovers of power. The former Malian president Alpha Oumar Konaré reportedly joked that he was retiring from office because "what Africa needs is more living ex-presidents."[4]

The beginnings of Mali's democracy can be traced back to a military coup in 1991. The coup toppled the leftist dictatorship of Moussa Traore, who had assumed power in 1968 and survived several coup attempts. His dictatorship was typical: A single party was in charge of the government, all media was tightly controlled, and there were few signs of political dissent until later in Traore's term. During his twenty-three years of rule, Traore enriched those closest to him while the standard of living in Mali steadily declined. His wife and her family controlled parts of the Malian economy.

When the present is gloomy, stories from a distant past often beckon. A former U.S. ambassador to Mali, Robert Pringle, recalls that his Malian driver would frequently listen to songs on the radio by griots, the musician-historian entertainers of West Africa, singing and chanting about Mali's ancient history. The griots often sang about the myth of Sundiata, the social outcast who later becomes the unlikely founder of the Malian Empire in 1240.[5] Sundiata laid the foundations for the modern nation of Mali, complete with an oral constitution known as the Kouroukan Fouga. The myth of Sundiata, bellowing from the radio as Pringle was driven to work, would prove prescient of events that would transpire in Mali in 1991.

In March of that year the fall of the Soviet Union and communist regimes across Eastern Europe sparked widespread protests by tens of thousands against Traore's corrupt rule. To contain the protests Traore ordered the military and the police to fire on the protestors.[6] During March alone, an estimated three hundred civilians were killed by government forces. That high death toll sparked mutiny among the soldiers, led by a prominent military commander, Colonel Amadou Toumani Touré, affectionately known as ATT. He instigated a coup and toppled Traore's dictatorship.

ATT, Mali's modern-day Sundiata, immediately vowed to relinquish power to elected government officials. "We didn't want to confiscate the power that wasn't ours," he explained.[7] He earned a reputation as a "soldier of democracy" when he refused to retain power and instead convened a national conference—similar to a constitutional convention—with nearly two thousand participants representing a wide range of Malian society. The National Conference laid the legal foundations for a democratic Malian republic. A new constitution was adopted and confirmed by referendum in January 1992. The Constitution was secular in nature, established a strong executive and a weaker legislature, limited presidential terms to two, and emphasized decentralization, resting real authority with previously disenfranchised local governments.

In April 1992, a little over a year after the coup, the Malian people held free and fair presidential elections for the first time in their history. ATT refused to run for president, citing his desire to avoid the appearance of a military power grab. He withdrew from political life until he ran for president as a civilian candidate ten years later. In the 1992 presidential elections, Konaré, a journalist and prominent pro-democracy activist, prevailed.

Mali's subsequent democratic record was far from perfect. The democratic institutions remained fragile, the judicial system was failing, the political parties were fragmented, and corruption remained systemic. But the new system was a substantial improvement over the past and had all the trappings of a democracy. "It is as if the people have learned to breathe," Mobido Diallo, the owner of a popular radio station, explained in an interview with the *Washington Post*. "For the first time, the people in power must think before they act, because there is now accountability that did not exist before."[8] The number of radio stations increased from a single tightly controlled government station in 1991 to forty in 1996, a meaningful jump in a nation long dependent on radio for information and entertainment. Likewise, for decades the only available newspaper was published by the government, but a few years after the 1991 coup the number of newspapers had increased to sixty. Mali also made significant progress in developing a market economy, privatizing most government-owned businesses, and opening to foreign investment. These developments led Freedom House to add Mali to its list of "free" nations.

After serving his two presidential terms, Konaré, instead of trying to dodge the constitutional term limits, peacefully stepped down in 2002. In his place ATT, who had retired from the army, ran for president and won, prompting a peaceful turnover of presidential power. Mali's democratic success story also reverberated in the United States, particularly because Mali is a majority-Muslim country located in a violent region threatened by Islamic extremism and civil war. The *Wall Street Journal* published a front-page article in 2004 touting Mali's rare democracy.[9] In the lead-up to presidential elections in 2012, ATT promised to respect the constitutional two-term limit and not run for reelection.

But then things took a turn for the worse. Northern Mali is home to the nomadic Tuaregs, an ethnic group spread across several countries. Mali has been an uncomfortable home for the Tuaregs, who feel culturally and politically marginalized. Until 1995 they were engaged in a bitter separatist rebellion against the Malian state after receiving training in Libya. To counter the Tuareg threat, in the early 1990s the Malian government had withdrawn its military from the North and offered autonomy to the Tuaregs.

Libya's liberation in 2011, enabled by NATO's cruise missiles, had dire consequences for Mali.[10] While intent on solving one problem, Western powers exacerbated another. After Gaddafi's fall in nearby Libya, the Tuaregs who had been fighting on behalf of the Gaddafi dictatorship returned to Mali along with the weapons they had seized from Gaddafi's armories. They used the opportunity created by the power vacuum in northern Mali to reinvigorate the long-simmering Tuareg rebellion. Gaddafi's weapons began pouring into Mali and allowed the Tuareg rebels to achieve surprising victories against the Malian Army.

These defeats prompted widespread disenchantment among the Malian soldiers. Many believed they were underfunded and underequipped to defend their homeland. In March 2012 the resurgence of the Tuareg rebellion prompted a coup just one month before what most observers assumed would be another democratic presidential election. ATT fell victim to the same device he had used in 1991 and was toppled by mutineering soldiers promising to fight the Tuareg rebels more effectively. Although the coup leaders transferred power to democratically elected leaders the following year, the 2012 coup cost Mali its status as a paragon of democracy in Africa.

As the 2012 coup illustrates, every seemingly grand idea—in this case, the NATO intervention in Libya—generates unforeseen, and sometimes disastrous, consequences. It also illustrates how a widely celebrated democratic coup against a dictatorship can awaken the wolves to their potential capabilities and prompt a nondemocratic coup against an elected government.

A Culture of Coups

In addition to awakening the wolves, a successful military intervention can also awaken the lambs. A coup can create a societal culture shift, with coups becoming an acceptable way of doing business and correcting deficiencies in civilian politics. The civilians may grow dependent on the military as a quick fix to solve their problems rather than using the mechanisms of democratic politics. The incumbent politicians causing you problems? Call your allies in the military. Violence on the streets? Ask the military to step in.

Of course the military is not the panacea to all of life's problems. Even if the military can solve civilians' problems quickly and efficiently, overreliance on the military can hinder rather than aid democratic progress over time. From the perspective of democratic development, dependence on the military is a poor substitute for long-term institution building. If the military is the all-purpose antibiotic for civilians' ailments, the polity may never develop the ability to fight political pathogens on its own.

We've already seen two examples of this phenomenon. In Egypt the same mechanism that was used in 2011 to get rid of Mubarak was deployed again in 2013 against the democratically elected Morsi, who had shown poor judgment in running the country, along with some authoritarian impulses. Instead of putting in the hard work of developing popular appeal and ousting Morsi through the ballot box, the opposition politicians relied on the military to do their dirty work for them. The military's quick fix short-circuited established democratic procedures and put the future of Egypt's democracy in jeopardy.

In Portugal, after the military upended the Estado Novo dictatorship in 1974 and planted the seeds for a democratic government, the prospects for democracy remained bleak.[11] Portugal's Communist Party appeared poised to assume power and establish a new dictatorship. The Communist Party had been banned during the defunct dictatorship but enjoyed five decades of underground existence. During the transition process, the Party behaved and acted very much like the authoritarian regime the military had just deposed and did not conceal its intention to install an antidemocratic communist regime in Portugal.

Elections for a Constituent Assembly, tasked with drafting a new constitution, were held on the first anniversary of the coup, April 25, 1975. Twelve major political parties participated in the elections, which were fair and free by all objective accounts. A center-left party, a center-right party, and a conservative party—whose agendas were dedicated to establishing a Western-style pluralist democracy—collectively won 72 percent of the vote. The Communist Party got only 12.5 percent.

Following its poor showing in the Constituent Assembly elections, the Communist Party, along with pro-communist factions in the military, attempted a coup on November 25, 1975. Having suffered a decisive electoral loss, the Communist Party opted to resort to less-than-democratic means and called upon its allies within the military to deliver a quick fix. But the military leadership, led by Lieutenant Colonel António Ramalho Eanes, successfully repelled the attempted coup. According to Eanes, November 25 represented the "moral rebirth of the armed forces" and the victory of a "democratic project over a totalitarian perversion that sought to destroy the military."

Although democracy triumphed in Portugal, its former colony, Guinea-Bissau, was not so lucky.[12] Guinea-Bissau is one of the world's poorest states with a long history of coups and unrest. Portugal's long colonial wars left Guinea-Bissau without a functioning political and economic marketplace and vulnerable to upheavals and coups. No president has had the luxury of completing a full term in office.

But one coup in Guinea-Bissau, staged in 2003, stands out from the rest. This coup toppled President Kumba Yala, who came to power through democratic elections in February 2000. After assuming office, Yala, a member of the country's dominant Balanta ethnic group, openly favored the Balanta in appointments to the military. He undermined checks and balances, refused to promulgate a draft constitution, removed Supreme Court judges from power, appointed his cronies to high-ranking positions within the military, jailed opposition activists, dissolved Parliament, and called for legislative elections but repeatedly postponed them. The delays in convening Parliament generated a budget crisis in the country. Salaries of public servants and the army went unpaid for months, creating a state of persistent political instability. By 2003 Yala was "at war with his own party, the opposition, the judiciary, the military, the media and society as a whole."[13] His excesses had turned former friends into foes, and few outside his own inner circle would have mourned his removal.

On September 14, 2003, Yala was ousted in a bloodless coup. The coup garnered widespread domestic and global support after the military agreed to quickly return power to a civilian interim government. With broad support, a businessman, Henrique Rosa, was appointed interim president.

The coup ushered in "a new era of democratic politics" in Guinea-Bissau,[14] with better government accountability. Legislative elections—declared free and fair by international observers—took place in March 2004, and the elected government took office that May. The legislature improved budgetary discipline, endorsed a reform program, and organized free and fair presidential elections. Twenty-two candidates from almost as many political parties entered the presidential election in 2005. João Bernardo Vieira won, marking the return to civilian rule and the end of the democratic coup against the Yala dictatorship.

Although the 2003 coup generated significant democratic progress, deeply entrenched ethnic rivalries between the dominant Balanta group and the minority Papel group continued to bubble underneath the surface. In addition the military continued to exert significant influence over civilian politics, which produced two centers of power: the civilian, led by President Vieira, a member of the minority Papel group, and the Balanta-dominated military, led by the chief of defense. President Vieira came to increasingly rely on the military when he found himself unable to fix the fragmentations in his own political party. He formed an alliance of convenience with a longtime nemesis, General Batista Tagme Na Waie, and appointed him chief of defense. In exchange Na Waie agreed to protect Vieira against his rivals from inside both his political party and the Balanta-dominated military. This alliance of convenience eventually frayed, as personal rifts trumped tactical considerations. Na Waie was assassinated on March 1, 2009, apparently on Vieira's orders. One day later soldiers loyal to Na Waie avenged his death and assassinated Vieira in his private home.

Elections were held to fill the seat vacated by Vieira's death. Malam Bacai Sanhá emerged victorious and assumed the presidential office in September 2009 after a run-off election against Yala, the dictator who was ousted in the 2003 coup.

But Yala refused to give up. He ran for president again in March 2012 and came in second. Because no presidential candidate got over 50 percent of the vote, run-off presidential elections were scheduled for April. But before they could take place, the military returned to the scene. On April 12 soldiers, equipped with Kalashnikov rifles and rocket-propelled grenades, stormed the headquarters of the ruling party and arrested Prime Minister Carlos Gomes Júnior, who had won the first round of the presidential elections and was a frontrunner for the run-off. Gomes was unpopular within the military because of his plans to prune the armed forces, build up the police force, and retire many senior military officers. He had also failed to appeal to the majority Balanta ethnic group, who dominated the military and who still saw Yala as their leader. In fact Yala was "suspected of involvement in the coup despite his avowed condemnation of the military action."[15] It took until April 2014 for democratic politics to return to normal, with fresh legislative and presidential elections.

As the Guinea-Bissau case illustrates, following a coup, politicians may begin to rely on the military as a means to topple unfriendly governments rather than attempting to spin the slow and uncertain wheels of democracy. In the case of Guinea-Bissau, Yala relied on the same military that overthrew him to help bring him back to power when he lost the first round of presidential elections.

But it's not just civilian politicians who lose their patience with democracy. At times democracy may turn into a hollow hope even for democratically minded military leaders.

22

Hollow Hope

Blessed is he who expects nothing, for he shall never be disappointed.
— Alexander Pope, letter to John Gay, October 6, 1727

Fool Me Once, Fool Me Twice

Nothing in his life could have prepared the Brazilian dictator Getúlio Vargas for not one but two military coups that toppled him at two different times during his rule.[1] Vargas had assumed power in 1930 and began ruling as dictator. He lacked the charm and drama of many of his twentieth-century contemporaries. But what he lacked in charms he made up for with intuition. Borrowing from the New Deal and European fascism, he relied heavily on both the military and technocrats to run the government, often buying the military's support with budget increases.

Initially Vargas was able to utilize the global depression to justify centralizing government and expanding his power. He quickly dissolved Congress, instituted emergency rule, and began ruling by executive decrees. Right before the November 1937 elections, Vargas, with military support, took complete control of the government. The military prevented congressmen from entering the Congress building in Rio de Janeiro, and Vargas announced to the Brazilian people that they were now living under the Estado Novo—a dictatorship that shared the name of its Portuguese counterpart established in 1933. Both Estado Novo regimes would suffer the same fate at the hands of their own militaries, with the Brazilian military ousting Vargas in 1945 and the Portuguese military ending the European dictatorship in 1974.

Vargas's Brazil was in shambles when the 1945 coup occurred. The nation had yet to industrialize. The economy was heavily reliant on coffee exports. The people were plagued with chronic disease and limited medical care, and the overall life expectancy was forty-six years. Brazil's infrastructure and education system were no match for the postwar population boom.

The last straw came when Vargas, incorrectly believing he still had the support of the people and the military, appointed his violent brother as police chief. On October 29 troops occupied Rio de Janeiro and threatened to isolate the presidential palace if Vargas didn't resign. With little resistance, he left office. But for Vargas the battle wasn't over. He was simply biding his time for an opportunity to return to power.

Remarkably the transfer of power from the military to civilians was quick and painless. Rather than seize the chance to take power for themselves, the military turned government control over to the president of the Federal Supreme Court. The temporary president immediately appointed a new cabinet to try to maintain order while the country awaited elections in December. The new electoral system implemented following the 1945 coup ensured free and fair elections through secret ballots and poll watchers. New municipal governments were created to reduce the power of long-ruling families, and the new autonomous court system gained the power to declare laws and executive decrees unconstitutional.

Despite these reforms, the old regime didn't completely disappear. Eurico Dutra, a military leader involved in the 1945 coup, had been a longtime supporter of the Estado Novo. He even served as war minister for Vargas for almost a decade. And with the political machine on his side, he was able to win the 1945 elections with 55 percent of the vote. He was perceived as "simple, unpretentious, silent, polite, and brave without being boastful."[2] Generally skeptical of nationalism and of communism, he tried to unify the nation behind a centrist ideology. He included representatives of the opposition in his decision making and respected democratic freedoms.

But Dutra faced significant practical and economic problems. The new multiparty system required stable political alliances, but these were not forthcoming. The economy remained in shambles. Dutra's government ran through the $700 million to $800 million in foreign reserves it had at the beginning of 1945.

Following the coup, Vargas's political rights—including his right to run for president—had been left intact. In 1950, only five years after his downfall, the former dictator seized on the failures of the Dutra administration and the divisions that still troubled it to launch a renewed bid for the presidency. Vargas won with 49 percent of the vote and returned to the office from which he had been expelled.

Absolute rulers don't become liberal democrats overnight. Vargas is a good case in point. Brazilians once again grew suspicious of his commitment to democracy, and his opponents in Congress began to accuse him of corruption.

The end of Vargas's presidency started with an assassination attempt and finished with his suicide. A member of Vargas's police force attempted to kill a prominent journalist and critic of the government outside of his Copacabana apartment. While Vargas may have had nothing to do with the attack, it cast a shadow across a government that was already distrusted by many. After public outcry, Congress and Vargas's own vice president suggested that he resign. When he refused, the military intervened and demanded his "unconditional resignation." Vargas shot himself in the heart and died the next day, August 24, 1954.

After Vargas's death, democracy would continue in Brazil for ten more years. But Vargas's suicide sparked an interventionist attitude in the Brazilian military that significantly diverged from the military's past behavior. As José Maria Bello, a prominent historian of Brazil, explains, "Since the founding of the Republic the military services had regarded themselves—and were identified in successive constitutions—as permanent national institutions responsible for preserving constitutional powers. It was further generally accepted that the military enjoyed the right, above the law, to intervene in the political process during moments of national crisis, when the basic institutions of the Republic appeared to be in jeopardy. This extralegal power had been used sparingly, however, and then only to transfer political control from one civilian regime to another."[3] This attitude changed as one president after another failed to establish stability. When João Goulart won the 1963 presidential election, military officers went on the offensive, perceiving Goulart to be a communist sympathizer. Fidel Castro had become president in Cuba, and the cold war was heating up. A crumbling economy and failing foreign relations pushed Brazil over the edge. In 1964, as protests and marches roiled the country, the military was drawn into its last and gravest intervention.

That year, 1964, would come to mark the beginning of twenty-one years of military totalitarianism in Brazil. The coup was staged by many of the same officers who had toppled Vargas in 1954. To the coup makers who once fought to protect it, "democracy seemed to permit and even encourage corruption, subversion, chaos, and demagoguery."[4] The military leaders quickly rid Brazil of any opposition and consolidated power into an alliance of military elites and technocrats. The government masked its brutality with "impressive economic growth,"[5] but make no mistake: Censorship, book burning, limited civil rights, and limits on political opposition were once again commonplace in Brazil. The military, having lost its optimism for democratic governance, instituted the very government it had tried to purge only two decades before.

Although militaries derive substantial benefits from democracy, coup makers may become disillusioned with democratic governance if democracy fails to live up to its promises. The transition from dictatorship to democracy may usher in a period of economic and social instability, with no segment of society spared its ravages. As democracy proves to be more of a foe than a friend, impatient military leaders, as in the case of Brazil, may morph from reformers to tyrants.

A Revolution Divided

A similar set of events unfolded in neighboring Argentina.[6] In 1955 the military toppled dictator Juan Domingo Perón and instituted democracy. But not long after, the military returned to power as the newly established Argentinian democracy remained unable to cope with the ghosts of its past.

After assuming power as president in 1946, Perón became increasingly authoritarian. When, for example, a bomb killed several people during one of his speeches, Peronists responded by setting opposition centers on fire. This incident was followed by widespread government brutality, including arrests of opposition leaders. After Perón's charismatic wife, the former radio actress Eva ("Evita"), died of cervical cancer in 1952, the national coalition that supported her husband began to crumble.

Things came to a head when Perón began targeting the Catholic Church in late 1954. He barred the Church from public procession, prohibited it from participating in education, and began to permit divorce. The military, previously placated by promotions and better benefits, became outraged by the increased authoritarianism of Perón's government and his attacks against the Church. On September 16, 1955, a coup toppled Perón and sent him to self-exile in Paraguay.

The initial euphoria that surrounded Perón's downfall was enough to conceal the deep divides that fractured Argentina. The revolutionaries' outrage against Perón was insufficient to unite them. One Argentina scholar, Celia Szusterman, explains that there was "no ideological consistency amongst the men who had variously contributed to Perón's downfall: military and civilians, Army and Navy, nationalists and liberals, were but some of the divisions that soon smashed the notion of 'revolutionary solidarity' to smithereens."[7]

The first few months after the coup were tumultuous. General Eduardo Lonardi, the leader of the coup, became provisional president. But despite leading the movement to overthrow Perón, Lonardi's goals for the revolution seemed too close to Peronism for the comfort of his contemporaries. He was ousted two months later by General Pedro Eugenio Aramburu, who had a clear vision of a free democratic government. He proposed sharing power with civilians and eventually relinquishing power completely to them.

Aramburu's government was decidedly anti-Peronist in its agenda. It became taboo to even mention the name of Perón. In a conspiracy that one might find in a Dan Brown novel, Aramburu orchestrated the kidnapping of Evita Perón's mummified corpse from Argentina and had it sent to a cemetery in Italy with the covert help of the Vatican.[8] Even dead Peróns were unwelcome in Aramburu's Argentina.

This personal animosity also assumed political dimensions. The 1949 Constitution was abolished, the Peronist Party dissolved, and workers' organizations and educational institutions purged of all Peronist ideology. But uniting the new government behind an anti-Peronist message was not quite so simple, particularly within the army. In 1956 pro-Peronist officers in the army attempted to overthrow the government. This move was met with cold-blooded violence, including executions to purge the army of Peronist support.

In February 1958 general elections were held as planned. Arturo Frondizi Ercoli, described as "an image of aloofness and coldness, a man almost without emotions," was the frontrunner.[9] Frondizi understood that he had to secure the Peronists' vote to win, so he entered into a pact with Perón. Though in exile, Perón still carried great weight with many Argentinians. Frondizi agreed to lift the prohibition of Peronism in exchange for Perón's support. The pact led to Frondizi's victory, and his party won a majority, both in Congress and in provincial governments. But Frondizi's Faustian bargain with Perón would plague him for the rest of his time in office.

In 1962, Frondizi buckled under Peronist pressure and allowed the party to participate in the gubernatorial and congressional elections. These Peronist policies frustrated the military officers who had ousted Perón only seven years before. After the Peronist party won in many provinces, including Buenos Aires, the military used the resurgence of Peronist power as an opportunity to remove Frondizi from office in a bloodless coup. The coup makers placed him in a military detention center and transferred power to José María Guido, president of the Senate.

Signaling what was to come, a growing divide emerged between military leaders on whether to maintain a military regime or transfer power to civilian politicians. Despite these divisions, the pro-democracy faction of the military prevailed. A new round of elections was held on July 1963. Because of the fractious state of the Argentinian party system, Dr. Arturo Illia won the presidency with only 25 percent of the vote. Illia's government was inefficient and quickly lost popular support. At the same time, the military underwent an ideological shift as "democracy began to appear as a liability for security."[10] With significant public support, the military deposed Illia on June 28, 1966, and General Juan Carlos Onganía became the new president.

General Onganía's government began with an "authoritarian shock treatment."[11] Congress was dissolved, legislative and executive powers were concentrated in the presidency, and political parties were banned. The number of ministries and staff was reduced, and economic and scientific issues fell under the purview of national security. Universities were targeted as bastions of critical thought and dissidence. The day after the coup, in an event known as the Night of the Long Batons (La Noche de los Bastones Largos), the police raided the University of Buenos Aires and used batons to beat up students and professors.

The new regime, still deeply anti-Peronist, was now also decidedly antidemocratic. Even this new authoritarianism was no match for the divisiveness of Argentine politics. When it became clear President Onganía couldn't fix the economy and resolve social conflicts, he was replaced in an internal coup by Marcelo Levingston in 1970. Levingston himself was replaced in 1971 by Alejandro Agustín Lanusse, another military dictator, who served until 1973.

Having failed to govern effectively through three successive military dictators, the military buckled under pressure to hold popular elections and return power to civilians. In the 1973 elections the same man that the military and political elites had tried to force out of Argentinian political and social consciousness for almost twenty years returned to power once again. Perón was elected president.

In the end Perón's legacy haunted the democratic presidents who tried to lead Argentina after his downfall. The military also was unable to escape the divides Perón had created within the armed forces. Ultimately it was the very anti-Peronist and exclusionary policies the military instituted to achieve its democratic aspirations that led to democracy's demise. Had this new democracy adopted a different course in the early years, the 1955 coup against Perón may have been able to unify a divided society, prevent his return in 1973, and avoid the years of violence and guerrilla warfare that followed. But in trying to combat him and save democracy, the military made Perón's legacy more powerful and credible than ever before.

Horror Vacui

Nature abhors a vacuum (Horror vacui).

—Aristotle

Steve Jobs, founder and CEO of Apple, took the stage in June 2010 wearing his usual jeans, sneakers, and black turtleneck to announce to a captivated audience Apple's revolutionary new technologies. One of these innovations, called FaceTime, made "the dream of video calling a reality" by allowing users to see their loved ones with wireless Internet access.[1] "We have been dreaming about [this breakthrough] for decades," Jobs added. Even in his wildest dreams he could not have imagined FaceTime would be used by a world leader to announce that a coup attempt was under way against his government.

On Friday, July 15, 2016, President Recep Tayyip Erdoğan of Turkey was vacationing in a resort in Marmaris, a tranquil town located on the coast of the Aegean Sea.[2] Taking advantage of Erdoğan's absence, hundreds of junior military officers began to execute what turned out to be an ill-fated coup attempt. Beginning Friday evening, key bridges and media stations were seized, major roads were blocked, and two dozen F-16 fighters thundered over Istanbul, triggering sonic booms strong enough to shatter windows in nearby buildings. Tanks surrounded the Parliament building in Ankara and opened fire. A news anchor for Turkish Radio and Television was forced to read on live television a statement by the coup makers. The statement declared, prematurely it turned out, that the government had been toppled, a "peace council" was running the country, and martial law was imposed. As the motive for the coup, the coup makers cited government corruption, erosion of human rights, and the government's loss of credibility both domestically and globally.[3] "The secular and democratic rule of law has been virtually eliminated," said the visibly anxious news anchor reading the statement under the watchful eye of armed soldiers.

Meanwhile a defiant Erdoğan appeared on television using FaceTime—an ironic act for a president who has long sought to censor the Internet—and called on his supporters to take to the streets and resist the military. The sounds of low-flying jets piloted by the coup makers were soon met with unscheduled calls to prayer from mosques, beckoning the faithful to heed Erdoğan's call to action. Erdoğan's supporters were quick to respond. Thousands flooded the streets and overwhelmed the coup makers, who were forced to decide between commencing a bloodbath against large groups of demonstrators and giving up their haphazard plan.

The coup failed with remarkable speed. By early Saturday morning, Erdoğan declared the coup attempt over, framing its failure as the triumph of democracy over antidemocratic factions within the military. The clashes prompted by the coup attempt left hundreds dead, and tens of thousands of people were arrested and detained during an ensuing state of emergency. The blame for the attempted coup fell on estranged military officers associated with Fetullah Gülen, an influential Islamist preacher living in self-exile halfway around the world in Pennsylvania, with a loyal following in Turkey. An alliance of convenience between Gülen and Erdoğan had broken down in recent years, as Erdoğan blamed Gülen's followers within the police and the military for a sweeping corruption investigation against Erdoğan and members of his cabinet in 2013. A clash of ideologies soon turned personal, locking the two men in an endless vendetta.

Although some media outlets speculated about whether the coup was democratic, it was not. President Erdoğan had been growing increasingly more authoritarian, but at the time of the coup attempt he was a democratically elected leader. As a result the ballot box, not a coup, was the proper way to dislodge him from his seat.

As coups go, the July 15 attempt will rank among the most incompetent in history. The coup plotters would all fail Coup Making 101. Although the details remain a mystery, the plotters were among hundreds of officers expecting imminent expulsion from the military for their ties to Gülen. The coup was sloppily planned and executed, with no real direction or coordination. A coup against the sitting executive, by definition, requires coup makers to neutralize that executive and other senior government officials. But the coup makers were apparently confused about basic facts—including President Erdoğan's whereabouts—even though the location of his resort was publicized in the media before the coup began. The junior military officers who attempted the coup also failed to garner support from the military's top brass. After the coup was launched, senior officers denounced it and ordered all personnel to return to the barracks.

The plotters also severely miscalculated the effort required to topple a stable government. Coups are always fraught with hazard, but coups against stable, popular governments are a fool's errand. Although Turkey had its share of turmoil in 2016 in the form of terrorist attacks and an influx of Syrian refugees in the millions, President Erdoğan was stronger than ever. The plotters hit one of the most stable governments in Turkish history. It would have taken nothing short of a civil war to oust Erdoğan from power.

What's more, having failed at their costly adventure, the coup makers emboldened the very man they set out to destroy. Erdoğan, a firm believer in the adage that a good crisis should never go to waste, authorized an immediate crackdown against so-called Gülenists. The numbers are dizzying: In less than a week after the coup attempt, the government detained 6,823 soldiers, 2,777 judges and prosecutors (including two judges on the Turkish Constitutional Court), and dozens of governors. To top it off, 49,321 civil servants were removed from their positions, and the teaching licenses of 21,000 private school teachers were terminated. Nearly 1,600 university deans were asked to resign, and academics at Turkish universities were required to return home and refrain from traveling abroad. The massive scale of the purge extended well beyond those who might have been connected to the coup attempt.

I watched this drama play itself out from my summer office in Nuremberg, Germany. I canceled two planned trips to Istanbul after reports of U.S.-based law professors being subject to interrogations before they were permitted to leave Turkey. My name, and the article I had written that served as a predecessor to this book, popped up in Turkish government emails leaked to WikiLeaks. In self-exile I observed and wrote about the events from a distance, with growing concern.

In the end, the failed coup attempt turned out to be Erdoğan's finest hour. Having emerged unscathed from a full-frontal confrontation with a powerful nemesis, he solidified his already tight hold on Turkish politics. In so doing he proved Nietzsche right: What doesn't kill us makes us stronger.

Nature, said Aristotle, abhors a vacuum (*horror vacui*). He argued that a vacuum, once formed, would be immediately filled by the dense material surrounding it. Aristotle's insights into vacuums in the physical world also apply to civil-military relations. When a vacuum exists in domestic politics because the political parties are weak, unstable, or underdeveloped, the dense material that is the military may fill the void by staging an intervention into domestic politics. But where, as in the July 2016 coup attempt in Turkey, the civilian leaders themselves hold densely concentrated authority—in other words, they are powerful, popular, and credible—their attempts to keep the military at bay are far more likely to succeed. Without a vacuum there is no void for the military to fill.

Conversely, when the military is divided, civilian leaders can be the ones who take advantage of the power vacuum. A divided military is a paralyzed military. Civilians can pit different factions against each other and fracture cooperation among those seeking to undermine democracy. Where competing military factions serve to neutralize each other, no one faction can marshal sufficient support to take over the government. The resulting stalemate can reduce the military's effectiveness as an instrument of political intervention.[4]

These theories map directly onto the rise and fall of military interventions in Turkey. Although the Turkish military staged two democratic coups in its history—the first in the 1920s against the Ottoman Empire and the second in 1960 against the Adnan Menderes government—these coups were followed by future nondemocratic coups against elected governments. How did the same institution that twice replaced tyranny with democracy come to present such impediments to civilian rule?

The answer is *horror vacui*.

The Strange Case of Dr. Jekyll, Mr. Hyde, and the Turkish Military

Between 1923, the year of Turkey's founding, and 1950, the Republican People's Party (Cumhuriyet Halk Partisi, CHP) governed Turkey in a single-party framework.[5] When Turkey transitioned to a multiparty system between 1946 and 1950, the Democrat Party (Demokrat Parti, DP) was established. CHP and DP split over cultural and political fault lines. CHP continued to represent the nation's secular elite, but DP emerged as a populist, antibureaucracy party, representing a largely rural constituency. In 1950 DP won a sweeping majority in the Parliament and evicted CHP from the government seat it had occupied for the previous twenty-seven years. Although CHP was no longer in power, both the military and the civil bureaucracy remained firmly loyal to it. The military's support was buttressed by the fact that CHP's leader, Ismet Inönü, had served alongside Turkey's founder, Mustafa Kemal Atatürk, as a well-respected general in the Turkish Independence War.

Well aware of the sturdy support CHP still enjoyed in many circles, DP quickly took an authoritarian and repressive turn. During the ten years it governed the Republic (1950 to 1960), DP suppressed the CHP-friendly press, forced disobedient civil servants, judges, and professors into early retirement, and passed laws to quell political opposition. It empowered the Ministry of Finance to audit CHP's internal finances and froze a substantial portion of its assets pending the audit. DP monopolized the state radio, the primary news source at the time, and prevented CHP from airing opposition commentary. It passed a law prohibiting university professors from engaging in political activities, which cut off political speech by a large portion of the intelligentsia, a constituency aligned primarily with CHP. It imposed criminal penalties on journalists whose writings were accused of damaging the government's prestige. In December 1954, shortly before the general parliamentary elections, the DP-led Parliament voted to confiscate all financial assets of CHP, which significantly curtailed CHP's ability to mount an election campaign. In part because of these authoritarian tactics, DP managed to win another term in office.

Despite the comfortable majority it enjoyed in Parliament, the DP government, led by Prime Minister Adnan Menderes, remained uncertain and uneasy about its political prospects. To ensure his political future, Menderes advocated a "new type of democracy" that would allow suppressing the opposition in the name of preserving national security and preventing "destructive activities."[6] Under Menderes's leadership, DP established a McCarthy-style parliamentary commission, composed entirely of DP members, to investigate "subversive activities" by the opposition parties. DP authorized the commission to censor the press and to impose criminal sanctions, including up to three years' imprisonment, against those who prevented or undermined the commission's activities. During its investigation, the commission prohibited all political activity by the investigated parties for three months and prohibited the press from reporting on the investigations.

The establishment of the investigatory commission prompted widespread protests beginning on April 19, 1960. On April 26 a group of law professors issued a declaration stating that the commission violated the Turkish Constitution. The next day, in a defiant attempt to flex its political muscles, DP passed a law increasing the commission's powers. DP then prohibited the leader of CHP, Inönü, from attending Parliament for twelve days on trumped-up charges of inciting the nation to revolt and violate the law. CHP, for its part, made the most out of the real dangers DP posed to the Republic and galvanized the public to rise up against the regime.

DP's witch-hunt against the opposition prompted protests in Istanbul and Ankara on April 28 and 29. In response DP declared martial law and ordered the military to fire on the protesters, forcing the military into domestic politics after more than three decades of civilian rule in Turkey. If the military sided with the DP government and obeyed the orders, it would enter politics on DP's behalf; if it refused, it would enter politics against it. Much to CHP's delight, the military picked the latter option, refused to fire on the protesters, and instead staged a coup, toppling the DP government.

After assuming power, the Armed Forces issued a communiqué stating that they staged the coup to "rescue the Turkish democracy from the unfortunate situation in which it has found itself." In the communiqué, the military promised to "hold fair and free elections as quickly as possible" and to relinquish power to the electoral victors.[7] During the transition period, thirty-eight officers ranging in rank from general to captain would govern the nation as part of the National Unity Committee. General Cemal Gürsel, a popular and highly respected military leader who "clearly showed his belief in a nonpolitical army," was selected to head the Committee.[8]

Following the coup, a group of law professors, handpicked by the ruling military leaders, prepared a new democratic constitution, which was ratified in 1961. Although drafted under military tutelage, the 1961 Constitution is widely accepted as the most liberal in Turkish history.[9] It established separation of powers, instituted checks and balances, and recognized judicial independence. Inspired by the global rights revolution—including the European Convention on Human Rights and the Universal Declaration of Human Rights—the Constitution expanded individual rights and liberties, expressly recognizing, for example, the right to privacy, the right to travel, the right to strike, and the freedoms of speech and assembly. The 1961 Constitution also expanded the right to freedom of association, which led to the establishment of numerous autonomous civil society organizations and political parties.

Ergun Özbudun, a Turkish constitutional law scholar and an ardent modern critic of the Turkish military, wrote in 1966 that the 1960 coup was "unquestionably a reformist coup," whose accomplishments in the field of democratic, social, and economic development cannot be minimized.[10] The military officers who staged the coup, observes Özbudun, sought to build a "healthy democracy" and effect a "more balanced economic growth" by making the previously excluded rural classes a more meaningful and effective part of Turkish politics.[11] Social reform, especially in rural areas, came to the political fore only after the coup, for which Özbudun credits the ruling military leaders.[12] The military also provided the impetus for economic development as well as social progress and stability. According to Özbudun, the effects of the military's reform agenda would have been substantial "had they not been reversed, halted, or watered down by the successor civilian administrations."[13] As the democratization expert Dankwart Rustow observes, Turkey's rapid return to constitutional government following a decade of autocracy "is itself a major achievement, for which President Gürsel and the moderate majority of his [National Unity Committee] deserve the fullest credit."[14] The political scientist Manfred Halpern echoes this view: "Within less than two years, [the military] had succeeded in establishing firmer constitutional, if not yet also political, foundations for Turkish democracy, and cautiously withdrew once more to its barracks." Following the 1960 coup, Turkey's score on the Polity IV database, which measures the quality of a country's democracy, increased from a 4 to a 9 out of 10.

After the coup the Turkish military also had a major influence in promoting socioeconomic development in rural cities surrounding military installations. For example, the location of an army headquarters in Erzurum in eastern Turkey prompted the establishment of a new university in that city to educate the children of military officers. Likewise the military leadership promoted the development of highways for their obvious military advantages, which also had the benefit of facilitating socioeconomic development. In addition, eleven thousand officer cadets assisted in the civilian government's education efforts to combat illiteracy.

On October 15, 1961, the military turned over power to democratically elected leaders following parliamentary elections. These elections produced a weak coalition government between two ideological rivals: the Republican People's Party and the Justice Party. Future parliamentary elections fared no better, and successive fragile coalition governments followed. As politicians remained unable to form stable governments—let alone effectively conduct legislative affairs—the military began to stage further interventions into the political arena to bolster what was envisioned as a one-shot intervention against the Menderes government. Just as Dr. Jekyll morphed into the evil, self-indulgent Mr. Hyde, the same Turkish military that championed democracy began to morph into its antithesis in a little over a decade.

An Unfinished Revolution

The late 1960s and early 1970s in Turkey were marked by an economic recession; social unrest; violence between left-wing, Islamist, and nationalist groups; and persistent strikes by factory workers.[15] On March 12, 1971, the chief of the general staff personally handed a memorandum to Prime Minister Süleyman Demirel that demanded the "formation, within the context of democratic principles, of a strong and credible government, which will neutralize the current anarchical situation and which, inspired by Atatürk's views, will implement the reformist laws envisioned by the [1961] Constitution."[16] The memorandum also demanded an end to "anarchy, fratricidal strife, and social and economic unrest."[17] If the demands were not met, the military would "exercise its constitutional duty to guard the Turkish Republic" and take control of the government.[18] In response to the memorandum, Prime Minister Demirel resigned his post with little protest, avoiding a military coup.

The parliamentary elections that followed Demirel's resignation also failed to produce a stable government. One government after another collapsed, and a deep stalemate ensued in political and economic life. The political deadlock was accompanied by terrorism and widespread political violence between the starkly polarized right-wing nationalists and left-wing socialists. The violence dramatically escalated in the late 1970s, resulting in the deaths of an estimated two thousand people between 1978 and 1979.

The military's stance toward the weak governments grew increasingly critical. But a military coup couldn't occur because competing factions within the military leadership served to neutralize each other. The resulting impasse reduced the military's effectiveness as an instrument of political intervention.

Eventually, as the civilians remained unable to cope with instability and widespread political violence, the stalemate within the military dissolved sufficiently to produce another coup. On September 12, 1980, the Turkish Armed Forces, led by General Kenan Evren, staged a coup to "protect the unity of the nation, prevent a possible civil war, restore the authority of the government," and "remove the obstructions to democracy."[19] Large segments of the Turkish public expressed popular support for the coup to restore domestic tranquility. The military junta overthrew the civilian government, declared martial law, suspended the Constitution, closed down all political parties and arrested their leaders, and prohibited all political activity. Numerous human rights violations ensued, including torture, arbitrary arrests, and extrajudicial killings.

By 1980 the Turkish military was a different institution than its 1960 counterpart, which had shifted the nation's political trajectory toward democracy. The military's top brass had been replaced, and their intentions morphed from democratic transition into long-term social transformation. The political environment was also different. In 1960, it was a political leader with authoritarian intentions who threatened Turkey's democracy. In 1980, the threat came from a different source: widespread political violence. The cure, from the military's perspective in 1980, was stability and unity—at all costs. The remedy also included a new, illiberal constitution that limited many of the rights and liberties in the 1961 Constitution in the name of national security. Viewing the rights created by their predecessors in retrospect, the coup makers in 1980 believed these freedoms were "luxuries" Turkey couldn't afford.

According to the 1980 coup makers, only a strong government could rescue the country from the calamity their more liberal counterparts had produced following the 1960 coup. To question the aims of this dystopian project became an unpardonable sin. The military could no longer sit idly by as the nation it was supposed to defend tore itself apart. Activism became the order of the day. Although the military held democratic elections and retreated to the barracks in 1982, the consequences of the 1980 coup would reverberate for decades to come.[20]

Exodus

In 1999 the tide began to turn against military interventions in Turkey with the onset of two developments.[21] First, the European Union (EU) officially designated Turkey a candidate country. Among the EU accession requirements was effective civilian control of the military. To advance Turkey's candidacy, the Parliament adopted numerous reforms to subordinate the military to civilian authorities.

Second, the weak coalition governments of the past gave way to strong, stable political majorities beginning in the early 2000s with the ascension to power of the Justice and Development Party (Adalet ve Kalkınma Partisi, AKP). Armed with a strong popular mandate, AKP sought to rein in the Turkish military. As then–Prime Minister Erdoğan put it, "The military intervened in politics only when there was a political vacuum; the military played a somewhat expanded role because the political will was weak."[22] With its popular mandate, the Erdoğan government managed to establish the most stable regime in recent Turkish history, altering the decades-long civil-military power imbalance.

Yet the military continued to resist. In 2007, after Erdoğan attempted to nominate one of his Islamist confidants, Abdullah Gül, as president, the military posted a cautionary memorandum on its website: "It should not be forgotten that the Turkish armed forces are a side in this debate and are a staunch defender of secularism. They will display their convictions and act openly and clearly whenever necessary."[23] In terms of iron will, the military had found its match in Erdoğan. He refused to back down, called for elections, won a popular mandate, and installed Gül as president.

The military's power continued to wane. Under AKP's reign, the military became a target of criminal investigations and charges. Under the Ergenekon and Sledgehammer prosecutions—which alleged a conspiracy to overthrow the AKP government by a coup—scores of military officers were imprisoned.[24] The clash between the AKP government and the military culminated in the mass resignation of Turkey's military high command in late July 2011. Yavuz Baydar, a Turkish columnist, explained that the resignations represented a "new phase, a sharp curve towards pushing the military to adapt to the current changes in Turkey," and "showed how toothless the military ha[d] become compared to the civilian authority."[25] Because the military leaders chose to resign rather than resist, Turkish politics expert Henri Barkey described the resignations as "the day the military threw in the towel."[26]

Although disenchanted factions within the military attempted to stage a coup on July 15, 2016, the stable AKP government managed to subdue them with little difficulty. All major political parties issued statements condemning the coup attempt. This time it was the united civilians facing down military tanks—literally and metaphorically—who tamed the wolf that attempted to roar back to life.

24

Synergy

The whole is greater than the sum of its parts.

—Aristotle

The word synergy is based on the Greek *synergia*, which means "working together." With synergy the forces of numerous individuals can create a combined effect greater than the sum of its individual components. In science a similar notion called emergent properties means that some qualities come into being only through the cohesion of a system.[1] Heart cells, for example, can beat on their own, but only erratically. It's only through their combination into united, interconnected layers of cells that the rhythmic beating of the heart, and the ensuing pumping of blood, becomes possible.

Balanced civil-military relations also emerge from synergy. In this case synergy refers to civilians setting aside their ideological differences, working together to build credible democratic institutions, and constructing a viable alternative to military rule. If the civilians themselves are divided on the future democratic trajectory of the nation or the military's exit from politics, the military may more easily exploit these divisions. Instead of trying for a quick power grab, civilians in an emerging democracy must shun any antidemocratic alternatives, including military interventions, to political rule.

The more effective the civilian politicians are in constructing a stable, robust democracy, the less likely power vacuums and military interventions will occur. If political parties have a real chance to compete and win in the electoral marketplace, they are more likely to play the democratic game rather than violate its rules and resort to tanks and guns to oust their opponents.[2] An empirical study of civil-military relations in eighteen Latin American countries in the twentieth century confirms this theory and establishes that healthy political competition decreases the risk of future coups.[3] It's only through a synergy of civilians that the emergent balance of civil-military relations materializes.

In Indonesia it was synergy between successive presidents that saved the country from the brink of collapse. In 1998 the dictator Suharto resigned from his post following three decades in office. His departure unleashed protests, insurgency, and deadly violence between religious groups.[4] Yet thanks to the country's post-Suharto presidents, Indonesia did not fall apart. Despite their various shortcomings, these leaders managed to fortify democracy, protected the rights of ethnic and religious minorities, and fended off antidemocratic influences from the military and religious movements.[5] According to Jonathan Tepperman, author and editor of *Foreign Affairs*, these leaders saved Indonesian democracy by definitively demonstrating that "democracy works."[6]

Consider also the following two examples.

United We Stand, Divided We Fall

General Gustavo Rojas Pinilla had his work cut out for him.[7] He came to power in Colombia in the 1950s through a coup. His presidency coincided with a period of civil war known as The Violence (La Violencia), which ended up claiming the lives of hundreds of thousands. The Rojas regime was corrupt and incompetent, and popular opposition mounted as he remained unable to cope with the civil war and the country's socioeconomic problems. The two major civilian political parties—the Liberals and the Conservatives—managed to set aside their ideological differences and call for a return to democratic rule through a coalition government. The parties issued a joint public manifesto advocating civilian two-party rule and free and fair elections for the presidency.

Rojas, threatened by the growing opposition to his power, moved to action. He tried, unsuccessfully, to place the parties' joint presidential candidate under arrest. In response to this act of cowardice, protests against Rojas erupted across Colombia on May 10, 1957. The protests were followed by a nationwide civic strike and shutdown of the country's major cities.

Throughout his term in office Rojas had managed to retain his hold on power primarily because the armed forces supported him. That loyalty began to fracture as the military displayed no interest in battling civilian protesters on the streets. Some military officers were also displeased with rampant corruption in the government and interpreted Rojas's nationalization efforts as a dangerous move toward socialism. Seizing on the vulnerability created by the nationwide protests and strikes, a five-man military junta staged a coup against Rojas, forcing him into exile.

Following the coup, Colombia's future hung in the balance. Rojas, sitting in exile, entertained delusions about the junta inviting him back to Colombia to reassume the presidential seat. Some military officers entertained not-so-passing thoughts about a dictatorial power grab of their own.

In the end this parade of horribles didn't materialize primarily because the democratic alternative was unassailable. *All* major political leaders supported the liberals' and conservatives' manifesto promising joint civilian rule and providing "mutual guarantees that neither [party] would be excluded from power." After the coup the liberals and the conservatives signed another pact agreeing to parity in Congress and in the cabinet for twelve years. The politicians' willingness to compromise resulted in large part from their less-than-pleasant experience under the Rojas regime and the horrors unleashed by La Violencia. They had no appetite for another dictatorship or a military government. Even as difficulties mounted—as they always do—during the transition process, civilians did not waver from their commitment to democracy nor resort to antidemocratic shortcuts.

Faced with a strong, united civilian opposition, the Colombian military was reluctant to act on any antidemocratic impulses that may have been looming among its ranks. Shortly after assuming power, the junta called for the formation of a bipartisan cabinet, reinstatement of the freedom of the press, and elections to replace the military in August 1958, which would have marked the end of Rojas's presidential term.

While maintaining a united front, civilians deftly avoided antagonizing the military. Instead they managed to march the military back to the barracks with its dignity and institutional autonomy intact. Although the armed forces had supported the Rojas dictatorship, civilians refrained from pointing fingers at them. They recognized that they would need the military's cooperation both during the transition process and in its aftermath. So they offered an alternative narrative for public consumption that uncoupled the armed forces from the Rojas regime. In this narrative, which the military leaders found much easier to swallow, it was the "presidential family" and a few corrupt civilians close to Rojas—not military officers—who were responsible for the regime's excesses.

For its part, the ruling junta ensured a relatively stable trajectory toward democratic rule and foiled a number of countercoup attempts by officers who remained loyal to Rojas. As Jonathan Hartlyn, a political scientist and an expert on Colombia, explains, the senior military officers, "impressed by the support for return to party rule by financial, industrial, and commercial elites, fearful of the loss of prestige of the armed forces and of the divisive currents within it, and confronted by civilians who appeared sensitive to their major fears, stood by their pledge to withdraw from power."[8] The officers in charge didn't feel threatened, personally or institutionally, by the liberal-conservative civilian alliance, which appeared poised to respect the military and provide the officers with golden parachutes in the form of autonomy in managing their internal affairs.

In the end democratic regime change was possible because the conservative and liberal parties, despite their policy differences, coalesced around a firm common commitment to democratic civilian rule. The resulting synergy left no power vacuums for the military to fill.

The Project and the Will

Most military leaders are notoriously reluctant to give interviews. But when noted political scientist Al Stepan came calling, a former Brazilian colonel answered. Among other things, Stepan asked the colonel why the civilians hadn't been able to subordinate the Brazilian military after the military regime ended in 1985. The colonel replied, "The military have a project and the will. The civilians have neither."[9]

In the colonel's pithy response lies the key to normalizing civil-military relations. Following a democratic coup, the military may continue to dominate a polity if the civilians lack a project of establishing a stable democracy and a will to play by the rules of the democratic game. Where the civilians are weak and fragmented, they will be poorly positioned to contain a military pining to insert itself into domestic politics.

Portuguese politicians managed to subordinate the military relatively quickly following the 1974 democratic coup against the Estado Novo dictatorship precisely because they had a plan and the political will to institute democratic reforms. Following the coup, the Council of the Revolution, primarily made up of military officers, was established with sweeping powers to make laws concerning the armed forces and veto laws passed by the Parliament. The civilians reluctantly agreed to the Council's majestic role largely to secure the military's cooperation and ensure its eventual exit from politics.

The implicit understanding during the democratic transition was that the president of the republic, who was also the chairperson of the Council of the Revolution, would be elected from among the senior military leadership.[10] Although the election of a military leader may appear antithetical to democratic development, a soldier-president who could invoke electoral legitimacy could also impose constraints on the Council of the Revolution's extensive prerogatives. By fusing civilian and military authority in the same office, the Constitution pitted soldier against soldier, which proved to be beneficial in consolidating the democratic regime. The juxtaposition of these two powers eventually ensured that the Council of the Revolution, the military organ, became subordinate to the civilian president as a mere advisory body.

General António Ramalho Eanes prevailed in the 1976 presidential elections, with an overwhelming 61.6 percent of the popular vote. Eanes, a political moderate, was widely viewed as the military leader best positioned to normalize and instill nonpartisanship in the armed forces. He believed that the "armed forces should not espouse a political role but should rather act as guarantors of a democratic system on a western model."[11] Under his leadership the military's focus would be on external, not internal, threats. Eanes also vowed to be a nonpartisan president who would remain "above the parties" and uncommitted to any political party or agenda.

The December 1979 and the October 1980 parliamentary elections handed a landslide victory to the Democratic Alliance coalition. That electoral triumph signaled that Portugal's civilian parties were ready to assume center stage in politics and ignited a period of stability and a process of institutional change that ended with the abolishment of the military's prerogatives. The Democratic Alliance coalition also sought to reinforce Portugal's ties to the European community, in part to ensure that Portugal mirrored the pattern of military subordination to civilian authority found in other democracies.

By 1982 the political parties and democratic institutions in Portugal had attained a "reasonable degree of stable existence."[12] A coalition of the existing political parties obtained the necessary supermajority to revise the Constitution. The constitutional amendments decreased the powers of the president, transferred those powers to other institutions, and abolished the Council of the Revolution. The amendments also created a legal framework for the subordination of the military to democratic civilian control.

The military officers on the Council of the Revolution were not universally content about being pushed out. Although many of them opposed the reforms, to their credit they complied with the changes and handed in their resignations. The abolishment of the Council might have prompted backlash by the military in the immediate aftermath of the 1974 coup, when civilian politicians were relatively weak, but the military acquiesced to the reforms advocated by the stable civilian government in power.

Although significant political instability also existed in post-1974 Portugal, the resulting political coalitions were much stronger than the weak and fragile coalitions in post-1961 Turkey. After the 1974 coup in Portugal, political parties "successfully infiltrated so many aspects of Portuguese society that one can imagine few public offices or social institutions not subject to their dictates."[13] It was the political parties, not military leaders, that filled any resulting power vacuums in Portugal. The result of this synergy was a robust democracy.

25

Cincinnatus

What was wanted was not only a strong man, but one who was free to act, unshackled by the laws. He should therefore nominate Lucius Quinctius Cincinnatus as Dictator, for he had the courage and resolution which such great powers demanded.

—Livy, *The History of Rome*

In 458 B.C. there lived in Rome a farmer named Lucius Quinctius Cincinnatus.[1] One day while Cincinnatus was tending to his farm, he raised his head to see on the horizon a group of riders thundering toward him. These weren't bandits or enemies. They were senators of the Roman Republic with an offer that Cincinnatus couldn't refuse.

Rome, the senators explained, was in dire straits. Its ancient enemies—the Aequians, Sabines, and Volscians—were launching devastating attacks and threatening the empire's continued existence. Desperate times called for desperate measures, prompting the Senate to invoke a law that permitted the appointment of a dictator with absolute power. The Senate, the riders told Cincinnatus, had appointed him dictator for six months in order to defeat Rome's rival tribes and restore order to the Republic. Cincinnatus had previously served as Rome's consul—the empire's chief magistrate responsible for administration—and had developed a reputation for fairness and equity. These qualities made him an ideal candidate to lead Rome in its hour of need.

Cincinnatus accepted the senators' offer, and in a mere fifteen days he saved Rome from near-certain defeat. But instead of completing his six-month term and enjoying the fruits of absolute power, he did something that most modern politicians would not do. He resigned his post and retreated to his farm. Nearly twenty years later, in 439 B.C., he came out of retirement once again to serve as dictator at the Senate's insistence to suppress a conspiracy by Spurius Maelius, who was plotting to become emperor. By now in his eighties, Cincinnatus accepted the nomination, swiftly put down Maelius's coup plot, and once again immediately resigned his post.

Cincinnatus became a legend in Rome and beyond, providing the name for the American city of Cincinnati and serving as partial inspiration for the character Maximus in the film *The Gladiator*. Although other men may have succumbed to the temptation of absolute power, he managed not to be corrupted by its lure. He held on to power not a moment longer than was necessary and returned to his farm uninterested in further political glory.

In this book we've learned about military officers reminiscent of Cincinnatus. They topple a dictator, assume absolute power during a temporary period, provide a steady hand during a turbulent transition, establish democratic procedures, and hand over power to elected leaders. We started our journey in Portugal, celebrating with carnations the 1974 coup against Western Europe's oldest dictatorship. We visited locations as diverse as Mali, Egypt, Colombia, Burkina Faso, Turkey, and the United States, and time periods ranging from Ancient Athens to modern Africa. We watched as ordinary soldiers were transformed into democratic politicians, some rising to the task and others falling short of its demands. We met unscrupulous and manipulative military leaders who betrayed their own people in the quest for absolute power and those who, like Cincinnatus, relinquished power to the people the moment the democratic transition was complete.

The reader may believe that characterizing these democratic coups as successes requires adopting an exceedingly broad definition of "success." After all, the democratic coups we covered involved failures of some form. In some cases the military exited politics only to roar back to life. In others the military engaged in various human rights abuses during its temporary term in power, ranging from suppressing protests to curtailing individual liberties. In still other cases, even after the military retreated to the barracks, the consequences of the coup reverberated for years, as the military continued to exert an influence on domestic politics.

Democratic does not mean unproblematic. All transitions to democracy, whether led by civilians or the military, are turbulent events and require a rethinking of our idealistic notions of success in moments of regime change. Even the legendary Cincinnatus, the farmer savior of Rome, had another side to him, as a hard-line opponent of commoners' rights. Democratic coups also have another side to them. The extreme therapy of a coup generates inevitable side effects even as it cures its authoritarian patient.

Despite these side effects, the objective that democratic coups accomplish— overthrowing a dictator and establishing the foundations of democracy—is nothing short of herculean. It was the military in Ancient Greece that stood up to the tyrannical coup of the Four Hundred that threatened to end democratic rule in the very state that invented the term "democracy." It was the military in England, with the help of William of Orange, that overthrew King James II and transitioned the country from absolute to constitutional monarchy. It was coups staged by citizen-soldier militias in the American colonies that paved the way for the American Revolution and the establishment of the modern United States. It was a coup in Turkey that ended a theocratic sultan's centuries-long rule, and a coup in Portugal that toppled Western Europe's oldest dictatorship.

This book will inevitably produce the same howls of outrage that my previous articles unleashed. It has become taboo to even think out loud about controversial ideas, to openly question popular wisdom, and to introduce nuance to a field dominated by ancient thinking. The experts reached a consensus that all coups are bad for democracy and told us to move along—there's nothing to see here—even though on-the-ground realities scream otherwise. But as John Adams put it, "Facts are stubborn things; and whatever may be our wishes, our inclinations, or the dictates of our passion, they cannot alter the state of facts and evidence."[2]

Despite the stubborn fact that some military coups build up democracies rather than destroy them, we have allowed theory to displace reality. We continue to cling to comfortable and emotionally reassuring mantras that cloud judgment and hide complexities. These mantras may have the benefit of being clean and simple, but they ultimately come at the expense of facts and good science. Physicist and Nobel laureate Richard Feynman put it bluntly: "If it disagrees with experiment, it's wrong. In that simple statement is the key to science. It doesn't make any difference how beautiful your guess is, it doesn't matter how smart you are who made the guess, or what his name is. If it disagrees with experiment, it's wrong. That's all there is to it."

The theory that all coups are bad for democracy disagrees with the experiments, which, in this context, are tangible facts about real historical events. These experiments show that a democratic transition is often possible only with the active or tacit approval of the domestic military. Where the military sides with the regime, as large sections of the Syrian military did in 2011, the dictatorship often reigns supreme. Where the military sides with the people, as it did in the democratic coups covered in this book, democracy becomes a possibility.

Ideally, of course, civilian, not military, leaders would spearhead democratic regime change. But as we saw, civilian leaders are often unable to shoulder the momentous task of overthrowing an entrenched dictator without the help of the domestic military. In many cases the only hope for democracy is to turn the domestic military against the very dictatorship it's tasked to defend. In our imperfect world, the second best may be the best we can do.

In the end we do militaries a disservice if we idolize them as much as if we vilify them. But ultimately we do ourselves a disservice if we ignore the decisive role they play in most transitions to democracy.[3]

ACKNOWLEDGMENTS

They say that writing a book is a solitary effort. For me, it was anything but. I was fortunate to receive help and input from numerous colleagues, friends, students, and family members who deserve acknowledgment here.

My extraordinary research assistants at Lewis & Clark Law School played an integral part in bringing this book together: Eric Brickenstein, Philip Thoennes, Katherine Krater, Kelsey Benedick, and particularly Elisabeth Rennick and Kelly Iler. Elisabeth and Kelly deserve special mention because they worked on this book in the year before its publication, devoting a substantial amount of time and energy to it when they should have been studying for their classes. This book is as much a product of their efforts as it is of mine.

During my short stint as a visiting assistant professor at Chicago-Kent College of Law, I found the best mentor one can imagine in Professor William Birdthistle. William encouraged me to pursue an academic career in comparative constitutional law, helped shape the proposal for this book and recommended it to Oxford University Press, and diligently answered my incessant stream of questions and doubts over the years. This book wouldn't exist without him.

Thank you to all of the colleagues who encouraged, challenged, and critiqued the ideas developed in this book, including Mark Tushnet, Rosalind Dixon, Tom Ginsburg, David Landau, William Partlett, Brad Roth, Mila Versteeg, Nathan Brown, Christopher Buccafusco, Tayyab Mahmud, John Parry, Kristen Stilt, Christopher Schmidt, Richard Kay, Kim Lane Scheppele, Lisa Bernstein, Francesca Bignami, Ran Hirschl, Samuel Issacharoff, and Miguel Schor. Special thanks to Richard Pildes for lending his support to the book proposal.

Thank you to Elizabeth Nishiura and her amazing red pen that helped clean up the mess my first drafts produced.

Thank you to Nelly Murariu for beautifully capturing the inherent paradox of the book in her cover design.

Thank you to the dedicated team of first readers who commented on advance drafts of this manuscript, including Viktor Gecas, Joshua Fortenbery, Jesse Neilson, Gokalp Gurer, Connor Adams, Philip Thoennes, Jobie Anderson, Katherine Krater, David Cerri, Craig Kussmaul, and Tucker Rossetto.

Thank you to the reference librarians at Lewis & Clark Law School, who were invaluable to this project, particularly Lynn Williams, Mari Cheney, and Wendy Hitchcock, and their student research assistants, Dwight Mears and Sam Williams.

Thank you to Ryan Holiday and Brent Underwood for their expert marketing guidance.

Thank you to Katharine Rowe of Smith, Gambrell & Russell LLP for her legal help.

Thank you to our Boston Terrier, Einstein, for providing endless entertainment as I wrote this book.

Thank you to the staff of Powell's Bookstore in Portland, Oregon, and Di Simo Caffè in Nuremberg, Germany, where much of this book was written.

Thank you to my better half, Kathy, for reading the early drafts, laughing at all the jokes, and never once complaining, only encouraging, as she shared the burden involved in this undertaking.

Hayatım boyunca kendi menfaatlerini düşünmeden beni şartsız destekleyen annem ve babam Yurdanur ve Tacettin'e gönülden teşekkür ederim.

CONTINUE THE CONVERSATION

To access bonus material related to the book, including documentaries and interviews with relevant actors, please text DEMOCRATIC to 444999 (for U.S.-based phone numbers) or navigate to http://ozanvarol.com/dcbonus. In addition to the bonuses, you'll also get regular updates on my writing. If you'd like to write to me, my email address is author@ozanvarol.com.

NOTES

Part I

1. *A Coup Is a Coup, There Could Not Be a Democratic Coup*, AK PARTİ (Aug. 26, 2013), https://www.akparti.org.tr/english/haberler/a-coup-is-coup-there-could-not-be-a-democratic-coup/51123#1.
2. *Tunisie: "L'armée a lâché Ben Ali,"* Le Monde Afrique, Jan. 16, 2011, http://www.lemonde.fr/afrique/article/2011/01/16/tunisie-l-armee-a-lachee-ben-ali_1466290_3212.html.
3. Wendall Steavenson, *On the Square: Were the Egyptian Protestors Right to Trust the Military?*, The New Yorker (Feb. 28, 2011), http://www.newyorker.com/magazine/2011/02/28/on-the-square-wendell-steavenson.

Chapter 1

1. The description of the Eurovision song contest is taken from *The Spectacle of the Eurovision Song Contest*, Boston.com (last visited December 6, 2016), http://archive.boston.com/news/world/gallery/051509eurovision/.
2. My analysis of the 1974 coup in Portugal rests on Kenneth Maxwell, *The Thorns of the Portuguese Revolution*, 54 Foreign Aff. 250 (1976); Douglas Porch, *The Portuguese Armed Forces and the Revolution* (1977); Lawrence S. Graham, *The Portuguese Military and the State: Rethinking Transitions in Europe and Latin America* (1993); John Hammond, *The Armed Forces Movement and the Portuguese Revolution: Two Steps Forward, One Step Back*, 10 J. Pol. & Mil. Soc. 71 (1982); Jose A. Santos, *Portugal: From Empire to Nation-State*, 9 Fletcher F. 125 (1985); Paul Christopher Manuel, *The Challenges of Democratic Consolidation in Portugal: Political, Economic, and Military Issues, 1976–1991* (1996); *Portugal: Cheers, Carnations, and Problems*, Time (May 13, 1974), http://www.time.com/time/magazine/article/0,9171,908577-1,00.html; Ozan O. Varol, *The Democratic Coup d'État*, 53 Harv. Int'l L.J. 292 (2012); Ozan O. Varol, *The Military as the Guardian of Constitutional Democracy*, 51 Colum. J. Transn'l L. 547 (2013).
3. *Portugal: Cheers, Carnations, and Problems.*
4. Samuel Huntington, *The Third Wave: Democratization in the Late Twentieth Century* (1991).
5. *Revolutionary Freedom Song Interrupts Parliamentary Debate*, Portugal News Online (Feb. 16, 2013), http://www.theportugalnews.com/news/revolutionary-freedom-song-interrupts-parliamentary-debate/27779.
6. See, e.g., Gregory H. Fox, *Internationalizing National Politics: Lessons for International Organizations*, 13 Widener L. Rev. 265, 265 (2007) (noting that the international

community has universally condemned military coups); Jonathan M. Powell, *An Assessment of the "Democratic Coup" Theory: Democratic Trajectories in Africa, 1952–2012*, 23 Afr. Security Rev. 213 (2014) (noting that "coups are almost invariably condemned"); Stephen E. Gottlieb, *Does What We Know about the Life Cycle of Democracy Fit Constitutional Law?*, 61 Rutgers L. Rev. 595, 604 n.43 (2009) (noting that a coup is a "non-democratic" form of regime change); Venkat Iyer, *Restoration Constitutionalism in the South Pacific*, 15 Pac. Rim L. & Pol'y J. 39, 39 (2006) (noting that coups often lead to "regimes antithetical to freedom and democracy"); Enrique Lagos & Timothy D. Rudy, *The Third Summit of the Americas and the Thirty-First Session of the OAS General Assembly*, 96 Am. J. Int'l L. 173, 175 (2002) (noting that a coup constitutes "undemocratic behavior"); Salvador Maria Lozada, *The Successful Appeal from Ballots to Bullets: The Herculean Hardships of Judicializing Politics in Latin America*, 25 N.Y.U. J. Int'l L. & Pol. 123, 125 (1992) ("The coup d'état extinguishes democratic government and establishes a military dictatorship, which implies the disappearance of legislative power."); Tayyab Mahmud, *Jurisprudence of Successful Treason: Coup d'Etat and Common Law*, 27 Cornell Int'l L.J. 49, 51 (1994) ("Since an incumbent regime forms part of the constitutional order, its extra-constitutional overthrow is not only illegal but amounts to the high crime of treason."); Andrew C. Janos, *The Seizure of Power: A Study of Force and Popular Consent*, in Res. Monograph No. 16, at 36 (Ctr. Int'l Studies, Woodrow Wilson Sch. Pub. & Int'l Affairs, Princeton Univ., 1964) (noting that a coup is "the reversal of the process of revolution"); Julio Rios-Figueroa, *Constitutional Courts as Mediators: Armed Conflict, Civil-Military Relations, and the Rule of Law in Latin America*, at 1 ("Coups kill the democratic rule of law.").

7. Nikolay Marinov & Hein Goemans, *Coups and Democracy*, 44 British J. Pol. Sci. 799 (2013). This does not mean, however, that 72 percent of all coups in the post–cold war era are democratic coups. For example, if a coup is staged against a democratically elected government (as opposed to an authoritarian government), that coup would fall outside this book's democratic coup framework, regardless of whether democratic elections followed the coup.

8. *Id.*

9. Powell (2014).

Chapter 2

1. Sydney J. Freedberg Jr., *Strategic Optimism and the Arab Spring*, Geo. J. Int'l Aff. (2011), http://journal.georgetown.edu/strategic-optimism-and-the-arab-spring/.

2. Woodrow Wilson, *Address to Congress Requesting a Declaration of War against Germany*, Miller Center, University of Virginia (April 2, 1917), http://millercenter.org/president/wilson/speeches/speech-4722.

3. *See* John Williamson, *What Washington Means by Policy Reform*, in *Latin American Adjustment: How Much Has Happened?* 7 (John Williamson ed., 1990).

4. *Towards a Community of Democracies*, 20 Electronic J. of the U.S. Dep't of State: Issues of Dem. (2000).

5. Second Inaugural Address of George W. Bush, The Avalon Project at Yale Law School (Jan. 20, 2015), http://avalon.law.yale.edu/21st_century/gbush2.asp.

6. President Barack Obama, Remarks by the President on the Death of Muammar Qaddafi (Oct. 20, 2011), https://www.whitehouse.gov/the-press-office/2011/10/20/remarks-president-death-muammar-qaddafi.

7. Max Boot, *The End of Appeasement*, Weekly Standard, Feb. 10, 2003, http://www.weeklystandard.com/the-end-of-appeasement/article/3458.

8. Thomas L. Friedman, *Postcard from a Free Egypt*, N.Y. Times, Feb. 11, 2011, http://www.nytimes.com/2011/02/11/opinion/11-web-friedman.html.

9. *Id.*

10. *See* Hannibal Travis, *Wargaming the "Arab Spring": Predicting Likely Outcomes and Planning U.N. Responses*, 46 Cornell Int'l L.J. 75 (2013); Saleem Kassim, *Twitter Revolution: How the*

Arab Spring Was Helped by Social Media, Policy Mic, July 3, 2012, https://mic.com/articles/ 10642/twitter-revolution-how-the-arab-spring-was-helped-by-social-media#.a7ohCeRQt; L. Gordon Crovitz, *Egypt's Revolution by Social Media: How Facebook and Twitter Let People Keep Ahead of the Regime,* Wall Street J., Feb. 14, 2011, http://www.wsj.com/articles/SB1 0001424052748703786804576137980252177072; Sam Gustin, *Social Media Sparked, Accelerated Egypt's Revolutionary Fire,* Wired, Feb. 11, 2011, https://www.wired.com/2011/ 02/egypts-revolutionary-fire/.

11. *Could the Internet Unleash Democracy in China?,* Wall Street Journal, Feb. 20, 2013, http:// www.wsj.com/video/could-the-internet-unleash-democracy-in-china/694586AD-D9A3- 40D3-8164-B64A7BFD4D0E.html.
12. Bruce Ackerman, *The Future of Liberal Revolution* 3 (1992).
13. The discussion on Sultan Abdulhamid II's restoration of the Ottoman Constitution relies on Stanford J. Shaw & Ezel Kural Shaw, *History of the Ottoman Empire and Modern Turkey: Volume 2, Reform, Revolution and Republic: The Rise of Modern Turkey 1809–1975* (1977).
14. Halide Edib, *Memoirs of Halide Edib* 258 (1926).
15. Shaw & Shaw (1977) at 273.
16. *See, e.g.,* Adam Przeworski, *Democracy and the Market: Political and Economic Reforms in Eastern Europe and Latin America* (1991); Sharun Mukand & Dani Rodrik, *The Political Economy of Liberal Democracy* (July 2015) (unpublished manuscript) (describing liberal democracy as a "rare beast"); Fareed Zakaria, *The Rise of Illiberal Democracy,* 76 Foreign Aff. 22 (1997); Howard J. Wiarda & Matthew Q. Clary, *Premature Democracy: Waking up to the Reality of Incomplete Democratic Transitions in Latin America,* 17 J. World Aff. 89 (2010).
17. Rebecca L. Schiff, *The Military and Domestic Politics: A Concordance Theory of Civil-Military Relations* 4 (2009).
18. Andrew Bacevich, *America's War for the Greater Middle East* 329–30 (2016).
19. *Id.* at 330.
20. *See* Ivan Krastev, *Why Did the Twitter Revolutions Fail?,* N.Y. Times, Nov. 11, 2015, http:// www.nytimes.com/2015/11/12/opinion/why-did-the-twitter-revolutions-fail.html?_r=0.
21. Alwaleed bin Talal, *The Lesson of the Arab Spring,* Wall Street Journal, Feb. 6, 2012, at A13.
22. Fareed Zakaria, *The Future of Freedom: Illiberal Democracy at Home and Abroad* (2003).
23. *What's Gone Wrong with Democracy,* The Economist (last visited Dec. 6, 2016), http://www. economist.com/news/essays/21596796-democracy-was-most-successful-political-idea- 20th-century-why-has-it-run-trouble-and-what-can-be-do.
24. *See, e.g.,* Alexander Keyssar, *Voter Suppression Returns: Voting Rights and Partisan Practices,* Harv. Mag., July–Aug. 2012, http://harvardmagazine.com/2012/07/voter-suppression-returns.
25. Schiff (2009) at 36.

Chapter 3

1. *See* Sharun Mukand & Dani Rodrik, *The Political Economy of Liberal Democracy* (July 2015) (unpublished manuscript).
2. The Federalist No. 10 (James Madison).
3. The Federalist No. 51 (James Madison).
4. Daryl J. Levinson, *Parchment and Politics: The Positive Puzzle of Constitutional Commitment,* 124 Harv. L. Rev. 657, 666–67 (2011).
5. Manfred Halpern, *Politics of Social Change: In the Middle East and North Africa* 260 (1963).
6. Paul Collier, *Let Us Now Praise Coups,* Wash. Post, June 22, 2008, http://www.washington- post.com/wp-dyn/content/article/2008/06/19/AR2008061901429.html.
7. Zoltan Barany, *How Armies Respond to Revolutions and Why* 8 (2016).
8. Richard Hamilton, *Who Voted for Hitler?* 443 (1982).
9. Collier (2008).

10. The discussion of the 1974 coup in Portugal is drawn from Douglas Porch, *The Portuguese Armed Forces and the Revolution* (1977).

11. Dankwart A. Rustow, *The Military: Turkey*, in *Political Modernization in Japan and Turkey* 352, 377 (Robert E. Ward & Dankwart A. Rustow eds., 1964).

12. *Id.*

13. *Id.*

14. Obaida El-Dandarawy, *Civil-Military Relations in Egypt: An Overview*, in *Security Sector Transformation in Southeastern Europe and the Middle East* (Thanos P. Dokos ed., 2007).

15. The discussion of the Tunisian military's role in the ouster of Ben Ali is drawn from Barany (2016) and Philippe Droz-Vincent, *The Military amidst Uprisings and Transitions in the Arab World*, in *The New Middle East: Protest and Revolution in the Arab World* (Farwaz A. Gerges, ed., 2014).

16. *Tunisie: "L'armée a lâché Ben Ali," Le Monde Afrique*, Jan. 16, 2011, http://www.lemonde.fr/afrique/article/2011/01/16/tunisie-l-armee-a-lachee-ben-ali_1466290_3212.html.

17. Hazem Kandil, *Soldiers, Spies, and Statesmen: Egypt's Road to Revolt* 226 (2012).

18. *Id.* at 229.

19. The discussion of the Serbian military's role in the ouster of Slobodan Milošević is drawn from Marina Ottaway, *Democracy Challenged: The Rise of Semi-Authoritarianism* 177 (2003).

20. The discussion of the ouster of Romanian dictator Nicolae Ceaușescu draws heavily from Gale Stokes, *The Walls Came Tumbling Down: The Collapse of Communism in Eastern Europe* (1993); Peter Siani-Davies, *The Romanian Revolution of December 1989* (2005); Clyde Haberman, *Upheaval In The East: Dictator's Flight; Pilot of Helicopter Describes Ceaușescu's Escape Attempt*, N.Y. Times, Jan. 1, 1990, http://www.nytimes.com/1990/01/01/world/upheaval-east-dictator-s-flight-pilot-helicopter-describes-ceausescu-s-escape.html; David Lauter, *Ceaușescu, Wife Reported Executed: Secret Trial Condemned Dictator; Bucharest Calm: Romania: The Army Announces Plans for a "Final Offensive" against the Security Forces Loyal to the Ex-ruler*, L.A. Times, Dec. 26, 1989, http://articles.latimes.com/1989-12-26/news/mn-981_1_security-forces.

21. Greg Scarlatoiu, *The Role of the Military in the Fall of Ceaușescu Regime and the Possible Relevance for a Post–Kim Jong-il Transition in North Korea*, KEI Exchange (2009), http://www.keia.org/sites/default/files/publications/02Exchange09.pdf.

22. *Id.*

23. *Id.*

24. *Id.*

25. D. E. H. Russell, *Rebellion, Revolution, and Armed Force* 12 (1974).

26. Hannah Arendt, *On Revolution* 112 (1965).

Chapter 4

1. Foreign Assistance Act, 22 U.S. § 8422 (2012); *see also* Max Fisher, *Law Says the U.S. Is Required to Cut Aid after Coups. Will It?*, Wash. Post, July 3, 2013, https://www.washingtonpost.com/news/worldviews/wp/2013/07/03/law-says-the-u-s-is-required-to-cut-aid-after-coups-will-it/?utm_term=.c08d400ff16e.

2. *Everybody Coups*, on *The Daily Show with Jon Stewart*, July 18, 2013, http://www.cc.com/video-clips/fzu4iq/the-daily-show-with-jon-stewart-everybody-coups.

3. Rebecca L. Schiff, *The Military and Domestic Politics: A Concordance Theory of Civil-Military Relations* 44 (2009).

4. Philippe Droz-Vincent, *The Military amidst Uprisings and Transitions in the Arab World*, in *The New Middle East: Protest and Revolution in the Arab World* 180, 183 (Farwaz A. Gerges, ed., 2014).

5. Peter D. Feaver, *Civil-Military Relations*, 2 Ann. Rev. Pol. Sci. 211, 214 (1999).

6. *Id.*

7. *See* Samuel Huntington, *Political Order in Changing Societies* 218 (2006); Jonathan Powell & Clayton Thyne, *Global Instances of Coups from 1950–2010: A New Dataset*, 28 J. of Peace Res. 249, 252 (2011).

8. Powell & Thyne (2011) at 251.

9. Ali Bozoğlu, *S/S Bandırma 1878–1924*, Deniz Haber (May 5, 2008), http://www.denizhaber. com/index.php?sayfa=yazar&id=28&yazi-id=100283 [Turk.]. The discussion on Mustafa Kemal's coup is drawn from Ozan O. Varol, *The Origins and Limits of Originalism: A Comparative Study*, 44 Vand. J. Transnat'l L. 1239 (2011). That article in turn relies on Manfred Halpern, *Politics of Social Change: In the Middle East and North Africa* 260 (1963); Adrien Katherine Wing & Ozan O. Varol, *Is Secularism Possible in a Majority-Muslim Country? The Turkish Example*, 42 Tex. Int'l L.J. 11 (2007); Hakan Yılmaz, *The Kemalist Revolution and the Foundation of the One-Party Regime in Turkey: A Political Analysis, in Essays in Honor of Ergun Özbudun* 535 (Serap Yazıcı et al., eds., 2008).

10. Bozoğlu (2008).

Chapter 5

1. Tom Ginsburg, *Egypt: Democratic Coup?*, I-Connect, July 5, 2013, http://www.iconnectblog. com/2013/07/egypt-democratic-coup/; Joshua Keating, *Can a Coup Ever be Democratic?*, Foreign Policy, July 3, 2013, http://foreignpolicy.com/2013/07/03/can-a-coup-ever-be-democratic/; Max Fisher, *The "Guardian Coup" Theory: Was Egypt's Coup Actually Good for Democracy?*, Wash. Post, July 5, 2013, http://www.washingtonpost.com/blogs/worldviews/wp/2013/07/05/the-guardian-coup-theory-was-egypts-coup-actually-good-for-democracy/; Alex Seitz-Wald, *Can Coups Be Democratic? Sometimes!*, Salon, July 3, 2013, http://www.salon.com/2013/07/03/can_coups_be_democratic_sometimes/; Mariano Castillo, *When a Coup Is Not Called a Coup*, CNN, July 6, 2013, http://www.cnn.com/2013/07/06/world/egypt-coup-debate.

2. Taha Kıvanç, *"Demokratik darbe" kuramının mucidini takdimimdir*, Star, July 8, 2013, http://haber.star.com.tr/yazar/demokratik-darbe-kuraminin-mucidini-takdimimdir/yazi-769551 [Turk.]

3. Özgür Öğret & Stefan Martens, *Pressing for Freedom: The Rise of a Party's Partisans*, Hurriyet Daily News, Sept. 6, 2010, http://www.hurriyetdailynews.com/pressing-for-freedom-the-rise-of-a-partys-partisans.aspx?pageID=438&n=part-v-the-rise-of-a-party8217s-partisans-2010-06-08.

4. *A Coup Is a Coup, There Could Not Be a Democratic Coup*, AK PARTİ (Aug. 26, 2013), https://www.akparti.org.tr/english/haberler/a-coup-is-coup-there-could-not-be-a-democratic-coup/51123#1.

5. 3 *Democracy in Developing Countries: Asia*, at xvii (Larry Diamond et al., eds., 1989).

6. *See, e.g.*, Larry Diamond, *Developing Democracy: Toward Consolidation* 8–15 (1999); Marc Morjé Howard & Philip G. Roessler, *Liberalizing Electoral Outcomes in Competitive Authoritarian Regimes*, 50 Am. J. Pol. Sci. 365, 366–67 (2006); Gerardo L. Munck, *Drawing Boundaries: How to Craft Intermediate Regime Categories, in Electoral Authoritarianism: The Dynamics of Unfree Competition* 27 (Andreas Schedler, ed., 2006); Andreas Schedler, *The Menu of Manipulation*, 13 J. Democracy 36 (2002).

7. *See* Samuel P. Huntington, *The Third Wave: Democratization In the Late Twentieth Century* 7 (1991).

8. *Id.* at 7–8.

9. *Id.* at 7.

10. Steven Levitsky & Lucan A. Way, *The Rise of Competitive Authoritarianism*, 13 J. Democracy, 51, 53 (2002).

11. *See generally id.* (discussing the rise of competitive authoritarian regimes after the cold war); William Case, *Manipulative Skills: How Do Rulers Control the Electoral Arena?*, in Schedler (2006) at 95 (electoral authoritarianism); Marina Ottaway, *Democracy Challenged: The Rise of*

Semi-Authoritarianism (2003). The term "hybrid regime" was first introduced by Terry Lynn Karl, who defines it as a regime that combines both democratic and authoritarian elements. *See* Terry Lynn Karl, *The Hybrid Regimes of Central America*, J. Democracy, July 1995, at 72, 73; *see also* Larry Diamond, *Thinking about Hybrid Regimes*, 6 J. Democracy, 21, 24–25 (2002); Kim Lane Scheppele, *Not Your Father's Authoritarianism: The Creation of the "Frankenstate,"* Eur. Pol. & Soc'y (Am. Political Sci. Ass'n), Winter 2013, at 5, 7.

12. Leah Gilbert & Payam Mohseni, *Beyond Authoritarianism: The Conceptualization of Hybrid Regimes*, 46 Stud. Comp. Int'l Dev. 270, 274 (2011).

13. David Landau, *Abusive Constitutionalism*, 47 U.C. Davis L. Rev. 189, 199 (2013).

14. Levitsky & Way (2002) at 54.

15. Juan J. Linz & Alfred Stepan, *Problems of Democratic Transition and Consolidation* 71 (1996).

16. *Id.* at 120; *see also* Giuseppe Di Palma, *To Craft Democracies: An Essay on Democratic Transition* 85 (1990).

17. *See* Thomas C. Bruneau, *From Revolution to Democracy in Portugal: The Roles and Stages of the Provisional Governments*, in *Between States: Interim Governments and Democratic Transitions* 152 (Yossi Shain & Juan J. Linz, eds., 1995).

18. Linz & Stepan (1996) at 120.

19. *Id.*

20. *See* Shaimaa Fayed & Patrick Werr, *Egypt Court Dissolves Mubarak's Former Ruling Party*, Reuters, Apr. 16, 2011, http://www.reuters.com/article/2011/04/16/us-egypt-politics-idUSTRE73F11X201 10416.

21. Douglas Porch, *The Portuguese Armed Forces and the Revolution* 233 (1977).

22. Julio Rios-Figueroa, *Constitutional Courts as Mediators: Armed Conflict, Civil-Military Relations, and the Rule of Law in Latin America* 1 (2016).

Part II

1. The relevant history of Egypt is drawn heavily from Hazem Kandil, *Soldiers, Spies, and Statesmen: Egypt's Road to Revolt* (2012). Other sources I rely on to describe the events include Tarek Osman, *Egypt on the Brink: From Nasser to Mubarak* (2011); Zoltan Barany, *How Armies Respond to Revolutions and Why* (2016); Adam Shatz, *Mubarak's Last Breath*, London Rev. of Books, May 27, 2010, http://www.lrb.co.uk/v32/n10/adam-shatz/mubaraks-last-breath; Charles Robert Davidson, *Reform and Repression and Mubarak's Egypt*, 24 Fletcher F. World Aff. 75 (2000); Alan W. Clarke, *Rendition to Torture: A Critical Legal History*, 62 Rutgers L. Rev. 1 (2009); Ozan O. Varol, *The Democratic Coup d'État*, 53 Harv. Int'l L.J. 292 (2012); Ozan O. Varol, *The Military as the Guardian of Constitutional Democracy*, 51 Col. J. Transn'l L. 547 (2013); Jack Shenker, *Egyptian Elections: Independents Fight for Hearts and Minds in "Fixed Ballot,"* Guardian (U.K.), Nov. 22, 2010; *Egypt Referendum Strongly Backs Constitution Changes*, BBC News, Mar. 20, 2011, http://www.bbc.co.uk/news/world-middle-east-12801125; Daniel Williams, *Egypt Extends 25-Year-Old Emergency Law*, Wash. Post, May 1, 2006, http://www.washingtonpost.com/wp-dyn/content/article/2006/04/30/AR2006043001039.html; Amro Hassan, *Mr. Mubarak and Son Go to Washington*, L.A. Times, Aug. 17, 2009, http://latimesblogs.latimes.com/babylonbeyond/2009/08/egypt-pessimism-amid-mubaraks-visit-to-washington.html; David D. Kirkpatrick, *Egypt Erupts in Jubilation as Mubarak Steps Down*, N.Y. Times, Feb. 11, 2011, http://www.nytimes.com/2011/02/12/world/middleeast/12egypt.html?pagewanted=all; Kareem Fahim & Mona El-Naggar, *Violent Clashes Mark Protests against Mubarak's Rule*, N.Y. Times, Jan. 25, 2011, http://www.nytimes.com/2011/01/26/world/middleeast/26egypt.html; David D. Kirkpatrick, *Mubarak Orders Crackdown, with Revolt Sweeping Egypt*, N.Y. Times, Jan. 28, 2011, http://www.nytimes.com/2011/01/29/world/middleeast/29unrest.html; Neil MacFarquhar, *Egypt's Military Is Seen as Pivotal in Next Step*, N.Y. Times, Jan. 28, 2011, http://www.nytimes.com/2010101/30/world/middleeast/30-egypt.html; David D.

Kirkpatrick, *Egyptians Defiant as Military Does Little to Quash Protests*, N.Y. Times, Jan. 29, 2011, http://www.nytimes.com/2011/01/30/world/middleeast/30-egypt.html; Anthony Shadid, *Obama Urges Faster Shift of Power in Egypt*, N.Y. Times, Feb. 1, 2011, http://www.nytimes.com/2011/02/02/world/middleeast/02egypt.html; David D. Kirkpatrick, *As Egypt Protest Swells, U.S. Sends Specific Demands*, N.Y. Times, Feb. 8, 2011, http://www.nytimes.com/2011/02/09/world/middleeast/09egypt.html; Anthony Shadid & David D. Kirkpatrick, *Mubarak Refuses to Step Down, Stoking Revolt's Fury and Resolve*, N.Y. Times, Feb. 10, 2011, http://www.nytimes.com/2011/02/11/world/middleeast/11egypt.html; *Hosni Mubarak Resigns as President*, Al Jazeera, Feb. 11, 2011, http://www.aljazeera.com/news/middleeast/2011/02/201121125158705862.html.

2. *See Voter Turnout Data for Egypt*, Int'l Inst. for Democracy & Electoral Assistance (last visited Dec. 6, 2016), http://www.idea.int/data-tools/country-view/100/40.
3. Kandil (2012) at 199.
4. Shatz (May 27, 2010).
5. Kandil (2012) at 198.
6. Kandil (2012) at 170.
7. Shatz (May 27, 2010).
8. Kandil (2012) at 217.
9. Interview with Maggie Morgan, Cairo, Aug. 3, 2011.
10. Kandil (2012) at 227.
11. Osman (2011).
12. Interview with Haytham Hammad, Cairo, Aug. 1, 2011.
13. You can follow Mohamed Elbaradei on Twitter (@ElBaradei).
14. Kandil (2012) at 227.
15. In his announcement Suleiman made a feeble attempt to portray Mubarak's decision to resign as voluntary: "Taking into consideration the difficult circumstances the country is going through, President Mohammed Hosni Mubarak has decided to leave the post of president of the republic and has asked the Supreme Council of the Armed Forces to manage the state's affairs." David D. Kirkpatrick, *Egypt Erupts in Jubilation as Mubarak Steps Down*, N.Y. Times, Feb. 11, 2011.
16. Kirkpatrick (Feb. 11, 2011).
17. Shakespeare, *The Life and Death of Julius Caesar*, act 3, sc. 2.
18. Barry Strauss, *The Death of Caesar* 75–76 (2015).

Chapter 6

1. John F. Clark, *Armed Arbiters: When Does the Military Step into the Electoral Arena?*, in *Electoral Authoritarianism: The Dynamics of Unfree Competition* 132 (Andreas Schedler, ed., 2006).
2. Boubacar N'Diaye, *The Challenge of Institutionalizing Civilian Control: Botswana, Ivory Coast, and Kenya in Comparative Perspective* 130 (2001).
3. Philippe Droz-Vincent, *The Military amidst Uprisings and Transitions in the Arab World*, in *The New Middle East: Protest and Revolution in the Arab World* 181 (Farwaz A. Gerges, ed., 2014).
4. N'Diaye (2001) at 129–30.
5. Boubacar N'Diaye, *How Not to Institutionalize Civilian Control: Kenya's Coup Prevention Strategies, 1964–1997*, 28 Armed Forces & Soc. 619 (2002).
6. Droz-Vincent (2014) at 186.
7. *Id.* at 194.
8. *Id.* at 194.
9. *See* Juan J. Linz & Alfred Stepan, *Problems of Democratic Transition and Consolidation* 67 (1996) ("As members of a situational elite who derive their power and status from the existence of a functioning state apparatus, the military-as-institution have an interest in a stable state.").
10. Clark (2006) at 135.

11. Mila Versteeg & David S. Law, *Constitutional Variation among Strains of Authoritarianism*, in *Constitutions in Authoritarian Regimes* 165, 168 (Tom Ginsburg & Alberto Simpser, eds., 2014).
12. *Id.* at 171.
13. The discussion on the relationship of France with its ex-colonies relies upon Clark (2006).

Chapter 7

1. Zoltan Barany, *How Armies Respond to Revolutions and Why* 32 (2016).
2. The discussion on the disenchantment of Portuguese soldiers with the Estado Novo dictatorship relies upon Douglas Porch, *The Portuguese Armed Forces and the Revolution* (1977); Eugene Keefe, *Portugal: A Country Study* (1993); John Hammond, *The Armed Forces Movement and the Portuguese Revolution: Two Steps Forward, One Step Back*, 10 J. Pol. & Mil. Soc. (1982); Juan J. Linz & Alfred Stepan, *Problems of Democratic Transition and Consolidation* (1996); Jose A. Santos, *Portugal: From Empire to Nation-State*, 9 Fletcher F. 125 (1985).
3. The discussion on the Romanian military's disenchantment with the Ceaușescu dictatorship relies on Peter Siani-Davies, *The Romanian Revolution of December 1989* (2005).
4. *Id.* at 125.
5. The discussion on the Egyptian military's relationship with King Farouk and Hosni Mubarak relies on Hazem Kandil, *Soldiers, Spies, and Statesmen: Egypt's Road to Revolt* (2012); Ozan O. Varol, *The Democratic Coup d'État*, 53 Harv. Int'l L.J. 292 (2012); Ozan O. Varol, *The Military as the Guardian of Constitutional Democracy*, 51 Col. J. Transn'l L. 547 (2013).
6. Kandil (2012) at 11.
7. Yezid Sayigh, *Egypt's Army Looks beyond Mubarak*, Financial Times, Feb. 3, 2011.
8. The discussion on the relationship between King James II and his military relies on Stephen Saunders Webb, *Lord Churchill's Coup: The Anglo-American Empire and the Glorious Revolution Reconsidered* (1995).
9. The sociological description of a popular uprising relies on Randolf S. David, *People Power and the Legal System: A Sociological Note*, in *Reflections on Sociology and Philippine Society* 241 (Randolf S. David, ed., 2001); Dante B. Gatmaytan, *It's All the Rage: Popular Uprisings and Philippine Democracy*, 15 Pac. Rim L. & Pol'y. 1 (2006); Randolf David, *The Third Time as Farce*, Phil. Daily Inquirer, Apr. 29, 2001, at A7.
10. Philippe Droz-Vincent, *The Military amidst Uprisings and Transitions in the Arab World*, in *The New Middle East: Protest and Revolution in the Arab World*, 180, 191 (Farwaz A. Gerges, ed., 2014).
11. Jack A. Goldstone, *Understanding the Revolutions of 2011*, Foreign Aff., May/June 2011, https://www.foreignaffairs.com/articles/middle-east/2011-04-14/understanding-revolutions-2011.
12. Steve Benen, *Obama: Egyptians "Bent the Arc of History toward Justice Once More,"* Wash. Monthly, Feb. 11, 2011, http://www.washingtonmonthly.com/archives/individual/2011_02/027961.Php.

Chapter 8

1. The discussion on the Muslim Brotherhood and its relationship with the Egyptian military relies on Tarek Osman, *Egypt on the Brink: From Nasser to Mubarak* (2010); Philippe Droz-Vincent, *The Military amidst Uprisings and Transitions in the Arab World*, in *The New Middle East: Protest and Revolution in the Arab World*, 180 (Farwaz A. Gerges, ed., 2014); Hazem Kandil, *Soldiers, Spies, and Statesmen: Egypt's Road to Revolt* (2012); Ozan O. Varol, *The Democratic Coup d'État*, 53 Harv. Int'l L.J. 292 (2012); Ozan O. Varol, *The Military as the Guardian of Constitutional Democracy*, 51 Col. J. Transn'l L. 547 (2013).
2. Gary C. Gambill, *What Is at Stake in Egypt's Referendum*, Jurist: Hotline, Mar. 19, 2011, http://jurist.org/hotline/2011/03/whats-at-stake-in-egypts-referendum-gary-c-gambill-editor-mideast-monitor.php; Michael Slackman, *Islamist Group Is Rising New Force in a New Egypt*,

N.Y. Times, March 24, 2001, http://www.nytimes.com/2011/03/25/world/middleeast/25egypt.html?pagewanted=all.

3. *Egypt: Torrid Post-Revolutionary Times,* Economist, July 30, 2011, http://www.economist.com/node/21524851 ("There are even whispers of a quiet alliance between the army and Islamist parties."); Slackman (2001) ("The Muslim Brotherhood, an Islamist group once banned by the state, transformed into a tacit partner with the military government.").

4. Nathan J. Brown & Kristen Stilt, *A Haphazard Constitutional Compromise,* Carnegie Found. for Int'l Peace (Apr. 11, 2011) http://carnegieendowment.org/publicationslindex.cfm?fa=view&id=43533.

5. *Id.*

6. *Id.*

7. Shahira Amin, *Muslim Brotherhood Undergoing Generational Rift in Egypt,* CNN, July 2, 2011, http://www.cnn.com/2011/WORLD/meast/06/30/egypt.muslim.brotherhood/; Mohamed Fadel Fahmy, *Egypt's Muslim Brotherhood to Field Presidential Candidate,* CNN, April 1, 2012, http://www.cnn.com/2012/04/01/world/meast/egypt-brotherhood-president/.

8. Jeffrey Fleishman & Reem Abdellatif, *Egypt President Purges Military Leaders,* L.A. Times, Aug. 12, 2012, http://articles.latimes.com/2012/aug/12/world/la-fg-egypt-morsi-military-20120813.

9. Basil El-Dabh, *Islamist Al-Nour Party Backs Al-Sisi,* Daily News Egypt, May 4, 2014, http://www.dailynewsegypt.com/2014/05/04/islamist-al-nour-party-backs-al-sisi/.

10. Emily Crane Linn & Nicholas Linn, *The Nour Party Goes Dim,* Foreign Pol'y (Nov. 21, 2015), https://foreignpolicy.com/2015/11/21/the-nour-party-goes-dim-egypt/.

Chapter 9

1. Stephen Saunders Webb, *Lord Churchill's Coup: The Anglo-American Empire and the Glorious Revolution Reconsidered* 159 (1995)

2. The discussion of the Glorious Revolution relies primarily on Stephen Saunders Webb, *Lord Churchill's Coup* (1995). Other sources that I consulted include Daron Acemoğlu & James Robinson, *Why Nations Fail: The Origins of Power, Prosperity, and Poverty* (2013); Richard Kay, *Glorious Revolution and the Continuity of Law* (2014); and Edward Vallance, *The Glorious Revolution,* BBC, June 2016, http://www.bbc.co.uk/history/british/civil_war_revolution/glorious_revolution_01.shtml.

3. Stephen Saunders Webb, *Lord Churchill's Coup* 134 (1995).

4. Acemoğlu & Robinson (2013) at 192.

5. *Id.* at 362.

6. *Id.* at 193.

7. *Id.*

Part III

1. The discussion of the Praetorian Guard is based on I. G. Spence et al., *Conflict in Ancient Greece and Rome: The Definitive Political, Social, and Military Encyclopedia* (2016); Patricia Southern, *The Roman Empire from Severus to Constantine* (2015); Sandra Bingham, *The Praetorian Guard: A History of Rome's Elite Special Forces* (2013); Franklin L. Ford, *Political Murder: From Tyrannicide to Terrorism* (1985); Evan Andrews, *8 Things You May Not Know about the Praetorian Guard,* History (July 8, 2014), http://www.history.com/news/history-lists/8-things-you-may-not-know-about-the-praetorian-guard.

Chapter 10

1. Alah Yuhas et al., *Turkey Coup Attempt: Erdogan Demands US Arrest Exiled Cleric Gulen amid Crackdown on Army—As It Happened,* Guardian (U.K.), July 16, 2016, https://www.theguardian.com/world/live/2016/jul/15/turkey-coup-attempt-military-gunfire-ankara?page=with:block-5789f65ce4b033b610b6e43e.

2. *Will Those Who Carried Guns and Lynched Soldiers Be Tried?* [*Silah taşıyanlar, askeri linç edenler yargılanacak mı?*], Cumhuriyet, July 16, 2016 [Turk.], http://www.cumhuriyet.com.tr/haber/turkiye/568583/Silah_tasiyanlar__askeri_linc_edenler_yargilanacak_mi_html; Ipek Yezdani, *Lynched Because of This Photograph* [*Bu fotoğraf yüzünden linç*], Hurriyet, July 17, 2016 [Turk.], http://www.hurriyet.com.tr/bu-fotograf-yuzunden-linc-40151617; *Brutal Moment Civilians Throw Stones and Stamp on a Turkish Tank Soldier before His Surrender*, Telegraph (U.K.), July 16, 2016, http://www.telegraph.co.uk/news/2016/07/16/brutal-moment-civilians-throw-stones-and-stamp-on-a-turkish-tank/.

3. Ian Krastev, *Paradoxes of New Authoritarianism*, 22 J. Democracy 1, 11 (2010); Steven Levitsky & Lucan A. Way, *Competitive Authoritarianism: Hybrid Regimes after the Cold War* 3 (2010).

4. Philippe Droz-Vincent, *The Military amidst Uprisings and Transitions in the Arab World*, in *The New Middle East: Protest and Revolution in the Arab World* 180, 181 (Farwaz A. Gerges, ed., 2014).

5. Morris Janowitz, *The Citizen Soldier and National Service*, Air University Review, December 1979.

6. Zoltan Barany, *How Armies Respond to Revolutions and Why* 29 (2016).

7. *Id.*

8. Narcís Serra, *The Military Transition: Democratic Reform of the Armed Forces* 207 (Peter Bush, trans., 2010).

9. *Id.*

10. Morris Janowitz, *The Professional Soldier: A Social and Political Portrait* 1 (1960).

11. *Id.*

12. *See* Deborah N. Pearlstein, *The Soldier, the State, and the Separation of Powers*, 90 Tex. L. Rev. 797, 842 (2012).

13. Richard H. Kohn, *Eagle and Sword: The Federalists and the Creation of the Military Establishment in America, 1783–1802*, 2 (1975); *see also* David C. Williams, *Civic Republicanism and the Citizen Militia: The Terrifying Second Amendment*, 101 Yale L.J. 551, 572 (1991); Pearlstein (2012).

14. Pearlstein (2012) at 842.

15. Rebecca L. Schiff, *The Military and Domestic Politics: A Concordance Theory of Civil-Military Relations* 56, 61 (2009).

16. *Id.* at 56, 58.

17. The Federalist No. 29 (Alexander Hamilton).

18. Bernard Bailyn, *The Ideological Origins of the American Revolution* 84 (1967).

19. The discussion on the coups in America draws on Owen Stanwood, *The Empire Reformed: English America in the Age of the Glorious Revolution* (2013); Owen Stanwood, *The Protestant Moment: Antipopery, the Revolution of 1688–1689, and the Making of an Anglo-American Empire*, 46 J. of Brit. Stud. 481 (2007); Charles McLean Andrews, *Colonial Self-Government* (1904); Stephen Saunders Webb, *Lord Churchill's Coup* 171–225 (1995); Stephen Saunders Webb, *The Strange Career of Francis Nicholson*, 23 William & Mary Q. 513 (1966); *Jacob Leisler: North American Colonist*, Encyclopedia Britannica (last visited March 21, 2017), https://www.britannica.com/biography/Jacob-Leisler.

20. Andrews (1904) at 74.

21. Stanwood (2013) at 96.

22. Erin Strogoff, *Connecticut's "Legend of the Charter Oak,"* ConnecticutHistory.org (last visited Dec. 7, 2016), http://connecticuthistory.org/connecticuts-the-legend-of-the-charter-oak/.

23. Webb (1995) at 522.

24. Andrews (1904) at 274.

25. *The Charter Oak—Connecticut's Most Famous* Tree, Charter Oak Figure Skating (last visited Dec. 7, 2016), http://www.charteroakfsc.com/TheCharterOak.pdf.

26. *Id.*

27. Craig Yirush, *Settlers, Liberty, and Empire: The Roots of Early American Political Theory, 1675–1775*, 74 (2011).

28. *The British and Their Laws in the Eighteenth Century* 210 (David Lemmings, ed., 2005).

29. Webb (1995) at 522.

30. Andrews (1904) at 104–5.

31. *Id.* at 287.

32. *Id.*

33. The Federalist No. 29 (Alexander Hamilton).

34. Dankwart A. Rustow, *The Military: Turkey*, in *Political Modernization in Japan and Turkey* 367 (Robert E. Ward & Dankwart A. Rustow, eds., 1964).

35. *Id.*

36. *Id.* at 367–68.

37. Nilüfer Narlı, *Civil-Military Relations in Turkey*, 1 Turk. Stud. 107, 117 (2000).

38. The discussion on the role of Portuguese conscripts in toppling the Estado Novo dictatorship relies on John Hammond, *The Armed Forces Movement and the Portuguese Revolution: Two Steps Forward, One Step Back*, 10 J. Pol. & Mil. Soc. 71 (1982); Jose A. Santos, *Portugal: From Empire to Nation-State*, 9 Fletcher F. 125 (1985); and Douglas Porch, *The Portuguese Armed Forces and the Revolution* (1977).

39. Porch (1977) at 31.

40. *Id.*

41. The discussion on how the Athenian Navy subverted the coup of the Four Hundred relies primarily on Martin Ostwald, *From Popular Sovereignty to the Sovereignty of Law: Law, Society, and Politics in Fifth-Century Athens* (1989). Other sources I consulted include Paul Gowder, *Democracy, Solidarity, and the Rule of Law: Lessons from Athens*, 62 Buffalo L. Rev. 1 (2014); *The Oligarchic Coup*, Livius (2016), http://www.livius.org/sources/content/aristotle/constitution-of-the-athenians/the-oligarchic-coup/; Thomas R. Martin, *An Overview of Classical Greek History from Mycenae to Alexander*, Perseus Digital Library (last visited March 21, 2017), http://www.perseus.tufts.edu/hopper/text?doc=Perseus%3Atext%3A1999.04.0009%3Achapter%3D12%3Asection%3D1%3Asubsection%3D17; Russell Meiggs, *Alcibiades*, Encyclopaedia Brittanica (last updated Nov. 21, 2012), https://www.britannica.com/biography/Alcibiades-Athenian-politician-and-general; Aristotle, *The Athenian Constitution* (last visited March 21, 2017), http://www.constitution.org/ari/athen_05.htm.

42. Ostwald (1989) at 387.

43. *Id.* at 389.

44. *Id.*

45. The discussion on Henri Tajfel and social identity theory relies on Kristen Monroe, *Ethics in an Age of Terror and Genocide: Identity and Moral Choice* (2011); Henri Tajfel, *Social Psychology of Intergroup Relations*, 33 Ann. Rev. Psych. 1 (1982); Henri Tajfel, *Human Groups and Social Categories: Studies in Social Psychology* (1981).

46. Janowitz (1960); Williams (1991).

47. Morris Janowitz, *The Military in the Political Development of New Nations* 64 (1964).

48. Timothy Brook, *Quelling the People: The Military Suppression of the Beijing Democracy Movement* 7 (1992).

49. Barany (2016) at 110.

50. *Id.* at 25.

51. *Id.* at 25–26

52. *Id.* at 144.

53. *Id.* at 144.

54. *Id.* at 146.

55. The discussion on military service in Bahrain relies on Droz-Vincent (2014); Barany (2016); Frederic Wehrey, *Bahrain's Lost Uprising*, Carnegie Endowment (June 12, 2012), http://

carnegieendowment.org/2012/06/12/bahrain-s-lost-uprising-pub-48475; Abdulhadi Khalaf, *Bahrain's Military Is Closely Tied to the Monarch*, N.Y. Times, Aug. 28, 2012, http://www.nytimes.com/roomfordebate/2012/08/28/the-staying-power-of-arab-monarchies/bahrains-military-is-closely-tied-to-the-monarch; *Sunni and Shia Muslims*, Pew Research Center (Jan. 27 2011), http://www.pewforum.org/2011/01/27/future-of-the-global-muslim-population-sunni-and-shia/.

56. The discussion on preferential recruitment within the Syrian military relies on Barany (2016) and Droz-Vincent (2014).

Chapter 11

1. Lucian W. Pye, *Armies in the Process of Political Modernization*, in *The Role of the Military in Underdeveloped Countries* 9 (John. J. Johnson, ed., 1962); Morris Janowitz, *The Military in the Political Development of New Nations* 53 n.17, 81 (1964).
2. Pye (1962) at 9.
3. Manfred Halpern, *Politics of Social Change: In the Middle East and North Africa* 260 (1963).
4. Pye (1962) at 84.
5. *Id.* at 81.
6. *Id.* at 10.
7. The discussion of meritocracy within the Turkish military relies on Janowitz (1964); Ergun Özbudun, *The Role of the Military in Recent Turkish Politics* (1966); James Brown, *The Military and Society: The Turkish Case*, 25 Middle E. Stud. 387 (1989); Daniel Lerner & Richard D. Robinson, *Swords and Ploughshares: The Turkish Army as a Modernizing Force*, 13 World Pol. 19 (1960); Ozan O. Varol, *The Turkish "Model" of Civil-Military Relations*, 11 Int'l J. of Con'l L. 727 (2013).
8. Paul Stirling, *The Structure of Turkish Peasant Communities* 165 (1951).
9. Dankwart A. Rustow, *The Military: Turkey*, in *Political Modernization in Japan and Turkey* 352, 385, 387 (Robert E. Ward & Dankwart A. Rustow, eds., 1964).
10. *Id.*
11. Lerner & Robinson (1960) at 36.
12. The discussion on the role of meritocracy within the Portuguese military draws on John Hammond, *The Armed Forces Movement and the Portuguese Revolution: Two Steps Forward, One Step Back*, 10 J. Pol. & Mil. Soc. 71 (1982); Eugene Keefe, *Portugal: A Country Study* (1993).
13. The discussion on the overthrow of the Ponce regime in Guatemala and its aftermath relies on Piero Gleijeses, *Shattered Hope: The Guatemalan Revolution and the United States, 1944–1954* (1991); Kenneth J. Grieb, *The Guatemalan Military and the Revolution of 1944*, 32 Americas 524 (1976); Donald Grant, *Guatemala and United States Foreign Policy*, 9 J. Int'l Aff. 64 (1955); Andrew J. Schlewitz, *Imperial Incompetence and Guatemalan Militarism, 1931–1966*, 17 Int'l J. Pol. Culture & Soc'y 585 (2004); Raymond Nunzio Ruggiero, *The Origins of a Democratic National Constitution: The 1945 Guatemalan Constitution and Human Rights* 95 (Apr. 8, 2013) (Ph.D. dissertation, Florida State University); Timothy J. Smith, *Reflecting upon the Historical Impact of the Coup*, in *After the Coup: An Ethnographic Reframing of Guatemala 1954* 1, 3 (Timothy J. Smith & Abigail E. Adams, eds., 2011).

Chapter 12

1. Manfred Halpern, *Politics of Social Change: In the Middle East and North Africa* 271 (1963).
2. Claude Welch & Arthur Smith, *Military Role and Rule* 10 (1974).
3. The discussion on the Spanish military relies heavily on Narcís Serra, *The Military Transition: Democratic Reform of the Armed Forces* (Peter Bush, trans., 2010).
4. Zoltan Barany, *How Armies Respond to Revolutions and Why* 30 (2016).
5. Morris Janowitz, *The Military in the Political Development of New Nations* (1964).

6. This is not universally true. In rare cases the police have sided with the rebellious populace against the government. *See* Edwin Lieuwen, *Militarism and Politics in Latin America*, in *The Role of the Military in Underdeveloped Countries*, 146 (1962) (citing Colombia in 1948 and Bolivia in 1952).

7. The discussion on the Egyptian military relies on Philippe Droz-Vincent, *The Military amidst Uprisings and Transitions in the Arab World*, in *The New Middle East: Protest and Revolution in the Arab World*, 180 (Farwaz A. Gerges, ed., 2014); Gary C. Gambill, *What Is at Stake in Egypt's Referendum*, Jurist: Hotline (Mar. 19, 2011), http://jurist.org/hotline/2011/03/whats-at-stake-in-egypts-referendum-gary-c-gambill-editor-mideast-monitor.php; David D. Kirkpatrick, *Mubarak Orders Crackdown, with Revolt Sweeping Egypt*, N.Y. Times, Jan. 28, 2011, htrp://www.nytimes.com/2011/01/29/world/middleeast/29unrest.html; Ozan O. Varol, *The Democratic Coup d'État*, 53 Harv. Int'l L.J. 292 (2012).

8. David D. Kirkpatrick, *Egyptians Defiant as Military Does Little to Quash Protests*, N.Y. Times, Jan. 29, 2011, http://www.nytimes.com/2011/01/30/world/middleeast/30-egypt.html.

9. The discussion on the Tunisian military's role in ousting Ben Ali relies on Beatrice Hibou, *The Force of Obedience: The Political Economy of Repression in Tunisia* (2011); Barany (2016); Droz-Vincent (2014); Steven Cook, *The Calculations of Tunisia's Military*, Foreign Pol'y, Jan. 20, 2011, https://foreignpolicy.com/2011/01/20/the-calculations-of-tunisias-military/.

10. Barany (2016) at 137.

11. *Id.*

Chapter 13

1. Steven Levitsky & Lucan A. Way, *Competitive Authoritarianism: Hybrid Regimes after the Cold War* 3 (2010); Ian Krastev, *Paradoxes of New Authoritarianism*, 22 J. Democracy 1, 11 (2010).

2. Lucian W. Pye, *Armies in the Process of Political Modernization*, in *The Role of the Military in Underdeveloped Countries* 78 (John. J. Johnson, ed., 1962).

3. Zoltan Barany, *How Armies Respond to Revolutions and Why* 38 (2016).

4. *Id.* at 39.

5. Pye (1964) at 67; Narcís Serra, *The Military Transition: Democratic Reform of the Armed Forces* 77 (Peter Bush, trans., 2010).

6. Metin Heper & Aylin Güney, *The Military and Democracy in the Third Turkish Republic*, 22 Armed Forces & Soc'y 619, 619 (1996); Metin Heper, *The European Union, the Turkish Military, and Democracy*, 10 S. Eur. Soc'y & Pol. 33, 34 (Apr. 2005); Ümit Cizre Sakallıoğlu, *The Anatomy of the Turkish Military's Political Autonomy*, 29 Comp. Pol. 151, 154 (Jan. 1997). The section on Young Turks draws on Edward Shils, *The Military in the Political Development of New States*, in *The Role of the Military in Underdeveloped Countries* (John J. Johnson, ed., 1962); Manfred Halpern, *The Politics of Social Change in the Middle East and North Africa* (1963); Eugene Rogan, *The Fall of the Ottomans: The Great War in the Middle East* (2015); Stanford J. Shaw & Ezel Kural Shaw, *History of the Ottoman Empire and Modern Turkey: Volume 2, Reform, Revolution and Republic: The Rise of Modern Turkey 1809–1975* (1977).

7. Heper & Güney (1996) at 619–20.

8. Rogan (2015).

9. *Id.* at 6.

10. The discussion on Western influence on the Turkish military relies on Kemal H. Karpat, *The Military and Politics in Turkey, 1960–64: A Socio-Cultural Analysis of a Revolution*, 75 Am. Hist. Rev. 1654 (1970); Daniel Lerner & Richard D. Robinson, *Swords and Ploughshares: The Turkish Army as a Modernizing Force*, 13 World Politics 30 (Oct. 1960); Dankwart A. Rustow, *The Military: Turkey*, in *Political Modernization in Japan and Turkey* 352 (Robert E. Ward & Dankwart A. Rustow, eds., 1964); Metin Heper, *Civil-Military Relations in Turkey: Toward a Liberal Model?*, 12 Turk. Stud. 241 (June 2011); Morris Janowitz, *The Military in the Political Development of New Nations: An Essay in Comparative Analysis* (1964); Dankwart A. Rustow,

Turkey's Second Try at Democracy, 52 Yale Rev. 518 (1963); Ozan O. Varol, *The Turkish "Model" of Civil-Military Relations*, 11 Int'l J. Con'l L. 727 (2013).

11. Rustow (1964) at 356.
12. Karpat (1970) at 1668.
13. Ergun Özbudun, *The Role of the Military in Recent Turkish Politics* 11 (1966).
14. The discussion on NATO officers in Portugal draws on Eugene Keefe, *Portugal: A Country Study* (1993); Douglas Porch, *The Portuguese Armed Forces and the Revolution* (1977); Vasco Fernando Ferreira Rato, *Reluctant Departure: The Politics of Military Extrication in Portugal, 1974–1982* (July 29, 2002) (Ph.D. dissertation, Georgetown University).
15. Porch (1977) at 147.
16. *Id.*
17. Susan B. Epstein et al., Cong. Research Serv., RL34296, *Democracy Promotion: Cornerstone of U.S. Foreign Policy?* 1 (2007).
18. The discussion of American influence on the coup against King Farouk relies on Hazem Kandil, *Soldiers, Spies, and Statesmen: Egypt's Road to Revolt* (2012).
19. *Id.* at 24.
20. Arthur Meier Schlesinger, *A Thousand Days: John F. Kennedy in the White House* 198 (2002).
21. Roger Owen, *Egypt and Tunisia: From the Revolutionary Overthrow of Dictatorships to the Struggle to Establish a New Constitutional Order*, in *The New Middle East: Protest and Revolution in the Arab World*, 264 (Farwaz Gerges, ed., 2014).
22. Barany (2016) at 142.
23. Press Statement from Jen Psaki, U.S. Department of State, Regarding U.S. Assistance to Egypt (Oct. 9 2013).
24. Amy Hawthrone, *What's Happening with Suspended Military Aid for Egypt? Part I*, Atlantic Council (Oct. 16. 2014), http://www.atlanticcouncil.org/blogs/menasource/what-s-happening-with-suspended-military-aid-for-egypt-part-i.
25. Spencer Ackerman, *Obama Restores US Military Aid to Egypt over Islamic State Concerns*, Guardian (U.K.), Mar. 31, 2015, http://www.theguardian.com/us-news/2015/mar/31/obama-restores-us-military-aid-to-egypt.
26. L. B. Ware, *Ben Ali's Constitutional Coup in Tunisia*, 42 Middle East J. 587, 593 (1988).
27. Barany (2016) at 39.
28. *Id.*
29. *Id.* at 148.

Chapter 14

1. The discussion on Madison's constitutional vision relies heavily on Daryl J. Levinson, *Parchment and Politics: The Positive Puzzle of Constitutional Commitment*, 124 Harv. L. Rev. 657 (2011).
2. Letter to Thomas Jefferson from James Madison (Oct. 17, 1788).
3. Federalist No. 10 (James Madison).
4. *See* David S. Law & Mila Versteeg, *Sham Constitutions*, 101 Calif. Law Rev. 863 (2013).
5. Daryl J. Levinson & Richard H. Pildes, *Separation of Parties, Not Powers*, 119 Harv. L. Rev 2311, 2386 (2006).
6. Charles M. Cameron, *Veto Bargaining: Presidents and the Politics of Negative Power* (2000); Levinson & Pildes (2006).
7. Levinson & Pildes (2006) at 2323.
8. Samuel Issacharoff, *Constitutional Courts and Democratic Hedging*, 99 Georgetown L.J. 961 (2011).
9. Levinson & Pildes (2006) at 2339.
10. Dankwart Rustow, *Transitions to Democracy: Toward a Dynamic Model*, 2 Comp. Pol. 337, 351 (1970).

11. Fareed Zakaria, *The Rise of Illiberal Democracy*, 76 Foreign Aff. 6 (1997) pp. 22–43.
12. Steven Levitsky & Lucan A. Way, *Competitive Authoritarianism: Hybrid Regimes after the Cold War* 3 (2010); Leah Gilbert & Payam Mohseni, *Beyond Authoritarianism: The Conceptualization of Hybrid Regimes*, 46 Stud. Comp. Int'l Dev. 270, 271 (2011).
13. David Landau, *Constitution-Making Gone Wrong*, 64 Ala. L. Rev. 923 (2013).
14. David Landau, *Abusive Constitutionalism*, 47 U.C. Davis L. Rev. 188 (2013).
15. Isobel Coleman & Terra Lawson-Remer, *A User's Guide to Democratic User Transitions*, Foreign Pol'y, June 18 2013, https://foreignpolicy.com/2013/06/18/a-users-guide-to-democratic-transitions/.
16. Levitsky & Way (2010).
17. Rustow (1970) at 355.
18. *See generally* Brian Lai & Ruth Melkonian-Hoover, *Democratic Progress and Regress: The Effect of Parties on the Transitions of States to and away from Democracy*, 58 Pol. Research Q. 551, 553–54 (Dec. 2005).
19. Levinson (2011) at 661.
20. Samuel Issacharoff, *Fragile Democracies: Contested Power in the Era of Constitutional Courts* (2015).
21. *Certification of the Constitution of the Republic of South Africa*, South Afr. Legal Info. Inst., Sept. 9, 1996, http://www.saflii.org/za/cases/ZACC/1996/26.html.
22. Landau, *Abusive Constitutionalism* 47 U.C. Davis L. Rev. 188 (2013).
23. Levinson (2011), at 733.
24. Matthew C. Stephenson, *When the Devil Turns . . . : The Political Foundations of Judicial Independence*, 32 J. Leg. Stud. 59 (2003).
25. Levinson (2011) at 741.
26. *Id.* at 733.
27. Brian Sheppard & David Landau, *Why Honduras's Judiciary Is Its Most Dangerous Branch*, N.Y. Times, June 25, 2015.
28. Levinson (2011).
29. The discussion on political pluralism in post-1974 Portugal draws on Nancy Gina Bermeo, *The Revolution within the Revolution: Worker's Control in Rural Portugal* (1986); Thomas C. Bruneau & Alex Macleod, *Politics in Contemporary Portugal: Parties and the Consolidation of Democracy* (1987); Vasco Fernando Ferreira Rato, *Reluctant Departure: The Politics of Military Extrication in Portugal, 1974–1982* (July 29, 2002) (Ph.D. dissertation, Georgetown University).
30. Philippe C. Schmitter, *Corporatism and Public Policy in Authoritarian Portugal* 62 (1975).
31. Robert A. Dahl, *Political Oppositions in Western Democracies* 397 (1966).
32. Juan J. Linz, *Crisis, Breakdown and Reequalibration*, in *The Breakdown of Democratic Regimes* (Juan Linz & Alfred Stepan, eds., 1978); Lai & Melkonian-Hoover (2005), at 551–53.
33. Ran Hirschl, *Dysfunctional? Dissonant? Démodé? America's Constitutional Woes in Comparative Perspective*, 94 B.U. L. Rev. 939, 951 (2014).
34. *Id.* at 950.
35. The discussion on political pluralism in post-1960 Turkey draws on Kemal H. Karpat, *The Military and Politics in Turkey, 1960–64: A Socio-Cultural Analysis of a Revolution*, 75 Am. Hist. Rev. 1654 (1970); Ergun Özbudun, *The Role of the Military in Recent Turkish Politics* (1966); Dankwart A. Rustow, *The Military: Turkey*, in *Political Modernization in Japan and Turkey* (Robert E. Ward & Dankwart A. Rustow, eds., 1964); Ozan O. Varol, *The Democratic Coup d'État*, 53 Harv. Int'l L. J. 291 (2012); Ozan O. Varol, *The Turkish "Model" of Civil-Military Relations*, 11 Int'l J. Con'l L. 727 (2013).
36. The discussion on the relationship between the Egyptian military and the Muslim Brotherhood relies on Mahmoud Hamad, *The Constitutional Challenges in Post-Mubarak Egypt*, 14 Insight Turk. 51 (2012); Nathan J. Brown, *Train Wreck along the Nile*, Foreign Pol'y, July 10, 2012; Jeremy M. Sharp, *Egypt: Transition under Military Rule*, Cong. Res. Serv., June 21, 2012; Ozan O. Varol, *The Military as the Guardian of Constitutional Democracy*, 51

Colum. J. Transn'l L. 547 (2013); Gary C. Gambill, *What Is at Stake in Egypt's Referendum,* Jurist: Hotline (Mar. 19, 2011), http://jurist.org/hotline/2011/03/whats-at-stake-in-egypts-referendum-gary-c-gambill-editor-mideast-monitor.php; Michael Slackman, *Islamist Group Is Rising New Force in a New Egypt,* N.Y. Times, March 24, 2001, http://www.nytimes.com/2011/03/25/world/middleeast/25egypt.html; David D. Kirkpatrick, *Egypt Islamists Demand the End of Military Rule,* N.Y. Times, Nov. 18, 2011, http://www.nytimes.com/2011/11/19/world/middleeast/egyptianislamists-rally-to-protest-military-rule.html; *Egypt Court Suspends Constitutional Assembly,* BBC News, Apr. 10, 2012, http://www.bbc.co.uk/news/world-middle-east-17665048; *Egypt: Administrative Judicial Court Suspends the Constitutional Panel,* Library of Cong. (Apr. 16, 2012), http://www.loc.gov/law/foreign-news/article/egypt-administrative-judicial-court-suspends-the-constitutional-panel/; David D. Kirkpatrick, *Egypt's Military Softens Tone as Vote Count Favors Islamist,* N.Y. Times, June 18, 2012, http://www.nytimes.com/2012/06/19/world/africa/islamist-candidate-is-apparent-victor-in-egypt-as-military-cements-itspowers.html.

37. Mahmoud Hamad, *The Constitutional Challenges in Post-Mubarak Egypt,* 14 Insight Turk. 51, 58 (2012).

38. The Assembly included "9 constitutional experts, 6 judicial officials, 5 from Al-Azhar, 4 from Egyptian churches, 7 professional syndicates' heads, 4 representatives of labour and farmers, 33 MPs from political parties, 3 representatives of the executive authority (Armed Forces, the Police and the government), 29 public figures and youth, 4 political parties chairmen, 7 representatives of women, 7 representatives of the uprising and the injured, 10 Islamic figures (including those from Al-Azhar), 8 representing the Copts, 28 legal experts, 10 thinkers and writers, 30 university professors, 4 representatives of the labour syndicates, one representative of the foreign-based Egyptians." Sherif Tarek & Hatem Maher, *Egypt's Constituent Assembly Unveiled amid Fears over Islamist Dominance,* Ahram Online (June 13, 2012), http://english.ahram.org.eg/NewsContent/1/0/44716/Egypt/0/Egypts-Constituent-Assembly-unveiled-amid-fears-ov.aspx.

39. Brown (2012); Haider Ala Hamoudi, *Democracy and the Supreme Constitutional Court of Egypt,* Jurist (June 28, 2012), http://www.jurist.org/forum/2012/06/haider-hamoudi-scc-parliament.php.

40. Brown (2012).

Chapter 15

1. Svetlana Boym, *The Future of Nostalgia* (2002).

2. Guillermo O'Donnell & Philippe C. Schmitter, *Transitions from Authoritarian Rule: Tentative Conclusions about Uncertain Democracies* 4 (1986).

3. *Egyptians Remain Optimistic, Embrace Democracy and Religion in Political Life,* Pew Research Center (May 8, 2012), http://www.pewglobal.org/2012/05/08/chapter-1-national-conditions-and-views-about-the-future/; *see also* Steven A. Cook, *It's Still Mubarak's Egypt,* Foreign Pol'y, June 13, 2012.

4. *Most Muslims Want Democracy, Personal Freedoms, and Islam in Political Life,* Pew Research Center (July 10, 2012), http://www.pewglobal.org/2012/07/10/most-muslims-want-democracy-personal-freedoms-and-islam-in-political-life/.

5. Neal Katyal, *Sunsetting Judicial Opinions,* 79 Notre Dame L. Rev. 1237, 1238 (2004); Hallie Ludsin, *Peacemaking and Constitution-Drafting: A Dysfunctional Marriage,* 33 U. Pa. J. Int'l L. 239, 258 (2011); Eric A. Posner & Adrian Vermeule, *Accommodating Emergencies,* 56 Stan. L. Rev. 605, 609 (2003).

6. *See, e.g.,* Marc Lynch, *The Battle for Egypt's Constitution,* Foreign Pol'y, Jan. 11, 2013, http://foreignpolicy.com/2013/01/11/the-battle-for-egypts-constitution/.

7. David D. Kirkpatrick & Kareem Fahim, *Egypt Islamists Expect Approval of Constitution,* N.Y. Times A1, Dec. 16, 2012.

8. David Smith, *Guinea's President Promises to Turn Country to Stable Democracy,* Guardian (U.K.), Sept. 24, 2012, https://www.theguardian.com/world/2012/sep/24/guinea-president-country-stable-democracy.

9. *Guinea Profile—Leaders: President, Alpha Conde*, BBC, Oct. 9, 2015, http://www.bbc.com/news/world-africa-13442053.

10. Suat Kınıklıoğlu, *Turks Chose the Devil They Know—and Stability over Freedom*, Huffington Post, Nov. 5, 2015, http://www.huffingtonpost.com/suat-kiniklioglu/turkey-election-stability_b_8472374.html.

11. *Id.*

12. Henry Steele Commager, *The Reconciliation of Liberty and Order*, 17 Austl. Q. 35, 25 (1945).

13. Niccolò Machiavelli, *The Prince*, chapter 18.

14. Adam Przeworski, *Democracy as a Contingent Outcome of Conflicts*, in *Constitutionalism and Democracy* 59, 65–66 (Jon Elster & Rune Slagstad, eds., 1988).

15. The discussion on Mohamed Morsi's rule in Egypt relies on AFP, *Egypt: Morsi's Rise to Power*, SBS, Aug 26, 2013, http://www.sbs.com.au/news/article/2013/07/04/egypt-morsis-rise-power; Abdeslam Maghraoui, *Egypt's Failed Transition to Democracy: Was Political Culture a Factor?*, E-Int'l Rel., April 29, 2014, http://www.e-ir.info/2014/04/29/egypts-failed-transition-to-democracy-was-political-culture-a-major-factor/; Mara Revkin, *Egypt's Untouchable President*, Foreign Pol'y, Nov. 21, 2012, http://foreignpolicy.com/2012/11/21/morsis-moment-on-gaza/.

16. Revkin (2012).

17. Przeworski (1988).

18. Adam Przeworski, *Democracy and the Market* 10 (1991).

19. *Id.* at 19.

20. Juan J. Linz & Alfred Stepan, *Problems of Democratic Transition and Consolidation: Southern Europe, South America, and Post-Communist Europe* 67 (1996); Alfred Stepan, *Inclusionary and Exclusionary Military Responses to Radicalism: With Special Attention to Peru*, in *Radicalism in the Contemporary Age* 221, 221 (Seweryn Bialer & Sophia Sluzar, eds., 1977).

21. Specifically the Council would be chaired by the president and comprise the chief of the general staff and his vice chief, the three branch chiefs of the military, the prime minister, and fourteen officers to be selected by the army, air force, and navy. *Constituição da República Portuguesa*, art. 142 (1976) [Port.].

22. Vasco Fernando Ferreira Rato, *Reluctant Departure: The Politics of Military Extrication in Portugal, 1974–1982*, 320 (July 29, 2002) (Ph.D. dissertation, Georgetown University).

23. *Id.*

24. See Morris Janowitz, *The Military in the Political Development of New Nations* 81 (1964).

25. Henry Cabot Lodge, *John Marshall, Statesman*, 172 N. Am. Law Rev. 191, 197 (1901).

26. 17 U.S. 316, 405 (1819).

27. David C. Williams, *Civic Republicanism and the Citizen Militia: The Terrifying Second Amendment*, 101 Yale L.J. 551, 580 (1991).

28. Dankwart A. Rustow, *The Military: Turkey*, in *Political Modernization in Japan and Turkey* 352, 384 (Robert E. Ward & Dankwart A. Rustow, eds., 1964).

29. *Egyptians Remain Optimistic, Embrace Democracy and Religion in Political Life*, Pew Research Center at chp. 2.

30. Thomas C. Bruneau & Alex Macleod, *Politics in Contemporary Portugal: Parties and the Consolidation of Democracy* 23 (1987).

31. Gregory A. Caldeira & James L. Gibson, *The Etiology of Public Support for the Supreme Court*, 36 Am. J. Pol. Sci. 635, 636 (1992), cited in Daryl J. Levinson, *Parchment and Politics: The Positive Puzzle of Constitutional Commitment*, 124 Harv. L. Rev. 657, 737 (2011).

32. Levinson (2011) at 742.

33. Frederic Wehrey, *Why Libya's Transition to Democracy Failed*, Wash. Post, Feb. 27, 2016, https://www.washingtonpost.com/news/monkey-cage/wp/2016/02/17/why-libyas-transition-failed/.

34. *Id.*

35. Elijah Zarwan, *Egyptians Making History*, Cairo Rev. Global Aff., June 9, 2012, http://www.aucegypt.edulgapp/cairoreview/Pages/articleDetails.aspx?aid=189.

36. *First the Stage Was Set, Then the Coup Followed* [Önce Ortam Hazırlandı, Sonra Darbe], Haber7.com, Sept. 12, 2005 [Turk.], http://www.haber7.com/siyaset/haber/111090-once-ortam-hazirlandi-sonra-darbe.

Part V

1. "Won't Get Fooled Again" Words and Music by Peter Townshend, Copyright (c) 1971 Fabulous Music Ltd. Copyright Renewed 1999. Published by Fabulous Music Ltd.

   Administered in the USA and Canada by Spirit Four Music (GMR) o/b/o Spirit Services Holdings, S.à.r.l., Suolubaf Music and ABKCO Music Inc. International Copyright Secured All Rights Reserved. Reprinted by Permission of Hal Leonard LLC.

Chapter 16

1. The discussion on the aftermath of King Farouk's ouster in Egypt relies on Yvonne Yazbeck Haddad, *Contemporary Islam and the Challenge of History* (1982) and Manfred Halpern, *Politics of Social Change: In the Middle East and North Africa* (1963).
2. Haddad (1982) at 25.
3. *Id.*
4. Halpern (1963) at 272.
5. The discussion on the coup against Juan Velasco Alvarado relies heavily on David P. Werlich, *Peru: The Lame-Duck "Revolution,"* Current Hist., Feb. 1970.
6. *Id.* at 63.
7. *See* Hamza Hendawi, *Mubarak Prosecutors Demand the Death Penalty*, Globe & Mail (Toronto), Jan. 5, 2012.
8. Jack Shenker, *Egypt Hit by a New Wave of Protests as Military Postpones Election,* Guardian (U.K.), July 13, 2011, https://www.theguardian.com/world/2011/jul/13/egypt-protests-military-postpones-election.
9. The discussion on the Egyptian military's repression of protestors draws on Hazem Kandil, *Soliders, Spies, and Statesmen: Egypt's Road to Revolt* (2012).
10. *Id.*
11. Christophe de Roquefeuil, *Egypt Protesters in Tahrir after Army Apology*, Ma'an News Agency, Feb. 26, 2011, http://www.maannews.com/Content.aspx?id=363652.
12. Uri Friedman, *How Indonesia Beat Back Terrorism—For Now,* The Atlantic, Sept. 25, 2016, http://www.theatlantic.com/international/archive/2016/09/indonesia-isis-islamic-terrorism/500951/; John Aglionby, *First East Timor, Now Aceh: Will Indonesia Fall Apart?,* Guardian (U.K.). Dec. 5, 1999, https://www.theguardian.com/world/1999/dec/06/indonesia.johnaglionby.
13. *The Sandinista War on Human Rights*, Heritage Found. (July 19, 1983), http://www.heritage.org/research/reports/1983/07/the-sandinista-war-on-human-rights.
14. Elke Larson & Kathleen Rustici, *Paradise Lost: Fiji's Failing Democratic Transition,* Cent. for Strat. & Int. Studies (April 11, 2013), https://www.csis.org/analysis/paradise-lost-fiji%E2%80%99s-failing-democratic-transition.
15. The discussion on the lack of available sanctions against the military during military rule is based on Ozan O. Varol, *The Democratic Coup d'État,* 53 Harv. Int'l L.J. 292 (2012).
16. *Cf.* Terry M. Moe, *The New Economics of Organization,* 28 Am. J. Pol. Sci. 767 (1984).
17. *See The Arab Awakening: Revolution Spinning in the Wind,* Economist, July 14, 2011, http://www.economist.com/node/18958237?fsrc=scn/fb/wl/ar/revolutioninthewind.
18. Interview with Haytham Hammad, Cairo, Aug. 1, 2011; *see also* David D. Kirkpatrick, *Egypt Erupts in Jubilation as Mubarak Steps Down,* N.Y. Times, Feb. 11, 2011, http://www.nytimes.com/2011/02/12/world/middleeast/12egypt.html.
19. Neil MacFarquhar, *Protestors Scold Egypt's Military Council*, N.Y. Times, Apr. 1, 2011, http://www.nytimes.com/2011/04/02/world/middleeast/02egypt.html.
20. Shenker (2011).

Chapter 17

1. Juan J. Linz & Alfred Stepan, *Problems of Democratic Transition and Consolidation: Southern Europe, South America, and Post-Communist Europe* (1996).

2. The discussion of the military's golden parachutes draws on Ozan O. Varol, *The Democratic Coup d'État*, 53 Harv. Int'l L.J. 292 (2012) and Ozan O. Varol, *Constitutional Performance in Transitions from Military Rule*, in *Assessing Constitutional Performance* (Tom Ginsburg & Aziz Huq, eds., 2016).

3. The discussion on the Portuguese military's golden parachutes relies heavily on Douglas Porch, *The Portuguese Armed Forces and the Revolution* (1977); Varol (2012); and Varol (2016).

4. Douglas Porch, *The Portuguese Armed Forces and the Revolution* (1977) at 171.

5. The line between direct and institutional entrenchment blurs with respect to institutions such as the National Security Council, which includes members of the military.

6. Tom Ginsburg, *Judicial Review in New Democracies: Constitutional Courts in East Asia* (2003); Ran Hirschl, *Towards Juristocracy: The Origins and Consequences of the New Constitutionalism* (2004).

7. Tamir Moustafa & Tom Ginsburg, *Introduction*, in *Rule by Law: The Politics of Courts in Authoritarian Regimes* (2008).

8. *Id.*; Alfred C. Stepan, *Rethinking Military Politics: Brazil and the Southern Cone* (1988).

9. The discussion on the Turkish Constitutional Court relies on Ozan O. Varol, *The Turkish "Model" of Civil-Military Relations*, 11 Int'l J. Const. L. 727 (2012); Varol (2016); Hootan Shambayati, *A Tale of Two Mayors: Courts and Politics in Iran and Turkey*, 36 Int'l J. of Middle East Stud. 253 (2004); Hootan Shambayati, *The Guardian of the Regime: The Turkish Constitutional Court in Comparative Perspective*, in *Constitutional Politics in the Middle East* (Saïd Amir Arjomand, ed., 2008); Ceren Belge, *Friends of the Court: The Republican Alliance and Selective Activism of the Constitutional Court of Turkey*, 40 L. & Soc. Rev. 653 (2006); Hootan Shambayati & Esen Kirdiş, *In Pursuit of "Contemporary Civilization": Judicial Empowerment in Turkey*, 62 Pol. Res. Q. 767 (2009); Sujit Choudhry et al., *Constitutional Courts after the Arab Spring: Appointment Mechanisms and Relative Judicial Independence* (2014); Dicle Koğacıoğlu, *Dissolution of Political Parties by the Constitutional Court in Turkey: Judicial Delimitation of the Political Domain*, 18 Int'l Soc. 258 (2003); Ersel Aydınlı et al., *The Turkish Military's March toward Europe*, 85 Foreign Aff. 77 (2006).

10. The discussion on Egypt's National Security Council relies on Hazem Kandil, *Soldiers, Spies, and Statesmen: Egypt's Road to Revolt* (2012).

11. Since its reintroduction in 2012, the Council's structure and authorities have slightly changed. The most recent version contains an equal number of civilians and military officers, but one of the civilian ministers (the minister of defense) must be a military officer, which gives the military the upper hand. The Council has exclusive oversight over the military's budget, and its opinion must be sought on pending legislation relevant to the armed forces. The president must consult with the Council before declaring war, sending armed forces to combat outside national territory, or dissolving the House of Representatives.

12. The discussion on the Turkish National Security Council relies on Shambayati (2008); Shambayati (2004); Varol (2012); Varol (2016); Aydınlı et al. (2006); Ümit Cizre Sakallıoğlu, *The Anatomy of the Turkish Military's Political Autonomy*, 29 Comp. Pol 151 (1997).

13. The discussion on the Egyptian military's procedural gamesmanship efforts draws on Varol (2012) and Varol (2016).

14. *See, e.g.*, Fouad Ajami, *Egypt and the Fruits of the Pharaohs*, Wall Street J., Nov. 29, 2011, at A19.

15. *Id.*

16. Ahmad Abed Rabbo, *Egyptian Political Parties and Parliamentary Elections 2011/2012*, Arab Ctr. for Res & Pol'y Stud. (2011), http://english.dohainstitute.org/release/f3e63fe9-eecb-49cc-884f-01bdc7a340eb.

Chapter 18

1. Ozan O. Varol, *The Democratic Coup d'État*, 53 Harv. Int'l L.J. 291 (2012).
2. Ozan O. Varol, *Constitutional Performance in Transitions from Military Rule*, in *Assessing Constitutional Performance* (Tom Ginsburg & Aziz Huq, eds., 2016).
3. For further analysis on temporal limitations on the military's golden parachutes, see Varol (2016) and Ozan O. Varol, *Temporary Constitutions*, 102 Calif. L. Rev. 409 (2014).
4. The discussion on the temporal limitations on the Portuguese military's authorities draws on Varol (2012) and Varol (2014).
5. Juan J. Linz & Alfred Stepan, *Problems of Democratic Transition and Consolidation: Southern Europe, South America, and Post-Communist Europe* (1996).
6. Vasco Fernando Ferreira Rato, *Reluctant Departure: The Politics of Military Extrication in Portugal, 1974–1982* (2002).
7. Hootan Shambayati, *The Guardian of the Regime: The Turkish Constitutional Court in Comparative Perspective*, in *Constitutional Politics in the Middle East* (Saïd Amir Arjomand, ed., 2008).
8. Alfred C. Stepan, *Rethinking Military Politics: Brazil and the Southern Cone* 100–101 (1988).
9. The Declaration of Independence para. 14 (U.S. 1776). For an excellent analysis of the constitutional implications of this question in the United States, see Deborah N. Pearlstein, *The Soldier, the State, and the Separation of Powers*, 90 Tex. L. Rev. 797 (2012).
10. Glenn Sulmasy & John Yoo, *Challenges to Civilian Control of the Military: A Rational Choice Approach to the War on Terror*, 54 UCLA L. Rev. 1815 (2007).
11. *Id.*
12. *Id.*
13. Pearlstein (2012) at 800.
14. Andrew Bacevich, *America's War for the Greater Middle East* 306, 308 (2016).
15. *Id.* at 312.

Chapter 19

1. Daniel Lametti, *If You Break It Do You Really Have to Buy It?*, Slate, July 28, 2012, http://www.slate.com/blogs/browbeat/2012/07/28/if_you_break_it_do_you_really_have_to_buy_it_.html.
2. David Samuels, *A Conversation with Colin Powell*, Atlantic, April 2007, http://www.theatlantic.com/magazine/archive/2007/04/a-conversation-with-colin-powell/305873/.
3. Philippe Droz-Vincent, *The Military amidst Uprisings and Transitions in the Arab World*, in *The New Middle East: Protest and Revolution in the Arab World*, 180, 197 (Farwaz A. Gerges, ed., 2014).
4. Farwaz Gerges, *Introduction*, in *The New Middle East* 27 (Farwaz Gerges, ed., 2014).
5. Barbara Geddes, *What Do We Know about Democratization after Twenty Years?*, 2 Ann. Rev. of Pol. Sci. 115, 131 (1999).
6. The discussion on the divisions within the Portuguese military following the 1974 coup relies on Eugene Keefe, *Portugal: A Country Study* (1993); Kenneth Maxwell, *The Thorns of the Portuguese Revolution*, 54 Foreign Aff. 250 (1976); John Hammond, *The Armed Forces Movement and the Portuguese Revolution: Two Steps Forward, One Step Back*, 10 J. Pol. & Mil. Soc. 71 (1982); Lawrence S. Graham, *The Portuguese Military and the State: Rethinking Transitions in Europe and Latin America* (1993); Douglas Porch, *The Portuguese Armed Forces and the Revolution* (1977).
7. Geddes (1999) at 126 (noting "a consensus in the literature that most professional soldiers place a higher value on the survival of the military itself than on anything else").
8. Graham (1993) at 40.
9. Porch (1977) at 236.

10. The discussion on the availability bias draws on Cass R. Sunstein, *What's Available? Social Influences and Behavioral Economics*, 97 Nw. U. L. Rev. 1295 (2003).
11. Geddes (1999) at 131.
12. *Id.* at 132.
13. Nikolay Marinov & Hein Goermans, *Coups and Democracy*, 44 British J. Pol. Sci. 799 (2013).
14. Geddes (1999) at 131.
15. Nathan J. Brown & Kristen Stilt, *A Haphazard Constitutional Compromise*, Carnegie Found. for Int'l Peace (Apr. 11, 2011), http://carnegieendowment.org/publicationslindex.cfm?fa=view&id=43533.
16. *Id.*
17. *Id.*
18. *Id.*
19. *Id.*
20. The discussion on Burkina Faso draws on Damien Glez, *An African Spring*, 32 World Pol. J. 77 (2015); Marie-Soleil Frére & Pierre Englebert, *Briefing: Burkina Faso—The Fall of Blaise Compaoré*, 114 Afr. Aff. 295 (2015); Kingsley Kobo, *Burkina Faso: Ghost of "Africa's Che Guevara,"* Al Jazeera, Oct. 31, 2014, http://www.aljazeera.com/indepth/features/2014/10/burkina-faso-thomas-sankara-africa-che-guevara-2014103017525682241.html; Ernest Harsch, *Citizens' Revolt in Burkina Faso*, Soc. Sci. Res. Council (Dec. 9, 2014), http://forums.ssrc.org/african-futures/2014/12/09/citizens-revolt-in-burkina-faso/; Rakotomalala & Nadia Karoui, *The Rise and Fall of Burkina Faso's Coup: What You Need to Know*, Guardian (U.K.), Sept. 24, 2015, https://www.theguardian.com/world/2015/sep/24/burkina-faso-coup-rise-and-fall-of-what-you-need-to-know; Simon Allison, *How the People of Burkina Faso Foiled a Military Coup*, Guardian (U.K.), Sept. 25, 2015, https://www.theguardian.com/world/2015/sep/25/burkina-faso-foiled-military-coup; Daniel Eizenga, *Burkina Faso Elections Mark Turning Point in Country's Recent Political Turmoil*, Wash. Post, Dec. 6, 2015, https://www.washingtonpost.com/news/monkey-cage/wp/2015/12/06/burkina-faso-elections-mark-a-turning-point-in-a-country-in-political-turmoil/.
21. Glez (2015) at 79.
22. Rakotomalala & Karoui (2012).
23. Hazem Kandil, *Soldiers, Spies, and Statesmen: Egypt's Road to Revolt* 232 (2012).

Chapter 20

1. The discussion on the 1952 coup against Farouk and its aftermath relies heavily on Hazem Kandil, *Soldiers, Spies, and Statesmen: Egypt's Road to Revolt* (2012); Tarek Osman, *Egypt on the Brink: From Nasser to Mubarak* (2011); and Richard Cavendish, *The Abdication of King Farouk*, 22 Hist. Today (July 2002), https://www.historytoday.com/richard-cavendish/abdication-king-farouk.
2. *Why Are Some Egyptians Pining Away for Their Long-Gone King?*, BBC, Aug. 23, 2015, http://www.bbc.com/news/blogs-trending-34017597.
3. Radio broadcast of Anwar Sadat, July 23, 1952, cited in Steven A. Cook, *The Struggle for Egypt: From Nasser to Tahrir Square* 11–12 (2012).
4. Kandil (2012) at 33.
5. *Id.*
6. Address by General Gamal Abdel Nasser in Alexandria, Oct. 26, 1954, cited in Joel Gordon, *Nasser's Blessed Movement: Egypt's Free Officers and the July Revolution* 179 (1992).
7. Kandil (2012) at 39.
8. The section on Napoleon's coup relies on Sally Waller, *France in Revolution, 1776–1830*, in *Heinemann Advanced History* (2000); H. Morse Stevens, *Recent Memoirs of the French Directory*, 1 Am. Hist. R. 473 (1896); Jocelyn Hunt, *Questions and Analysis in History: The French Revolution* (1998); Wayne Hanley, *The Genesis of Napoleonic Propaganda, 1796–1799*

(2005), http://www.gutenberg-e.org/haw01/haw07.html; Sir Walter Scott, *Prose Works: Life of Napoleon Bonaparte* (2016).

9. Hanley (2005).

10. *Id.*

11. *The Correspondence of Shelby Foote and Walker Percy* 169 (Jay Tolson, ed., 1997).

12. The discussion on Nasser's pan-Arabism relies on Saïd K. Aburish, *Nasser: The Last Arab* (2013) and Kandil (2012).

Chapter 21

1. Ozan O. Varol, *Constitutional Performance in Transitions from Military Rule*, in *Assessing Constitutional Performance* (Tom Ginsburg & Aziz Huq, eds., 2016).

2. Fabrice Lehoucq & Anibal Pérez-Liñan, *Breaking Out of the Coup Trap*, 47 Comp. Pol. Stud. 1105, 1110 (2014); John B. Londregan & Keith T. Poole, *Poverty, the Coup Trap, and the Seizure of Executive Power*, 42 World Pol. 151 (1990); Robert D. Putnam, *Explaining Military Intervention in Latin American Politics*, 20 World Pol. 83 (1967); Adam Przeworski et al., *Democracy and Development: Political Institutions and Well-Being in the World, 1950–1990* (2000); Aaron Belkin & Evan Schofer, *Toward a Structural Understanding of Coup Risk*, 47 J. of Conflict Res. 594 (2003); Rosemary H. T. O'Kane, *A Probabilistic Approach to the Causes of Coups d'État*, 11 Brit. J. Pol. Sci. 287 (1981).

3. The section on Africa's spring and fall relies on Robert Pringle, *Mali's Unlikely Democracy*, 30 Wilson Q. 31 (2006); Jane Turrittin, *People Topple Traoré*, 52 Rev. Afr. Pol. Econ. 97 (1991); Susanna D. Wing, *Briefing Mali: Politics of a Crisis*, 112 Afr. Aff. 476 (2013); Enrico Sborgi, *Assessing Democracy in Mali: A Procedural Analysis,* Il Politico 63(3) (1998); Steve McDonald, *Africa's Long Spring*, Wilson Q., Winter (2013); Yaroslav Trofimov, *Islamic Democracy? Mali Finds a Way to Make It Work*, Wall Street Journal, June 22, 2004, http://www.wsj.com/articles/SB108785720026143450; Stephen Buckley, *Mali: Tuned in and Democratic,* Wash. Post, Mar. 24, 1996, https://www.washingtonpost.com/archive/politics/1996/03/24/mali-tuned-in-and-democratic/45f7299f-c772-4ca0-859f-ff29e47c7774/; Adam Nossiter, *Soldiers Overthrow Mali Government in Setback for Democracy in Africa,* N.Y. Times, March 22, 2012, http://www.nytimes.com/2012/03/23/world/africa/mali-coup-france-calls-for-elections.html?_r=1&pagewanted=all.

4. Pringle (2006) at 32.

5. *Sunjata,* Myths Encyclopedia (last visited Dec. 7, 2016), http://www.mythencyclopedia.com/Sp-Tl/Sunjata.html.

6. According to the 1991 CIA World Factbook, there was no conscription in Mali at the time of the coup.

7. Trofimov (2004).

8. Buckley (1996).

9. Trofimov (2004).

10. Ross Douthat, *Libya's Unintended Consequences,* N.Y. Times, July 7, 2012, http://www.nytimes.com/2012/07/08/opinion/sunday/libyas-unintended-consequences.html.

11. The discussion on Portugal relies on Samuel P, Huntington, *After Twenty Years: The Future of the Third Wave*, 8 J. Democracy 3 (1997); Vasco Fernando Ferreira Rato, *Reluctant Departure: The Politics of Military Extrication in Portugal, 1974–1982* (July 29, 2002) (Ph.D. dissertation, Georgetown University); Thomas C. Bruneau, *From Revolution to Democracy in Portugal: The Roles and Stages of the Provisional Governments*, in *Between States: Interim Governments and Democratic Transitions* 144 (Yossi Shain & Juan J. Linz, eds., 1995); Juan J. Linz & Alfred Stepan, *Problems of Democratic Transition and Consolidation: Southern Europe, South America, and Post-Communist Europe* 121 (1996); Nancy Gina Bermeo, *The Revolution within the Revolution: Workers' Control in Rural Portugal* 171 (1986); Ozan O. Varol, *The Democratic*

Coup d'État, 53 Harv. Int'l L.J. 292 (2012); Ozan O. Varol, *The Military as the Guardian of Constitutional Democracy*, 51 Colum. J. Trans'l L. 547 (2013).

12. The section on Guinea-Bissau relies on Barry Boubacar-Sid & Quentin Wodon, *Conflict, Growth, and Poverty in Guinea-Bissau*, in *Conflict, Livelihoods, and Poverty in Guinea-Bissau* 11 (G. E. Creppy et al., eds., 2007); Marina Padrão Temudo, *From "People's Struggle" to "This War of Today": Entanglements of Peace and Conflict in Guinea-Bissau*, 78 J. Int'l Afr. Inst. 245 (2008); Birgit Embaló, *Civil-Military Relations and Political Order in Guinea-Bissau*, 50 J. Mod. Afr. Stud. 253 (2012); Estanislao Gacitua-Mario et al., *Institutions, Social Networks, and Conflicts in Guinea-Bissau: Results from a 2005 Survey*, in *Conflict, Livelihoods, and Poverty in Guinea-Bissau* 23 (G. E. Creppy et al., eds., 2007); *Guinea-Bissau Election Derailed by Coup*, 49 Afr. Res. Bull. 19219 (2012); *Guinea-Bissau President Shot Dead*, BBC, Mar. 2, 2009, http://news.bbc.co.uk/2/hi/africa/7918061.stm; *Update Report on Guinea-Bissau*, Sec. Council Rept. (May 4, 2012), http://www.securitycouncilreport. org/update-report/lookup-c-glKWLeMTIsG-b-8079461.php; *Polity IV Country Report 2010: Guinea-Bissau*, Polity IV Project (2010), http://www.systemicpeace.org/polity/ GuineaBissau2010.pdf.
13. Embaló (2012) at 269.
14. Polity IV Project (2010).
15. *Guinea-Bissau Election Derailed by Coup* (2012) at 19220.

Chapter 22

1. The discussion on the 1945 coup in Brazil draws on E. Bradford Burns, *A History of Brazil* (1993); Thomas E. Skidmore, *Brazil: Five Centuries of Change* (1999); and José Maria Bello, *A History of Modern Brazil: 1889–1964* (James L. Taylor, trans., 1966).
2. Bello (1966) at 310.
3. *Id.* at 325.
4. Burns (1993) at 446.
5. *Id.* at 445.
6. The discussion on Argentina relies on Gary W. Wynia, *Argentina in the Post War Era: Politics and Economic Policy Making in a Divided Society* (1978); Luis Alberto Romero, *A History of Argentina in the Twentieth Century* (1994); 2 Robert A. Potash, *The Army and Politics in Argentina 1945–1962: Perón to Frondizi* (1980); 3 Robert A. Potash, *The Army and Politics in Argentina 1962–63: From Frondizi's Fall to the Peronist Revolution* (1996); Celia Szusterman, *The "Revolución Libertadora," 1955–58*, in *The Political Economy of Argentina, 1946–83* (Guido di Tella & Rudiger Dornbusch, eds., 1989).
7. Szusterman (1989) at 89.
8. http://www.bbc.com/news/magazine-18616380.
9. Potash (1980) at 272.
10. Romero (1994) at 152.
11. *Id.* at 174.

Chapter 23

1. *Apple Presents iPhone 4*, Apple.com (June 7, 2010), https://www.apple.com/pr/library/ 2010/06/07Apple-Presents-iPhone-4.html.
2. The discussion on the July 15, 2016, coup attempt in Turkey draws on Ozan Varol, *Irony and Tragedy in Turkey's Coup Attempt*, Huffington Post, July 17, 2016, http://www.huffingtonpost. com/entry/irony-and-tragedy-in-turkeys-coup-attempt_us_578b29e2e4b0e7c873504ca2 and Ozan Varol, *Turkey's Reichstag Fire*, Huffington Post, July 22, 2016, http://www.huffing- tonpost.com/entry/turkeys-reichstag-fire_us_5791f215e4b0a1917a6e71e3.

3. *The Soldiers Are in the TRT Building: Here's the "Coup" Declaration* [*Asker TRT Binasinda: İşte "Darbe" Bildirisi*], Haber 3, July 16, 2016 [Turk.], http://www.haber3.com/asker-trt-binasinda-iste-darbe-bildirisi-3977124h.htm.

4. Richard H. Dekmejian, *Egypt and Turkey: The Military in the Background*, in *Soldiers, Peasants, and Bureaucrats: Civil–Military Relations in Communist and Modernizing Societies* 28, 47 (Roman Kolkowicz & Andrzej Korbonski, eds., 1982).

5. The section on "The Strange Case of Dr. Jekyll, Mr. Hyde, and the Turkish Military" relies on Ceren Belge, *Friends of the Court: The Republican Alliance and Selective Activism of the Constitutional Court of Turkey*, 40 Law & Soc'y Rev. 653 (2006); Ozan Ergül, *Türk Anayasa Mahkemesi ve Demokrasi* [The Turkish Constitutional Court and Democracy] (2007); Feroz Ahmad, *Demokrasi Sürecinde Türkiye 1945–1980* [Turkey on the Path to Democracy 1945–1980] (1994); Dankwart A. Rustow, *The Military: Turkey*, in *Political Modernization in Japan And Turkey* 352 (Robert E. Ward & Dankwart A. Rustow, eds., 1964); Ozan O. Varol, *The Democratic Coup d'État*, 53 Harv. Int'l L.J. 325 (2012); Ozan O. Varol, *The Turkish "Model" of Civil-Military Relations*, 11 Int'l J. Con'l L. 727 (2013); Kemal H. Karpat, *The Military and Politics in Turkey, 1960–64: A Socio-Cultural Analysis of a Revolution*, 75 Am. Hist. Rev. 1654 (1970); Dankwart A. Rustow, *Turkey's Second Try at Democracy*, 52 Yale Rev. 518 (1963); Ergun Özbudun, *The Role of the Military in Recent Turkish Politics* 10, 26 (1966); Nilüfer Narlı, *Civil-Military Relations in Turkey*, 1 Turk. Stud. 107, 113 (2000); Daniel Lerner & Richard D. Robinson, *Swords and Ploughshares: The Turkish Army as a Modernizing Force*, 13 World Pol. 38 (1960); Morris Janowitz, *The Military in the Political Development of New Nations: An Essay in Comparative Analysis* 82 (1964); Manfred Halpern, *Social Change in Middle East and North Africa* 266 (1963).

6. Ahmad (1994) at 132; Rustow (1964) at 366; Dekmejian (1982).

7. Varol (2013).

8. Özbudun (1966) at 26.

9. *Id.* at 1; Rustow (1963) at 536.

10. Özbudun (1966) at 3; Samuel P. Huntington, *The Soldier and the State: The Theory and Politics of Civil-Military Relations* 83 (1957); Samuel P. Huntington, *Political Development and Political Decay*, 17 World Pol. 386, 421 (1965).

11. Özbudun (1966) at 42.

12. *Id.* at 26.

13. *Id.*

14. Rustow (1963) at 536.

15. The section titled "Unfinished Revolution" relies on George S. Harris, *Military Coups and Turkish Democracy, 1960–1980*, 12 Turk. Stud. 205 (2011); Erik-Jan Zürcher, *Turkey: A Modern History* (2004); Engin Şahin, *Siyaset ve Hukuk Arasında Anayasa Mahkemesi* [Between Politics and Law: The Turkish Constitutional Court] (2010); James Brown, *The Military and Society: The Turkish Case*, 25 Middle Eastern Stud. 387 (July 1989); Dekmejian (1982); Varol (2013); Narlı (2000); Ersel Aydınlı, *A Paradigmatic Shift for the Turkish Generals and an End to the Coup Era in Turkey*, 63 Middle East J. 581 (2009).

16. Zürcher (2004) at 258.

17. *Id.*

18. Şahin (2010) at 354.

19. *Id.* at 82.

20. On February 28, 1997, after a seventeen-year hiatus, the Turkish Armed Forces staged a coup-without-arms during a National Security Council meeting. Concerned about the continued instability caused by weak coalition governments and the rise of political Islam in Turkey, the military presented to Prime Minister Necmettin Erbakan, a member of the Islamist Welfare Party, a list of "recommendations" to curb antisecular activity by his party. Narlı (2000); Angel Rabasa & Stephen Larrabee, *The Rise of Political Islam in Turkey* 37 (2008). Following the

February 28 meeting of the Council, Erbakan resigned his post without bloodshed or political upheaval, leading many to dub the 1997 coup the "postmodern coup" in Turkey. Hootan
Shambayati, *The Guardian of the Regime: The Turkish Constitutional Court in Comparative
Perspective,* in *Constitutional Politics in the Middle East* 99, 102 (Saïd Amir Arjomand,
ed., 2008).

21. The section titled "Exodus" draws on Metin Heper, *The European Union, the Turkish Military,
and Democracy,* 10 S. Eur. Soc'y & Pol. 33 (2005); Narlı (2000); Amberin Zaman, *Receding
Power of Turkey's Military: A Leap for Democracy or Another Power Struggle?,* Hürriyet Daily
News, July 30, 2009, http://www.hurriyetdailynews.com/n.php?n=receding-power-
ofturkey8217s-military-a-leap-for-democracy-or-another-power-struggle-2009-07-28.

22. Metin Heper, *The Justice and Development Party Government and the Military in Turkey,* 6 Turk.
Stud. 215, 223 (June 2005).

23. Dexter Filkins, *Turkey's Thirty Year Coup,* New Yorker, Oct. 17, 2016, http://www.newyorker.
com/magazine/2016/10/17/turkeys-thirty-year-coup.

24. *Ten Percent of Generals Jailed* [*Generallerin Yuzde 10'u Hapiste*], Hürriyet, Feb. 15, 2011, http://
www.hurriyet.com.tr/gundem/17024835.asp.

25. Gul Tuysuz & Liz Sly, *For Turkish Military, a Telling Change of Tactics,* Wash. Post, July 31,
2011, https://www.washingtonpost.com/world/middle-east/for-turkish-military-a-telling-
change-of-tactics/2011/07/30/gIQAjZevjI_story.html?utm_term=.16455af72938.

26. *Id.*

Chapter 24

1. *Emergence,* PBS: NOVA (last visited Dec. 9, 2016) http://www.pbs.org/wgbh/nova/science-
now/3410/03-ever-nf.html.

2. Fabrice Lehoucq & Anibal Pérez-Liñan, *Breaking Out of the Coup Trap,* 47 Comp. Pol. Stud.
1105, 1122 (2014).

3. *Id.*

4. Uri Friedman, *How Indonesia Beat Back Terrorism—For Now,* Atlantic, Sept. 25, 2016, http://
www.theatlantic.com/international/archive/2016/09/indonesia-isis-islamic-terrorism/
500951/.

5. *Id.*

6. *Id.*

7. The section titled "United We Stand, Divided We Fall" relies heavily on Jonathan Hartlyn,
*Military Governments and the Transition to Civilian Rule: The Colombian Experience of 1957–
1958,* 26 J. of Interam. Stud. & World Aff., 245 (1984).

8. *Id.* at 267.

9. Alfred C. Stepan, *Rethinking Military Politics: Brazil and the Southern Cone* (1988).

10. The discussion on Portugal relies on Vasco Fernando Ferreira Rato, *Reluctant Departure: The
Politics of Military Extrication in Portugal, 1974–1982* (July 29, 2002) (Ph.D. dissertation,
Georgetown University); Kenneth Maxwell, *The Making of Portuguese Democracy* (1997);
Ozan O. Varol, *The Democratic Coup d'État,* 53 Harv. Int'l L.J. 339 (2012); Ozan O. Varol,
The Military as the Guardian of Constitutional Democracy, 51 Colum. J. Trans'l L. 547
(2013); Jost M. Magone, *European Portugal: The Difficult Road to Sustainable Democracy*
28 (1997); Thomas C. Bruneau & Alex Macleod, *Politics in Contemporary Portugal: Parties
and the Consolidation of Democracy* 8 (1987); Paul Christopher Manuel, *The Challenges of
Democratic Consolidation in Portugal: Political, Economic, and Military Issues, 1976–1991*
(1996).

11. Maxwell (1997) at 87.

12. Bruneau & Macleod (1987) at 8.

13. *Id.* at 7.

Chapter 25

1. The discussion on Cincinnatus relies on Mary Beard, *SPQR: A History of Ancient Rome* (2016); Dionysius of Halicarnassus, *Roman Antiquities*, 19(1); Titus Livius [Livy], *The History of Rome*, http://mcadams.posc.mu.edu/txt/ah/Livy/; *Lucius Quinctius Cincinnatus*, Wikipedia (last visited Dec. 7, 2016), https://en.wikipedia.org/wiki/Lucius_Quinctius_ Cincinnatus; Clinton Rossiter, *Constitutional Dictatorship: Crisis Government in the Modern Democracies* (1948).
2. http://thefederalistpapers.org/founders/john-adams.
3. The final sentence of the book was inspired by the closing sentence in Beard (2016).

INDEX